REGISTER OF NEW ZEALAND RAILWAYS STEAM LOCOMOTIVES 1863-1971

(AND BEYOND)

W. G. LLOYD

Copyright Second Edition: Text W. G. Lloyd; Chapter 11, W. W. Prebble; Chapter 12, R. D. Grant. Layout and design, Triple M Publications. All rights reserved. No part of this book may be reproduced in any manner whatsoever without written permission of the copyright holders, except in the case of brief quotations embodied in critical articles and reviews, and for the purposes of private study and research.

FIRST PUBLISHED IN 1974 BY THE NEW ZEALAND RAILWAY AND LOCOMOTIVE SOCIETY (OTAGO BRANCH) INC.

THIS EDITION PUBLISHED IN 2002 JOINTLY BY THE OTAGO RAILWAY AND LOCOMOTIVE SOCIETY INC., P. O. BOX 1297, DUNEDIN, 9015,

AND

TRIPLE M PUBLICATIONS, P. O. BOX 166, WELLINGTON, 6015.

PRINTED IN NEW ZEALAND BY ROGAN-M^CINDOE PRINT LTD., DUNEDIN.

ISBN 0-9582072-1-6

ABOVE: J^A 1274, the last steam locomotive built for New Zealand Railways, steams out from Hillside Workshops, brand new, 20 December 1956. (G. W. Emerson)

IN MEMORIAM

GEORGE WEST EMERSON PhD, QSM

6 MARCH 1935 - 24 MARCH 2002

CONTENTS

Chapter		Page
	FOREWORDS	I
	INTRODUCTION	II
	ACKNOWLEDGEMENTS	III
ONE	Mr. WERRY'S PROBLEM "I cannot find any trace of the system...."	1
TWO	THE BROAD-GAUGE LOCOMOTIVES	3
	The Oreti Railway	3
	The Bluff Harbour and Invercargill Railway	3
	The Canterbury Provincial Railways	4
	The Auckland and Drury Railway	5
THREE	THE PUBLIC WORKS DEPARTMENT NUMBERING	6
	The Classification of Locomotives	8
	North Island Railways	9
	South Island Railways	16
FOUR	THE ANSWER TO THE PROBLEM	31
FIVE	THE PURCHASES	44
SIX	STEAM LOCOMOTIVE NUMBERING 1890-1971	46
	Notes to Steam locomotive Numbering 1890-1971	108
SEVEN	LOCOMOTIVE NAMES	119
EIGHT	THE MAKERS OF NZR LOCOMOTIVES	126
NINE	DISPOSAL OF LOCOMOTIVES FOR INDUSTRIAL AND OTHER RAILWAY USE	144
	Locomotive sales prior to 1890	144
	Locomotive sales after 1890	147
TEN	NOSTALGIA	163
	Preserved locomotives	
ELEVEN	NUMBER PLATES AND MAKER'S PLATES OF THE NZR STEAM LOCOMOTIVE (W. W. Prebble)	179
	Cabside Number Plates	179
	Smokebox Door Number Plates	183
	The NZR Maker's Plate	185
TWELVE	A GOOD MANY BRAINS AT WORK (R. D. Grant)	192
	PHOTOGRAPH INDEX	201

FOREWORD
(First Edition)

T. A. BLYTH
Former Chief Mechanical Engineer, NZR.

In a highly competitive transport world, any organisation involved in the mass movement of goods and commodities must concern itself basically with increasing efficiency within the organisation and with economical improvements to its tools of trade.

However, unfortunately for posterity, these developments and improvements have so often been made in the past with little thought for the record book, and the New Zealand Railways Department is one organisation which has been the victim of such circumstances in the earlier years.

I think it can be claimed, with some sense of pride, by railwaymen and women and also by railway enthusiasts throughout the country, that the steam locomotive reigned supreme as the workhorse of the world for over a century, and perhaps our forebears could be forgiven any shortcomings in their failure to keep fully documented records of their rolling stock, if their thoughts were such during the early years of railways that they were unable to visualise any development that would supplant the steam locomotive in its major transport role as prime mover.

This, and the fact that each locomotive in service would be known in detail to the small number of staff involved in its operation, control and maintenance, would be the main reasons for the lack of early organisation and method in recording the numbers and types of this class of stock in service.

In addition, some records which have been kept over such a lengthy period (and many would have been written longhand) do become bulky and after many years of storage without use, would be destroyed as a means of providing space for the more important documents in current use.

The herculean task of anyone attempting to trace, analyse and correctly document in chronological order, the records of every steam locomotive that has been used by the New Zealand Railways Department can well be imagined and the extreme patience and painstaking research that has been displayed and undertaken by W. G. Lloyd in producing such an historical document will provide a lasting record of the proud steam era of the New Zealand Railways.

There are few who have lived in this era who have not thrilled to the high-pitched whine of the turbo-electric generator while an express train was standing at a country station awaiting a crossing during the night hours, or who have not found something to enthuse at over the commanding blast of a chime whistle as a train was speeding towards a level crossing and it is only fitting that a fully documented and well illustrated record of these workhorses should be available.

I congratulate Mr. Lloyd on the production of this register. I am sure it will prove a worthy addition to any collection of material associated with New Zealand Railway working.

FOREWORD
(Revised Edition)

E. J. McCLARE
NZR Locomotive Researcher and Historian

Unravelling the locomotive numbering systems of our early railways is a fascinating and somewhat daunting task which requires great determination and perseverance. To finally complete a Register that is 100% accurate is the goal, but there are so many side issues that cannot be resolved because early P.W.D. records are far from complete, with a large proportion being lost in the Hope Gibbons fire of 1952. Bill Lloyd has made a great attempt to put the record straight and has to be congratulated for his contribution to our knowledge of the early New Zealand Railways numbering of locomotives.

This writer first corresponded with Bill Lloyd in the 1960s and many letters have been exchanged since in the search for information to help in compiling his Register. There are lists of numbering and renumbering of locomotives mentioned in P.W.D. correspondence files but these are only headings of memos and until the actual complete documents surface, the information therein will remain a tantalising vision. In the interim he has done his best in interpreting the sometimes conflicting evidence that is contained in the early P.W.D. and Railway Statements.

This second edition of the Register is as complete as possible and further additions or alterations are expected to be minimal, unless of course more vital information should come to light.

INTRODUCTION

The identification of the railway locomotive is a diverse study of interest to many people for a variety of reasons. To the builder, the works number provides a ready means of referring to an engine for the subsequent supply of spare parts; to the railway officer, the road or running number is useful for maintenance, operating and accounting purposes; to the railway amateur, engine numbers serve many interests.

When I first became acquainted with New Zealand's railways in the mid-1950s the major source of information on the subject was found in the pages of the journal of the New Zealand Railway and Locomotive Society, *The New Zealand Railway Observer*. Enquiry revealed that a complete list of NZR locomotives was not readily available. Discussion with Society Officers suggested that such a list might prove useful to members. Accordingly, I prepared *Supplement N⁰ 5, 1957; NZR Steam Locomotive Lists 1880 - 1957*.

Supplement N⁰ 5 was not entirely satisfactory because it by no means told all of the story. During research traces of earlier systems of identification of locomotives had emerged, as did the fact that in 1918 the Chief Draughtsman of the NZR Locomotive Department had essayed a compilation of names and numbers from earlier times. Just what aroused Mr. Jenkinson's interest is not known but the Chief Clerk's reason 37 years earlier was plainly stated. After a decade of research it proved possible to sketch out schemes of numbers from the early days. A process of elimination and permutation of the collected details allowed reconstructed lists to be published as the first edition of this Register in 1974.

Much more information has been uncovered in the succeeding quarter-century. The methodology of the Public Works Department numbering is now demonstrated, Mr. Werry's problem is solved and dated North and South Island locomotive lists provided. Even so, the story is not yet complete; only one of the Canterbury Railway's narrow-gauge locomotives is matched to the maker's works list, how the Wellington section identified its engines between 1874 and 1877 is not known and there are still tantalising glimpses of number systems prior to 1877. In recent history the pedigree of the class K^A locomotives is discussed, whilst developments and alterations in appearance of the variant classes J and K are noted.

By 1971 the steam locomotive, to all intents and purposes, had gone from the NZR system. What has happened to the surviving locomotives is set out in detail. As relics are still being recovered from bush and riverbed this story will continue.

The reconstructed Public Works Department List is necessarily a creature of deduction. Although the best sources available have been used there may yet be items of information discovered which could lead to alternative conclusions. I shall be very pleased to receive any such items and to undertake debate on the subject.

W. G. Lloyd,
15 Scotia Street,
Port Chalmers,
Otago, 9005

September 2002

ACKNOWLEDGEMENTS

It would have been impossible to have undertaken the revision of this Register without the considerable support and encouragement of many friends. It gives me great pleasure to record their services.

The members of the Otago Railway and Locomotive Society Inc. cajoled me more than six years ago to undertake the task. The original version had been annotated in a desultory fashion over the previous quarter-century, mostly for my own edification.

George Emerson gave tremendous enthusiasm, encouragement and drive to the project. He supplied numerous photographs and gave considerable advice on the selection of illustrations. In his last days he saw and critiqued some of the proof pages. George keenly wished to see the project completed, alas that was not to be.

For their contributions thanks are due to Ron Grant *(A Good Many Brains at Work)* and to Bill Prebble *(The Number and Maker's Plates of NZR Steam Locomotives)*. Don Selby provided an extensive selection of material on the heritage railway locomotives. Thanks are also due to the officers of the many preservation schemes and heritage railways who reported progress on their activities and contributed information as to what others were doing.

Juliet Scoble has spent many hours searching early files of the Public Works and Railways Departments held at National Archives in Wellington and very graciously offered the results. These were of great assistance in the compilation of the PWD North Island numbering list and in the establishment of the methodology of the PWD/NZR classification system.

In the acknowledgements to the First Edition I noted the contribution made by newspaper correspondents and editors. One name must be singled out; Charles Rous-Marten, sometime editor of the *Wellington Evening Post* and the *New Zealand Times* newspapers, dispatched a series of letters to the *English Mechanic* magazine between 1878 and 1885. These New Zealand letters are a mine of information on our pioneer railways, their locomotives and train running, mostly gleaned from official information and personal observation. Because of some hearsay material included this mine became a minefield which needed to be trod warily, for herein lay the origins of the quasi-official classification of S 52 and the phantom Barclay locomotive *Carrickfergus*, which ghost Ron Grant laid to rest a century later.

Ron Grant and Jack M[c]Clare were most generous in the supply of fact, comment and argument.

Bill Cowan, Euan M[c]Queen and Toija Saniainen made useful comments on the text. Brian Pearce proof read and questioned aspects of the text.

Karl Morris spent many hours at his computer setting the text and laying out the book.

Barry O'Donnell put in considerable time and effort designing the new dust cover and the fly-sheet illustration layouts.

The illustrations were masterminded and sought out by Reid M[c]Naught who also edited the captions. A considerable number of photographs from their cameras were supplied by Jack Creber, Richard Croker, Keith Cullen, George Emerson, Les Hostick, Jack M[c]Clare, Reid M[c]Naught, Graham Radcliffe, David Sims, Trev Terry and Denys Whyte. The Godber Collection held at the Alexander Turnbull Library, National Library of New Zealand, as well as the E. J. M[c]Clare, T. A. M[c]Gavin, S. A. Rockliff and W. W. Stewart Collections provided a great many images.

The Directors of the Hocken Library, Dunedin and the Port Chalmers Museum assisted greatly in providing access to their files of the *Otago Daily Times* newspaper and to the Journals of the Otago Provincial Council and the Appendices to the Journals of the House of Representatives. The Editors, past and present, provided a great deal of information from the files of the magazines, *The New Zealand Railway Observer, New Zealand Railfan, The New Zealand Model Railway Journal* and *Rails*, thereby assisting in the revision of the Register.

To all of these people and to any others I may have inadvertently omitted my very considerable thanks are due.

CHAPTER ONE

MR. WERRY'S PROBLEM

"Mr. Maxwell.
I cannot find any trace of the system of which the North Island stock has been numbered in the past, and before dealing with this I think it would perhaps be as well to ask managers to send in returns of stock as numbered, when some clue might be obtained as to how the numbers run."

This brief memorandum to the General Manager of the newly formed Railways Department was made by Mr. W. N. Werry (probably Chief Clerk) on 18 March 1881 to a request from the District Manager of the Auckland section for locomotive and rolling-stock numbers. The suggestion found favour and a circular letter was despatched to the managers of the several sections asking for the details. These duly came to hand setting out the numbering as at 31 March 1881.

Eighty-five years later the replies were rediscovered. Whether Mr. Werry made a tabulated statement cannot be established from the file. Had he done so, the system would have become evident and thus his problem would have been solved.

Apart from a list of the Hurunui-Bluff section engines published in the 1880 Appendix to the Journals of the House of Representatives, these are the earliest authentic lists known. Since so much of the reasoning to be found in these pages is based on the replies, it is worth quoting the consolidated list in full.

LOCOMOTIVE NUMBERS AS AT 31 MARCH 1881

SOUTH ISLAND RAILWAYS
HURUNUI-BLUFF SECTION

Class	Numbers	Class	Numbers	Class	Numbers	Class	Numbers
O	1, 2	E	23-26	G	55-58	L	91
M	3, 4	B	27	P	59	K	92-97
C	5	R	28-30, 32, 33	A	60-71	F	98-100
A	6	F	34, 35, 38	O	72-74	T	101-106
O	7-10	O	39-45	F	75-79	J	107-110
F	11-14	D	46-50	O	80	O	111
D	16, 18	S	52	J	81-86	R	112
O	19-21	C	53	K	87-88	J	115-124
R	22	P [1]	54	M	89-90	R. & A.F.R. [2]	1, 2

N° 15 sent to Nelson. N° 17 sent to Picton. N° 31 sent to Greymouth. N° 51 sent to New Plymouth, Numbers 36 and 37 with Public Works Department (PWD). N° 113 Hakataramea Company's engine. N° 114 "missing number".

PICTON SECTION	WESTPORT SECTION
D 17 C 11 C 125	C 126 C 127
NELSON SECTION	**GREYMOUTH SECTION**
D 15 D 128 D 129	R 31 C 131 C 132

[1] The Manager of this section recorded N° 54 as a class D locomotive. The 1880 Appendix lists it as a P and P 54 was sold in 1885. The classification has been amended accordingly.

[2] Rakaia and Ashburton Forks Railway locomotives numbers 1 and 2 later became Q 51 and Q 17 respectively.

LOCOMOTIVE NUMBERS AS AT 31 MARCH 1881

NORTH ISLAND RAILWAYS

Class	Class Total	Locomotive Numbers	Class	Class Total	Locomotive Numbers
AUCKLAND SECTION			**PATEA-MANAWATU SECTION**		
F	9	1, 2, 4, 5, 6, 7, 8, 9, --	E	3	23, 24, --
B	1	10	F	6	25, 26, 27, 28, 29, --
L	4	11, 12, 13, 14	L	1	30
R	2	Not numbered	R	5	Not numbered
WHANGAREI SECTION			--	2	Small locomotives built in Wellington, not numbered
F	2	3 (from Auckland) --	**WELLINGTON SECTION**		
KAIPARA SECTION			C	2	32, --
			D	3	33, 34, --
C	1	15	H	4	35, 36, 37, 38
D	1	16	L	4	39, 40, 41, 42
			R	3	Not numbered
NAPIER SECTION			**NEW PLYMOUTH SECTION**		
C	3	1, 2, 4	A	2	43, 44
D	2	Not numbered	C	2	45, 46
F	4	18, 19, 46, 47	D	3	51, --, --

A dash (--) indicates an engine without a number.

Two valuable pieces of information can be taken from this tabulation. Firstly, there was a separate list of locomotive numbers for each island. However, the more interesting point is that the lists reveal that there were earlier sequences of numbers. The oldest locomotives do not have the lowest numbers and there is some duplication. How, when and where did the earlier numbers arise? These were the basic questions. It is hoped that the succeeding pages will throw more than a glimmer of light on the problems.

In the interests of chronology, the methods adopted by the Railways Department to identify its rolling stock will be discussed at a later point. Our attention is now turned to the earliest locomotives used in the country.

CHAPTER TWO

THE BROAD-GAUGE LOCOMOTIVES

The steam locomotive made its debut in New Zealand six decades after Richard Trevithick demonstrated the first locomotive at Penydarren in 1804, or thirty-four years after George and Robert Stephenson showed it to be a practical proposition and just twenty-three years after the founding of the colony. The Invercargill wharf was the venue for the demonstration of *Lady Barkly* on 8 August 1863, whilst *Pilgrim* arrived at Ferrymead, Canterbury, on 6 May in the same year, and was in use working ballast trains in mid-November. Newspaper reports provide the sole evidence for these names and there is considerable doubt that they were actually carried on the locomotives.

THE ORETI RAILWAY

The Oreti Railway was opened between Invercargill and Makarewa on 18 October 1864. It was beset by misfortune, both financial and physical: the physical, wooden rails, being a consequence of the financial. It was moribund by early 1867. There were four locomotives, only once was more than one in steam at any one time. Indeed, one was not placed in service on the line at all. Two are known to have been numbered and three are reported as having names.

Road Number	Type	Builder	Year Built	Name
	2-2-0	Hunt and Opie	1861	*Lady Barkly*
2	2-2-0	Robinson Thomas and Co.	1864	
3	2-2-0	Robinson Thomas and Co.	1864	
	2-4-0		1865	

Lady Barkly was demonstrated on the Invercargill wharf on 8 August 1863. It was used by the contractor until 7 April 1865, then worked trains after this date. Later it was sold and worked for Massey and Company, sawmillers, Woodend, about 1886 as a 3ft 6in gauge 0-4-0 locomotive. The locomotive was originally built to 5 feet 3 inch gauge and the railway to 4 feet 8½ inch, inevitably the wooden rails were damaged.

N⁰ 2 commenced work hauling ballast trains on 6 September 1864 and was photographed on the opening day of the railway, 19 October 1864. In May 1865 the track was declared not fit to carry this locomotive; it did, however, receive a further trial run in December 1866 when five wooden rails were broken.

N⁰ 3 was never put into service on the Oreti Railway.

Both numbers 2 & 3 were sold to the sawmilling industry about 1869. One was hauled by bullock team from Invercargill to Makarewa on 10 April 1869. The other was moved in similar manner from Hare and Pratt's mill at Invercargill to the railway station *en route* to Sykes and Tulloch's mill, Makarewa, in December 1873. One was in use on a bush tramway about 1880 and its boiler was in stationary use between 1903 and 1917.

R. M. Marchant, the Southland Provincial Engineer and J. R. Davies, contractor, concocted the fourth locomotive from the frame of the tender of the unused N⁰ 3 engine and a portable steam engine. It was put into service as a locomotive on 21 September 1865. Suffering a broken crankshaft on 23 October 1865 it did not run again as a locomotive on the railway.

THE BLUFF HARBOUR AND INVERCARGILL RAILWAY

Southland's other railway venture was contemporary with the ill-fated wooden line. Construction commenced in 1863 and the line opened between Bluff and Invercargill on 5 February 1867. All three locomotives were shipped by *Charlotte Jane* from London on 26 February 1864 and landed at Bluff on 3 and 4 August 1864. The first landed, one of the Hudswells, was christened *The Bluff*. The derelict Oreti Railway was rebuilt with iron rails

4 - The Broad-Gauge Locomotives

by 1869 and extended to Winton, where the first train arrived on 22 September 1870. A fortnight later the Provinces of Otago and Southland were united and the railway was subsequently operated as Otago Railways. The gauge of the line was altered from 4 feet 8½ inches to 3 feet 6 inches over the weekend of 18-20 December 1875. Thereafter the three locomotives were stored until sold to the New South Wales Government Railways. They left Southland in the barque *Cezarewitch* and were lost with the wreck of the vessel at Big Bay on the remote west coast of the South Island.

\multicolumn{5}{c}{**BLUFF HARBOUR AND INVERCARGILL RAILWAY LOCOMOTIVES**}
Road Number	Type	Builder	Maker's Number	Notes
1	2-4-0T	Slaughter, Gruning	?/1864	Probably maker's Nº 531
2	0-4-0ST	Hudswell and Clarke	23/1864	One christened *The Bluff*
3	0-4-0ST	Hudswell and Clarke	24/1864	Both altered to 0-4-2ST

BELOW: Southland broad-gauge. Bluff Harbour and Invercargill Railway Nº 1 (Slaughter, Gruning 531 of 1863). (S. A. Rockliff Collection)

CANTERBURY PROVINCIAL RAILWAYS

Ten locomotives were delivered to the broad-gauge lines of the Canterbury province. The *Lyttelton Times* of 7 May 1863 suggests that the first engine was named. However, a photograph taken in 1863 shows the locomotive known as *Pilgrim* plainly identified as "Nº 1" and without any trace of a name.

The last portion of the broad-gauge railway was converted to the New Zealand standardised gauge of 3 feet 6 inches on 21 December 1877. Following the change of gauge the rolling stock was sold to the South Australian Railways, leaving Lyttelton on the ships *Hydrabad* on 22 July 1878 and *Bulwark* on 5 September 1878. *Hydrabad* ran aground on Waitarere Beach near Foxton, but the cargo was subsequently salvaged. The locomotives were all put into service on the South Australian Railways between 1879 and 1882 and ran for many years.

CANTERBURY PROVINCIAL RAILWAYS LOCOMOTIVES							
Road Number	Type	Builder	Maker's Number	Date of Arrival	SAR Number	SAR Class	Date Condemned
1	2-4-0T	Slaughter, Gruning	488/62	4-1863	56	Ez	12-12-1904
2	2-4-0T	Slaughter, Gruning	532/63	4-1864	51	E	8-4-1929
3	2-4-0T	Avonside	699/66	3-1867	50	E	17-10-1900
4	2-4-0T	Avonside	742/67	5-1868	42/49	E	19-4-1929
5	0-4-2WT	Avonside	740/67	5-1868	44	M	29-4-1916
6	0-4-2WT	Avonside	741/67	5-1868	46	M	2-2-1917
7	0-4-2T	Avonside	855/71	8-1872	45	M	3-2-1917
8	0-4-2T	Avonside	964/73	3-1874	43	M	23-12-1913
9	0-4-0T	Neilson	1798/73	1-1874	38/48	I	10-1905
10	0-4-2T	Avonside	1021/74	6-1874	47	M	16-5-1917

Nº 1 was bought unused from the Melbourne and Essendon Railway, Australia. Its boiler was in stationary use at the Addington Workshops in 1876. The frame was sold to the South Australian Railways.
Nº 4 which became SAR 42 was renumbered 49 in 1880.
Numbers 5, 6, 7, 8, & 10 (SAR 43-47) were broken up in 1922.
Nº 9 which became SAR 38 was renumbered 48 in 1880. It was sold to the South Australian Harbour Works Construction Department in 1906 and was dismantled in 1909.

THE AUCKLAND AND DRURY RAILWAY

Fortune smiled faintly on the pioneer railway in the North Island, the 4 feet 8½ inch gauge line south from Auckland. The first locomotive was steamed for demonstration purposes on 5 February 1866. However, by the end of the year work had ceased due to a lack of finance and the engine spent the next five years in storage. Nº 2 arrived too late to be of use on construction trains and joined *Driver* in storage. Work recommenced in 1872 and Nº 2 was employed hauling ballast trains. A year later a third rail had been laid between the tracks and a new narrow-gauge locomotive replaced Nº 2.

There is no evidence that either locomotive carried a number. In the maker's record the name *Auckland* against MW 162 has been crossed out and *Driver* substituted. MW 201 is recorded as Nº 2. A photograph taken when this locomotive was working at the Parnell tunnel reveals that it had a nameplate. It is of interest to note a possible derivation for the name *Driver*. The first steam ship to visit New Zealand was H. M. Steam Sloop *Driver* which was stationed at Auckland.

The locomotives were sold to the Bay of Islands Coal Company, Kawakawa, MW 162 in 1871 and MW 201 in June 1874. They were used on the company's railway until 1877 and the boilers were then adapted for powering winding machinery.

AUCKLAND AND DRURY RAILWAY LOCOMOTIVES				
Number	Type	Builder	Maker's Number	Name
--	0-6-0ST	Manning Wardle	162/65	*Driver*
2	0-6-0ST	Manning Wardle	201/66	

CHAPTER THREE

THE PUBLIC WORKS DEPARTMENT NUMBERING

The passing of the Railways Act 1870 set the scene for a considerable increase in the pace of construction, mainly by contractors, with design and operation of railways undertaken by the colonial Public Works Department. Subject to an overriding control from the PWD Head Office the Provincial Councils of Otago and Canterbury had some part in the construction, particularly of branch lines, and operated the railways of those provinces as Otago Railways and Canterbury Railways. Just a year after the first government locomotives arrived an official mind realised that there should be order in the identification of engines and issued this instruction.

Public Works Office,
Wellington.
6th January 1874

Circular to Engineers,

New Zealand Railways
Instruction for the naming and numbering of engines.

8 inch cylinder engines to be named after animals, "Fox", "Ferret", etc.
9½ inch cylinder engines, four wheels, to be named after towns in New Zealand, "Wellington", "Auckland", etc.
9½ inch cylinder, six wheels, to be named after English counties, "Kent", "Essex", "Sussex", etc.
10½ inch cylinder engines to be named after names in Sir W. Scott's works, "Ivanhoe", etc.
14 inch cylinder engines to be named after classical names, "Ajax", "Diana", etc.

Besides the name, each class of engine must be numbered on both buffer beams "Nº" being placed on one side of the buffer and the "Figure" on the other.

No engine must be named without such name and number being submitted to the Engineer-in-Chief for approval.

(Signed) John Carruthers
Engineer-in-Chief.

At the date of this instruction only locomotives of the future classes C (9½ inch cylinder, 4 wheels) and F (10½ inch cylinder) had arrived in the colony. The first arrival of the 8 inch (Dubs A) locomotives was three days later, whilst classes D (9½ inch cylinder, 6 wheels) and J (14 inch cylinder) were six months and a year respectively from delivery.

Soon after the Railways Department was created in 1880, the attention of its General Manager was drawn to a lack of knowledge as to how locomotives had been numbered in the past. The steps taken to rectify this matter are related in Chapter One. The lists gathered by Mr. Werry in 1881 show that while most of the PWD system for identifying engines still existed, its composition had been lost. (References - '1881 List' or 'in 1881').

The Annual Statements of the Public Works and Railways Departments presented to Parliament, as contained in the Appendices to the Journal of the House of Representatives, contain valuable detail as to the ordering, quantity, working and numbering of locomotives. (Reference - 'AJHR, year, paper, table and page').

A recently discovered source of information is contained in the Correspondence Registers of the Public Works and Railways Department held by National Archives, Wellington. These record the receipt and brief details of the content of letters from the Managers of, mostly North Island, sections of railway. (Reference - HOCR).

These sources, together with details taken from the Railways Department's locomotive records and newspaper reports provide evidence to reconstruct entirely and to date the Public Works Department number lists, The only matter that is assumed is that locomotives were allocated numbers in the system at the time an order was placed.

Tabled are locomotive details extracted from the Inwards Correspondence Registers of the Constructed Railways and Public Works Departments. Each entry is quoted in full as in the Registers. The Registers have been treated selectively with only those entries giving locomotive details being noted.

DATE	FROM	SUBJECT
21 Jan 1874	Napier	Answer to circular regarding naming engines.
27 Apr 1875	Oamaru	Wants instructions as to the naming and numbering of engines and rolling stock.
18 Sep 1875	Wanganui	Items deficient in Nº 2, 12 ton locomotive ex-*Hindostan*.
21 Oct 1875	Foxton	Report on engine Nº 1.
27 Oct 1875	Picton	Engine *Waitohi* has been overhauled and repaired (an engine ran off the line about 3 September 1875).
7 Dec 1875	Napier	Wanting to know the number and name of new locomotive.
1 Aug 1876	Dunedin	Alterations in names of engines.
16 Aug 1876	Auckland	The General Manager wants tracings of detail work of new engines -classes B, C, D, E and F.
22 Sep 1876	Auckland	Tracing showing patches on tube plate of F 1 and F 5.
25 Sep 1876	Napier	Broken spring link, engine F 18.
28 Sep 1876	Auckland	Spark catcher of F 3.
23 Oct 1876	Foxton	Spring links class F broken.
30 Oct 1876	Foxton	Spring links for *Helen McGregor* too long, are broken.
15 Nov 1876	Foxton	Springs for ballast engine urgently required. One of *Skunk's* springs again broken.
21 Nov 1876	Foxton	*Helen McGregor* left rails, slight damage, near Feilding.
23 Nov 1876	Auckland	Tracings required of axlebox brasses, locomotive class D.
22 Feb 1877	Greymouth	Asking for tracing locomotive sandboxes, class C.
10 Apr 1877	Auckland	Mr. Stewart includes the Taupiri engine F 8 on his return.
4 June 1877	Greymouth	Alterations made in numbers of locomotives.
4 June 1877	Foxton	Alterations made in numbers of locomotives.
19 June 1877		Classification of locomotives on the Canterbury Railways.
26 June 1877	Wanganui	Alterations in numbers of engines.
27 June 1877	Napier	Renumbering locomotives.
9 July 1877	Auckland	Name of maker of air brake engine - *Marmion,* F 6 Stephenson.
24 Aug 1877	Auckland, Napier & Wanganui	Class F engines with radial axleboxes.
27 Aug 1877	Foxton	Class F engines with radial axleboxes.
10 Apr 1878	Auckland	Defective firebox of class B Fairlie engine.
16 July 1878	Head Office	Enclosing proposed alterations re classification and numbering of locomotives and rolling stock.
7 Aug 1878	Picton	Asking for lithos of method of fixing bogies under class C engines.
22 Nov 1878	Head Office	Tables showing the alteration in numbering rolling stock on the North Island railways.
16 Jan 1879	Head Office	List of alterations in numbering locomotives on the North Island sections.
25 July 1879	Head Office	Single Fairlies to be R class.

The Correspondence Registers show that an alphabetic classification for locomotives was in use on the North Island Railways as early as August 1876 and on the South Island Isolated Sections by January 1877. The first evidence of class letters on the South Island Hurunui-Bluff Section appears in May 1877.

THE CLASSIFICATION OF LOCOMOTIVES
1874 - 1971

Implicit in the Engineer-in-Chief's instruction on the naming and numbering of locomotives is the fact that before most of the types had arrived in the country, a system of classification had evolved. This, a long descriptive form based on the physical characteristics of each type, was extended to cover locomotives ordered to 1879.

The Head Office Correspondence Registers show that, by mid-1876, perhaps even as early as mid-1874, an alphabetic system of classification was in use in parallel with the cumbersome long form. Initially class letters A to J, except I which was never used, were assigned to types on order by April 1874; with cylinder diameter in ascending order as the first principle adopted, supplemented if necessary by the number of wheels where types shared a common cylinder size.

Thereafter, the allocation of class letters was chronological. Each new or acquired type was almost invariably given the next available letter. By early 1877 new classes on order became K and L; mid-1877 former Otago provincial locomotives were allocated classes M, N, O and P; 1879 saw classes Q and R added, and so on. Canterbury local custom seems to have been responsible for the 1877 nomination of the letter S to the Hughes *Robina* and for the retention of the letter O for five Avonside locomotives (F) 75-79 until 1885, four years after its official deletion. Deleted letters were available for issue to new types. The Fairlie *Lady Mordaunt*, at first class N, was reclassified to B with its twin *Snake*. The letter N was taken by an 1883 specification for 2-6-2 passenger locomotives; of the two groups built, the Americans retained class N and those of English make were reclassified to V certainly and also probably class U. Similarly, with the 2-8-0 goods locomotives, the Americans retained the O classification and the English were given the class letter P.

Rebuilding and development of existing classes D, F, L and W led to the adoption of the multiple letter system. The letter W then became the portmanteau label, suitably suffixed, for subsequent tank locomotive classes. The earliest example known is found on a contract drawing where the Scott built locomotives of 1887/8 are shown as class D^A; the 1893 Working Timetable also records this classification.

After the turn of the Twentieth Century the availability of single letters for new types was becoming scarce. The new compound passenger locomotives of 1906 were class A and with no letters available between the corresponding goods locomotives of 1908 received the next vacant letter-X. Consequently, a suffix letter was allocated to locomotives of similar specification and characteristics. For instance the 'English' U and the 'American' U became in 1903 respectively classes U^A and U^B. Locomotives acquired with the Wellington and Manawatu Railway and the New Zealand Midland Railway were suffixed at near similar types.

Although outside the bounds of this work, it is of interest to note that when the first electric locomotives were introduced in 1923 the next available letter was quite fortuitously E. It seems likely that overseas trends in motive power had been noted in 1938 and the letter D was reserved for diesel locomotives.

With the issue of suffix letters there was never any need to allocate letters Y and Z to steam locomotives. However, the last type, three small 0-6-0 tank locomotives acquired from the Public Works Department in 1938 and 1942, were given the class letter Y in 1952, skipping nine vacant letters.

NORTH ISLAND RAILWAYS

By September 1876 the Auckland section had a numerical list of locomotives from 1 to 10 with a name for each. In 1918 an old engine driver, Jack Sargent, made a list for Mr. W. W. Stewart of the early Auckland locomotives showing for each the road number, name, maker and works number. Other than for the reversal of two numbers it is not faulted. Included were class L locomotives at numbers 11-14 (not named) and two class R locomotives as R 1 and R 2.

The concept for the class L locomotives was sketched on PWD plan 5403 dated 25 November 1876. The approved design was signed in May 1877. It is concluded that some of these, the Auckland four, were interpolations into this scheme of numbers and that locomotives on order had been allocated to these numbers initially. The only locomotives on order were the Avonside class F machines covered by PWD Memorandum 55/74 of September 1874. Two parts of this order were two for Kaipara which were delivered to Napier; and five for Auckland - Ohaupo, two of which went to the Bay of Islands Coal Company at Kawakawa and the rest delivered elsewhere.

A complete sequence of numbers from 1 to 19 had been made by September 1876.

SECTION NUMBERS

Auckland 1-10	Ten locomotives in service by October 1875. It is known that numbers had been altered prior to this date. Photographs exist of *Snake* as Nº 1 and later as B 10, whilst *Ada* at first was not numbered, later becoming F 1.
10-14	Allocated for five Avonside class F locomotives, none remained in Auckland.
Kaipara 15-17	Three locomotives, C 15 and D 16, so numbered in 1881, and E 17, an Avonside Fairlie double locomotive, arriving there in March 1876. It was later transferred to Wanganui in May 1878.
Kaipara/Napier 18-19	Two Avonside class F locomotives ordered for Kaipara were delivered to Napier. One was F 18 by September 1876 and the other, by inference from its 1881 number, was F 19. The numbers may have been issued for Kaipara when the order was placed.

BELOW: *Snake*, Avonside 1022-3 of 1874, outside the Auckland workshops is carrying the original Auckland section Nº 1. This was the first British built locomotive to be fitted with Walschaert valve gear. (Cedric Green Collection)

10 - The Public Works Department Numbering

ABOVE: The same locomotive (from page 9), this time at the Pukekohe road crossing about 1879, having been renumbered B 10. (S. A. Rockcliff Collection)

BELOW: In the 1882 system of numbering *Snake* was B 51, finally becoming B 238 in 1889. The locomotive was posed with the crew outside the Auckland running shed. (S. A. Rockcliff Collection)

The second part of the North Island List was made about June 1877 when the Correspondence Register records that renumberings took place at Napier, Wanganui and Foxton.

SECTION NUMBERS

Napier
20-23

What happened at Napier is easily understood. It was the proposed elimination of an earlier set of numbers which seems not to have been carried into practice. In December 1875 the manager sought a number and name for his new locomotive, the fourth on the section. He had received two Neilson class C locomotives in November 1873, a Neilson class D a year later and finally the Dubs C. In 1881 the class C locomotives were numbers 1, 2 and 4 whilst the D locomotive, sent to Wellington in April 1879, would have been Nº 3.

Some, if not all, of the Napier locomotives were named. The *Hawke's Bay Herald* reported, among other details, the naming of locomotives: 13 October 1874, the *Hastings*, either Nº 1 or 2; 5 September 1876, *Die Vernon* - properly *Diana Vernon*, a character who appears in Scott's Waverley novel *Rob Roy* - one of the new Avonside engines F 18 or F 19.

This gem taken from the *Otago Daily Times* of 2 July 1877 identities another, the *Eel*. "Napier by telegraph. So many sheep and cattle have been killed by the engines on the Hawke's Bay Railway that it is said that three of the engines are to be re-christened. The *Eel* is to be renamed the *Cleaver* and the other two are to be named the *Sausage Machine* and the *Butcher*."

An interesting speculation is that perhaps Napier's answer to the Engineer-in-Chief's naming circular of 6 January 1874 was to suggest a substitution of 'fish', as a generic name in place of English counties for the class D locomotives. At least four of the first Neilson batch of seven were so named. At Kaipara was *Schnapper*, at Napier, *Eel* and Nelson had *Trout* and *Kingfish*.

Wanganui
24-26

There were only three locomotives at Wanganui when the renumbering was made in June 1877; in 1881 these were E 24 (*Pelican*), F 25 and F 26. The Head Office Register reference of 18 September 1875 notes that one of the class F locomotives just landed was Nº 2. Two further class E Fairlies came to Wanganui by 1879, having been transferred from Kaipara and Wellington.

Foxton
27-29

Two small locomotives, built by E. W. Mills of Wellington, arrived at Foxton in August 1875, followed by a third two months later. One, named *Opossum*, was transferred to Greymouth via Wellington in February 1877. The Section Manager made a report on "Nº 1 engine" in October 1875. Thereafter until 1877 he referred to his charges by name only. In 1881 he listed "Two small locomotives built in Wellington - not numbered" and his complement of Avonside class F locomotives, which arrived in September 1876 and January 1877 as F 27 - F 29.

Wellington
30-35

How Wellington identified its early locomotives is an enigma; a few names and no numbers survive to tell the story. Two Neilson class C locomotives were received in September 1873, one of which was *Belmont* (C 32 in 1881) and the other transferred to New Plymouth in August 1878, would have been the adjacent C 31 from 1877. Then followed two Neilson class D in 1881, D 33 and D 34. E 30 was an Avonside Fairlie double locomotive which arrived in December 1875, transferring to Wanganui in May 1879. Finally, the four Rimutaka Fell locomotives, H 35 - H 38 had 'Mount' names and were delivered in early 1876.

Auckland
11-14
Wellington
39-42
Wanganui
30

An order was placed with the Avonside Company before the end of June 1877 for ten class L locomotives. The only reference found in the Public Works Statement, June 1877 (AJHR 1877, E 1, table 6, page 31) is that ten were on order. No other information is given and the intended disposition is not known. Between July and September 1878 both Wellington and Auckland each received four. At Auckland they were numbered in the vacant series 11-14 and those in Wellington took the next available 39-42. Wanganui received one L class locomotive about March 1879, listed in 1881 as L 30. The tenth locomotive always worked in the South Island.

New Plymouth
43-46:
The original equipment at New Plymouth, *Fox* and *Ferret*, delivered in June 1874 became A 43 and A 44, so listed in 1881. These were joined by class C locomotives: one, transferred from Wellington in August 1878 was C 45 in 1881; the other, C 46 came from Westport on 23 January 1879.

Napier
46-47
Provision was made in the scheme for two Dubs class F locomotives on order by January 1878 and delivered to Napier in April 1879 as F 46 and F 47.

Renumberings, Transfers and Aberrations.
The North Island Locomotive List was complete to number 47 by August 1878, but this is not the end of the story since the Head Office Registers note proposed alterations to locomotive numbers in July 1878 and issued a list of alterations on 16 January 1879. No official action on identification appears to have been taken after the Head Office List was promulgated until the enquiries were made leading up to the Railways Department scheme of 1882.

The first locomotives of class R were delivered in April 1879, when the vessel *Peri* brought two for Wellington and one for Wanganui. They were to be known as class R by dictate of 25 July 1879. Two at Auckland were said to be R 1 and R 2. The 1881 list does not substantiate this as all class R engines in the North Island are shown "Not numbered".

The 1881 lists have vacant numbers at 17, 20-22, a duplication at 46 and aberrations which are not original numbers at 23 and 30.

The renumbering of locomotives at Napier seems to have been an unfulfilled proposal to eliminate the original numbers 1 - 4 by the issue of new numbers 20 - 23.

Kaipara E 17 was transferred to Wanganui on 5 May 1878, prior to the proposed renumbering of July 1878. It qualifies to be E 23.

Wellington C 31 was transferred to New Plymouth on 13 August 1878, within the period of the proposed and actual numbering. It qualifies to be C 45.

Napier N° 3, possibly D 23, transferred to Wellington on 5 April 1879; and Wellington E 30 transferred to Wanganui on 24 May 1879. Both fall after the date of the Head Office List and were not numbered in 1881.

New Plymouth C 46 was transferred from Westport on 23 January 1879. It thus postdated the Head Office list. This was much later than the order placed for Napier's F 46 and F 47. Therefore, C 46 is the interloper.

It is likely that numbers E 23 and L 30 at Wanganui and C 46 at New Plymouth were initiated by the local supervisors.

It can be deduced how the North Island locomotives were numbered before 1876-7. Evidence shows that Napier had a numeric system early in 1874, having enquired how locomotives should be numbered and named on 21 January and with those numbers still extant in 1881. Wanganui had a N° 2 locomotive, and by inference, a N° 1 in September 1875, as soon as these locomotives arrived there. Foxton, likewise, had a N° 1 locomotive. Auckland's sequence, probably commenced in October 1874 since it was not in the same order as the arrival of the locomotives, almost certainly became the first part of the North Island List. It is inconceivable that the district closest to Head Office would not be aware of the directive on identification or that its number system should differ from other North Island sections; as yet no trace of the early numbers for the locomotives at Wellington has been found.

NORTH ISLAND LOCOMOTIVE LIST 1876 and 1877

Section & Number	Name	Maker	Maker's Number	Renumberings and Transfers	1882 Number
Auckland		List created by September 1876			
1	*Snake*	Avonside	1022-3	Renumbered to B 10.	
F 1	*Ada*	Stephenson	2086	Not numbered at first.	F 52
F 2	*Ivanhoe*	Neilson	1706		F 51
F 3	*Lady of the Lake*	Yorkshire	239		F 55
F 4	*Lord of the Isles*	Yorkshire	240		F 56
F 5	*Flora McIvor*	Stephenson	2085		F 53
F 6	*Marmion*	Stephenson	2087		F 54
F 7	*Madge Wildfire*	Vulcan	735		F 57
F 8	*Jeanie Deans*	Vulcan	737		F 59
F 9	*MacCallum Mhor*	Vulcan	736		F 58
10-14				Five Avonside F not retained in Auckland	
B 10	*Snake*	Avonside	1022-3		B 51
L 11-14		Avonside	1208/2/3/4	Ordered by 30-6-1877	L 51-4
Kaipara					
C 15	*Kaihu*	Dubs	800		C 51
D 16	*Schnapper*	Neilson	1843		D 51
E 17	*Albatross*	Avonside	1070-1	To Wanganui, E 23, 5-5-1878	---
Kaipara/ Napier					
F 18	} *Diana Vernon*	Avonside	1086	Ordered for Kaipara, delivered to Napier.	F 41
F 19		Avonside	1089	Ordered for Kaipara, delivered to Napier.	F 42
		List created by June 1877			
Napier 20-23				Allocated for No's 1-4 next.	
1	} *Hastings*	Neilson	1770	To South Island, C 6, 11-1881.	
2		Neilson	1771	To South Island, C 31, 11-1881.	
3	*Eel*	Neilson	1844	To Wellington, 5-4-1879 (not numbered).	
4		Dubs	802	To Westport, 10-1881.	
Wanganui					
E 23	*Albatross*	Avonside	1070-1	From Kaipara, E 17, 5-5-1878.	E 21
E 24	*Pelican*	Avonside	1068-9		E 22
F 25	*Guy Mannering*	Yorkshire	245		F 22
F 26	*Meg Merrilies*	Yorkshire	244		F 21
Foxton					
1	*Skunk*	Mills		No 1 may or may not have been *Skunk*.	
	Wallaby	Mills			
	Opossum	Mills		To Greymouth 13-2-1877.	
F 27	*Helen McGregor*	Avonside	1084		F 23
F 28	*Dougal*	Avonside	1136		F 24
F 29	*Black Dwarf*	Avonside	1135		F 25
Wanganui					
L 30		Avonside	1207	Ordered by 30-6-1877, Delivered to Wanganui c. 3-1879	L 21

14 - The Public Works Department Numbering

NORTH ISLAND LOCOMOTIVE LIST 1876 and 1877 (continued)					
Section & Number	Name	Maker	Maker's Number	Renumberings and Transfers	1882 Number
Wellington					
E 30		Avonside	1066-7	To Wanganui, 24-5-1879.	E 23
C 31		Neilson	1765	To New Plymouth, C 45, 13-8-1878.	
C 32	*Belmont*	Neilson	1764	Sold 3-10-1882.	C 1 (?)
D 33		Neilson	1846		D 1
D 34		Neilson	1845		D 2
H 35	*Mont Cenis*	Avonside	1075		H 1
H 36	*Mount Cook*	Avonside	1074		H 2
H 37	*Mount Egmont*	Avonside	1072		H 3
H 38	*Mount Tongariro*	Avonside	1073		H 4
L 39-42		Avonside	1200/1/5/6	Ordered by 30-6-1877.	L 1-4
New Plymouth					
A 43	*Fox*	Dubs	646		A 21
A 44	*Ferret*	Dubs	645		A 22
C 45		Neilson	1765	From Wellington, C 31, 13-8-1878.	C 21
C 46		Dubs	801	From Westport, 23-1-1879.	C 22
Napier					
F 46		Dubs	1169	On order by 1-1878.	F 43
F 47		Dubs	1170	On order by 1-1878.	F 44

BELOW: *Ada* worked the first train to Onehunga and was named at Auckland on 20 December 1873. The nameplate, temporarily fixed to the handrail, was later placed in the position occupied by the maker's plate which was then moved to the sandbox. (W. W. Stewart Collection)

The Public Works Department Numbering -15

ABOVE: *Jeanie Deans*, Vulcan 737 of 1875, was numbered F 8 in the North Island list. (S. A. Rockcliff Collection)

BELOW: L 12, Avonside 1202 of 1877, clearly displays an early Auckland section number. Later it became Auckland L 52 in 1882 and finally L 265 in the 1890 List. (S. A. Rockcliff Collection)

16 - The Public Works Department Numbering

SOUTH ISLAND RAILWAYS

There was a fundamental difference between the railways of Otago and Canterbury as opposed to those elsewhere. These two provinces operated their railways as separate entities, indeed, both councils built several branch lines. A large degree of autonomy was taken, subject to an overriding control by the PWD. Each province had, amongst other matters, a separate locomotive list approved by the Engineer-in-Chief.

After the abolition of the Provinces in 1876 a brief interim arrangement of numbers appears to have had currency in Canterbury. However, all was replaced by a completely new scheme for these combined railways in 1877.

Parliament debated the question of railway gauge in 1870. At this time there were three sections of railway already built using two track gauges. These were the English and World Standard of 4 feet 8½ inches (1435mm) and the Irish gauge of 5 feet 3 inches (1600mm). The Railways Act specified 'narrow-gauge', permitting a maximum width of 3 feet 6 inches (1067mm). In the light of the country's rugged terrain the adoption of the latter gauge was a wise decision.

THE DUNEDIN AND PORT CHALMERS RAILWAY COMPANY LIMITED

The Port Chalmers Railway, the first built to the newly adopted New Zealand gauge, was constructed by a private company and opened for traffic on 31 December 1872. It was purchased by the Colonial Government in April 1873 and immediately vested in the Otago Provincial Council. The two eight-wheeled Fairlie double locomotives were landed from *Wave Queen* at Port Chalmers on 28 August 1872. In due course they were numbered in the Otago Railways list.

DUNEDIN AND PORT CHALMERS RAILWAY LOCOMOTIVES							
DPCR Number	Name	Type	Builder	Maker's Number	Steam Trial	Otago Railways Nº
1	*Rose*	0-4-4-0T	Vulcan	636/72	14-9-1872	6
2	*Josephine*	0-4-4-0T	Vulcan	637/72	10-9-1872	7

BELOW: Dunedin and Port Chalmers Railway Nº 2 locomotive, *Josephine*, at Wickliffe Terrace, Port Chalmers, probably photographed while on a trial run in September 1872. (Burton Brothers)

OTAGO RAILWAYS

Otago Railways comprised lines at Invercargill, Dunedin and Oamaru. Those at Invercargill were the broad-gauge tracks between Bluff and Winton, which until the purchase of the Port Chalmers Railway in April 1873 comprised the whole of the Otago system.

The key to the solution of the Otago Railways Locomotive List was found in two documents. The first, a handwritten list, was discovered attached to the inside of an old cupboard which presumably had belonged to the Provincial Railways Department. (Reference - 'The Dunedin Locomotives List').

\multicolumn{8}{c}{**LOCOMOTIVES ON THE DUNEDIN DISTRICT RAILWAY LINES 19 APRIL 1876**}

Number of Engine	Name of Engine	Kind of Engine	Number of Wheels	Number of Cylinders	Diameter of Cylinders	Weight in Tons Loaded for Work	Name of Importing Ship
6	*Rose*	Fairlie	8	4	10 inch	28 ⎫	Bought with the Port
7	*Josephine*	Fairlie	8	4	10 inch	28 ⎭	Chalmers Line.
18		Fairlie	8	4	9 inch	25	Imported by the Superintendent.
23		Fairlie	8	4	10 inch	35	*Zealandia*
24		Fairlie	8	4	10 inch	35	*Zealandia*
25		Fairlie	8	4	10 inch	35	*Mataura*
8	*Edie Ochiltree*		6	2	10½ inch	17	*Palmerston*
10	*Rob Roy*		6	2	10½ inch	17	*Asia*
11	*Waverley*		6	2	10½ inch	17	*Asia*
17	*Peveril*		6	2	10½ inch	17	*Nelson*
12			6	2	10½ inch	17	*Atrato*
9			4	2	9½ inch	14	*Rokeby Hall*

Pencilled additions to the list were: against N° 12 the name *Dandie Dinmont*, and to the foot of the name column *Nigel*, *Pinute* (sic), and *Roderick Dhu*.

The second document is an old correspondence register. It appears that a majority of the letters noted came from the Oamaru district of the former Otago Railways, which was physically linked to the former Canterbury Railways in February 1877. The Provinces and Provincial Councils were abolished in November 1876 and subsequently the railways came under the control of the Public Works Department. (Reference - Canterbury Correspondence Register - 'CCR').

This Register contains references to four series of numbers; Otago Railways, Canterbury Railways, a Canterbury interim list and a new list of engines noted on 3 December 1877 but certainly commenced in the previous July. Any number above 51 belongs to the new list. The problem was to unravel the numbers belonging to the other three series. These extracts of references from the Register provide clues to locomotive identification at Oamaru.

THE INWARD CORRESPONDENCE REGISTER OF THE CANTERBURY ENGINEERING DEPARTMENT (Abridged)

DATE	SUBJECT
4-5-1877	Engine N° 23 unsuitable, Waiareka Branch.
5-5-1877	N° 31 engine, broken spring.
8-5-1877	Re numbers 27 and 31.
14-5-1877	Stores, numbers 19, 20 and 13.
20-5-1877	Re classification of engines.
23-5-1877	Numbers 26 and 27 at Oamaru.
25-6-1877	Re bogie engine N° 3.
16-5-1877	Re firebars 21 and 24.
8-6-1877	Differences in class F & O engines.
22-7-1877	Re engines N° 57 and 31.
17-8-1877	Repairs G 2 engine.
25-9-1877	Re C 53, N° 28 and N° 51, Oamaru.
29-9-1877	Forward N° 28 small engine for repairs (Oamaru)
13-10-1877	Re 57 unfit for Breakwater line.
30-10-1877	Visit to Oamaru with A 10 engine.
7-11-1877	N° 31 'O' engine requires ports facing.
1-12-1877	From Engineer Invercargill, re two locos ex-*Hopeful*.
3-12-1877	Re new numbers on engines and list of engines.
8-12-1877	Re engine P 54 setting fire to gorse.
11-12-1877	Re F 19 exhaust pipes.
11-12-1877	Re mileage worked by numbers I and 2, Invercargill engines.
10-1-1878	Flanges on *Mazeppa* and *Corsair*.
13-5-1878	M 89 (ex-Invercargill N° 2) repairs.

In 1918 a similar essay to the present was attempted and some of the correspondence from both the Public Works Department officers and senior Railways' officers has survived. In the main this consists of lists of photographs but there are letters written by elderly locomotive drivers. Whilst these letters of reminiscence do contain errors they are valuable because they were written by men who worked with the locomotives from the very earliest days. Men who, because of the long hours of work and lengthy periods spent in travelling to and from work, had little time for other interests.

Other sources are photographs, particularly those showing a legible maker's number plate, newspaper reports and government papers.

The new series of numbers made in July 1877 is set out in Chapter Four. This was made before any of the Otago sections of line were linked together. In this renumbering it appears that a block of numbers was allocated to each section, Invercargill from 1 up, Dunedin 21 up, and Canterbury (including Oamaru) from 51 up. Concluding that any locomotive found in a block of numbers was an original locomotive on that section it is possible to reconstruct the Otago Railways locomotive list.

NUMBERS

1 - 3   These are quoted in the 1873 Otago Provincial Council Reports. Since there were no narrow-gauge lines open at this time, these must be the broad-gauge locomotives. There is no reason to suspect that the Bluff Harbour and Invercargill Railway numbers were altered.

4, 8   The 1874 Otago Council Reports quote an additional number, that being N° 4, together with a statement that the "Woodlands" section was opened for traffic. The "Woodlands" section was the first stage of narrow-gauge main trunk railway from Invercargill. There being only three broad-gauge locomotives, the new number must belong to a narrow-gauge engine. Three locomotives arrived at Dunedin from Glasgow in the ship *Palmerston* on 6 December 1872. There is no doubt that these were the Neilson built locomotives, maker's numbers 1691, 1692 and 1706. Two were sent from Dunedin almost immediately, 1706 to Auckland and the other to Invercargill. Neilson

The Public Works Department Numbering - 19

1691 was at Invercargill in 1877 and was presumably N° 4, leaving 1692 as the contender for N° 8 at Dunedin.

The name of N° 8 is recorded in the Dunedin Locomotives List of April 1876 as *Edie Ochiltree*. The *Otago Daily Times* of 19 May 1873 recorded "A very satisfactory trial of the new engine *Clutha* was made on Saturday afternoon on the Southern Trunk Line...."

5, 9   By similar reasoning these are Neilson 1768 and 1769 respectively. "A second toy engine mounted on a truck arrived at Winton... it is called *The Rat*..." from the *Southland Times*, 25 October 1875. And "I do not think that from eight to ten miles an hour would be too fast to drive the engine which is termed a grasshopper engine - a four-wheeled coupled engine... I thought that the engine was too heavily weighted behind, that it hung over the back wheels too much... There is another engine of the same type in Southland..." Evidence from an inquest reported in the *Otago Daily Times*, 17 May 1877.

6, 7   The Dunedin Locomotives List records that these were the two locomotives of the Dunedin and Port Chalmers Railway, *Rose* and *Josephine*.

10 - 12   Three six-coupled locomotives, built in 1873, two by Neilson and the other by Black Hawthorn were delivered to the Dunedin section. N° 10, *Rob Roy*, is known from newspaper and photographic evidence to be Neilson 1842. Neilson 1841, which also arrived on the ship *Asia* is N° 11, *Waverley*. The remaining engine N° 12, built by Black Hawthorn, is known to have been shipped by *Atrato*. *The Bruce Herald*, 21 August 1874, noted that the locomotive working on the Waihola section had been christened *Ivanhoe*. Photographs reveal that this was the distinctive Black Hawthorn locomotive. It is noted that in the original compilation of the Dunedin Locomotives List no name was shown against this locomotive, subsequently *Dandie Dinmont* was pencilled in on the list. The Head Office Correspondence Register notes on 1 August 1876 alterations of names to Dunedin locomotives.

13   Oamaru newspapers gave comprehensive reports which provide useful references to the names, numbers and types of locomotives used for the opening of the railway between Oamaru and Moeraki on 4 November 1876.

"The first train into Oamaru left Moeraki at 7:30 a.m drawn by *Talisman* (one of Brogdens engines)... The train from the junction (Waiareka) drawn by N° 13 bogie engine known as *Possum* arrived soon after. Shortly after 9 a.m. the engines *Possum* and *Bothwell* drew nine carriages and a van up to the station platform... This train departed at 9:30 a.m.... The second train of ten carriages and a van drawn by *Roswal* and *Talisman* left Oamaru at 11:05 a.m...."

All of the locomotives at Oamaru were either four-coupled or six-coupled machines except Neilson 1848, a 2-4-0T. This locomotive was the only one of its type in Otago or Canterbury. It had previously worked for contractors building the Invercargill to Mataura railway at Kamahi, north of Woodlands.

14 - 17
(18)
19 - 20   By Public Works Memorandum 28/73 of 2 June 1873, seven six-coupled saddle tank locomotives were ordered from the Yorkshire Engine Company for Otago Railways. It was intended that four would be delivered to Oamaru and three to Invercargill. One of the Oamaru locomotives was kept on the Dunedin section and was photographed both at Stirling and Balclutha as *Peveril*, N° 17 on the Dunedin Locomotive List. Yorkshire 248 was the only locomotive of this make in the Dunedin portion of the 1877 renumbering. It can be deduced from the Dunedin Locomotives List and the Canterbury Correspondence Register which numbers were used in Dunedin and Oamaru; thus by inference numbers 14-16 were at Invercargill. N° 14 was the leading locomotive of three which drew an excursion train from Invercargill at the opening of the Mataura line of railway. Numbers 14-16 of Otago Railways, Yorkshire 241-243, became F 12-14 in the Invercargill portion of the 1877 renumbering. It is not known which maker's number matched the Otago running number.

In 1877 all of the Oamaru locomotives were numbered into the Canterbury portion of the new list, with the three Yorkshires 246, 247 and 249 becoming O 72-74. Otago Nº 20, *Saladin,* is known from a photograph to be Yorkshire 247. Another pair of photographs show that *Roswal*, F 32 in the interim scheme of numbers, was of the same manufacture. F 19, also of the interim numbering noted in the Canterbury Register matches the name *Talisman* as the third of the Yorkshire trio.

This leaves the question. What was the Otago Railways number allocated to *Roswal*? Assuming that numbers were allocated when locomotives were ordered the whole batch would be 14 - 20, with *Roswal* at Nº 18. However, this locomotive was delivered new to and erected by contractors and thus probably did not carry the number. Consequently it was available for reissue.

18   The Dunedin Locomotives List shows Nº 18 as a Fairlie locomotive smaller than the remainder and noted as "Imported by the Superintendent". It was ordered by the Otago Provincial Council on 24 September 1873 from the Avonside Company. Delivered by the *Wild Deer* at Port Chalmers in February 1875 and was erected in Dunedin, where it remained. Avonside issued two works numbers to every Fairlie double locomotive it made. Avonside 1044-5 was widely and commonly known as *Lady Mordaunt.* The name never appeared on the locomotive and is said to have been bestowed by driver Thomas Gallaway at Burkes Brewery on the occasion of a trial run.

1 - 3 & 22   The broad-gauge locomotives were stored after December 1875. Four six-coupled locomotives were ordered by the Otago Provincial Council from the Hunslet Engine Company. Arriving in August and November 1875 they were given the numbers vacated by the broad-gauge locomotives and the next lowest available, Nº 22. There is no mention of Nº 22 in either the Dunedin Locomotives List or the Canterbury Correspondence Register.

23 - 25   The Dunedin Locomotives List notes these as three Fairlie locomotives. Other than the addition of the class letter the numbers were not altered when the PWD made its new South Island list in 1877. They were ordered by the PWD for the Lawrence branch line railway in April 1874. The *Otago Daily Times* of 26 May 1877 notes complaints from Lawrence concerning the rundown condition of locomotives used on that line and enquired as to the whereabouts of the Fairlie locomotives named *Tuapeka* Nº 1 and *Tuapeka* Nº 2 imported for the line.

21, 26 - 28   The Otago Provincial Council purchased four small locomotives which were all stationed at Oamaru. Of the two wharf locomotives imported by the contractors, Walkem and Peyman, the small one, a vertical-boilered machine built by Chaplin of Glasgow (their number 1455), was bought by the Otago Provincial Council on 26 January 1876. The larger Hughes machine named *Robina* arrived at Port Chalmers on 29 April 1876 and, as agreed, was purchased by the Council on its arrival. Two locomotives put together by Davidson of Dunedin, *Weka* delivered on 13 May and *Kiwi* delivered on 15 October 1876 complete the quartet. The numbers 21 and 26 to 28, noticed in the Canterbury Correspondence Register, are allocated to these four locomotives.

The next, and last, locomotives ordered by the Public Works Department specifically for Otago Railways were nine 0-6-0 saddle-tanks from the Avonside Company. Public Works Memo 55/74 of 25 September 1874 scheduled these as five for Dunedin - Invercargill and four for Winton - Kingston. There is some justification for an assumption that the Dunedin five were intended to be Numbers 29-33, with the Southland four following.

29 - 32,   Among the references to Otago locomotives in the engine drivers' reminiscences are "... Nº 29, *Nigel,* later F 40 (Avonside 1090), Nº 30, *Pirate* and Nº 32, *Roderick Dhu...*" These names were also added in pencil at the foot of the Dunedin Locomotives List. *Nigel* was photographed on two separate occasions at Stirling. Two more of the first batch of Avonsides, maker's numbers 1091 and 1093, are found in the Dunedin portion of the 1877 List. Reminiscences also note "*Rothwell* (sic) was transferred from Oamaru to Dunedin in 1878. This engine was afterwards F 80..." The Canterbury Correspondence Register quoting "Nº 31" and "Nº 31 'O' engine...." together with the name *Bothwell* taken from Oamaru newspapers provide clues to the earlier identity of the locomotive F 80 in 1877 (Avonside 1085).

33 onwards Hereafter a paucity of references preclude a further reconstruction. In addition more Avonsides came to Otago than were ordered. The four Avonsides of the second batch at Dunedin were maker's numbers 1140, 1142-1144. Avonside 1144 arrived at Port Chalmers on board *Wanlock* on 22 July 1877, after the first of the new 1877 numbers had been placed on an engine (Reference CCR 2-7-1877 Nº 57).

The six Southland locomotives were Avonside 1094, 1095, 1133, 1134, 1137 and 1141. The only reference to numbers of Invercargill locomotives is found in the *Southland Times* of 17 May 1878 which reported heavy snow conditions on the Kingston line. "The gallant little F 1,... at Elbow (now Lumsden) engine Nº 37..." F 1 was certainly of the new 1877 PWD numbering scheme and with F 2 would not have become so until after the departure of the former Invercargill numbers 1 and 2 locomotives to Christchurch in December 1877.

Shanks Two small locomotives built by Alexander Shanks and Son, Arbroath, came into PWD ownership in November 1876. These had been ordered by contractor David Proudfoot for use on the Western Districts Railways in Southland at the expense of the Otago Provincial Council, and were delivered at Bluff in January 1876. David Proudfoot was released from his contract in the same month as the Provinces were abolished. *Kangaroo* was sent from Bluff to Greymouth in April 1877 for use on harbour construction works. *Mouse* remained in Southland and became A 6 in the 1877 PWD South Island List.

BELOW: Otago Railways Nº 20, *Saladin*, Yorkshire 247 of 1874, at Oamaru about 1875. The style of lettering and cartouche are unusual. (S. A. Rockcliff Collection)

22 - The Public Works Department Numbering

OTAGO RAILWAYS LOCOMOTIVE LIST

Road Number	Type	Name	Builder	Maker's Number	1877 number
1	2-4-0T		Slaughter, Gruning	531/64	--
2	0-4-2ST		Hudswell & Clarke	23/64	--
3	0-4-2ST		Hudswell & Clarke	24/64	--
4	0-6-0ST		Neilson	1691/72	F 11
5	0-4-0ST	*Rat*	Neilson	1768/73	C 5
6	0-4-4-0T	*Rose*	Vulcan	636/72	E 27
7	0-4-4-0T	*Josephine*	Vulcan	637/72	E 26
8	0-6-0ST	*Edie Ochiltree*	Neilson	1692/72	F 36
9	0-4-0ST		Neilson	1769/73	C 22
10	0-6-0ST	*Rob Roy*	Neilson	1842/73	F 37
11	0-6-0ST	*Waverley*	Neilson	1841/73	F 38
12	0-6-0ST	*Dandie Dinmont*	Black Hawthorn	277/73	F 34
13	2-4-0T	*Possum*	Neilson	1848/74	D 51
14 *	0-6-0ST		Yorkshire	241/74	F 12
15 *	0-6-0ST		Yorkshire	242/74	F 13
16 *	0-6-0ST		Yorkshire	243/74	F 14
17	0-6-0ST	*Peveril*	Yorkshire	248/74	F 35
(18)	0-6-0T	*Roswal*	Yorkshire	249/74	F 74
19	0-6-0ST	*Talisman*	Yorkshire	246/74	F 72
20	0-6-0ST	*Saladin*	Yorkshire	247/74	F 73
18	0-4-4-0T	*Lady Mordaunt*	Avonside	1044-5/74	B 21
21 *	0-4-0VBT		Chaplin	1455/71	--
1 *	0-6-0T	*Corsair*	Hunslet	141/75	M 90
2 *	0-6-0T	*Mazeppa*	Hunslet	142/75	M 89
3 *	0-6-0T	*Werner*	Hunslet	143/75	M 3
22 *	0-6-0T	*Manfred*	Hunslet	144/75	M 4
23	0-4-4-0T		Avonside	1060-1/75	E 23
24	0-4-4-0T		Avonside	1064-5/75	E 24
25	0-4-4-0T		Avonside	1062-3/75	E 25
26 *	0-6-0ST	*Weka*	Davidson	1/76	P 54
27 *	0-6-0ST	*Kiwi*	Davidson	3/76	P 59
28 *	0-4-0ST	*Robina*	Hughes	not known	S 52
29	0-6-0ST	*Nigel*	Avonside	1090/76	F 40
30	0-6-0ST	*Pirate*	Avonside	1091 or 1093/76	F 44 or 19
31	0-6-0ST	*Bothwell*	Avonside	1085/75	F 80
32	0-6-0ST	*Roderick Dhu*	Avonside	1091 or 1093/76	F 44 or 19

Number 33 onwards. Nine more Avonside 0-6-0ST locomotives were numbered in the Otago Railways list.

* These numbers are computed as explained in the text.

The Head Office Correspondence Register records..."1 August 1876 - Dunedin, alterations in names of locomotives".
Nº 8 was *Clutha* by report of the *Otago Daily Times*, 19 May 1873. It was, however, according to the Dunedin Locomotives List *Edie Ochiltree*.
Nº 12 was *Ivanhoe* by report of *The Bruce Herald* on 21 August 1874, but was, according to a pencilled note on the Dunedin Locomotives List, *Dandie Dinmont*.

CANTERBURY RAILWAYS

The numbering of the Canterbury narrow-gauge locomotives still remains an enigma. There are four photographs showing engines bearing the Canterbury style of number. Of these only Nº 21 can be identified as the sole C class locomotive in the province. Some evidence of the Canterbury scheme of numbers has been obtained from the Correspondence Register: "Bogie engine Nº 3", G 2 (later than the new number 57), A 7, A 8, A 10, J 16 and in a newspaper report of a fatal accident "Nº 17 engine and tender..." can be found. The scheme set out in the table encompasses the available evidence. It is not known which road number related to particular maker's numbers; both are listed in numerical order. The relationship of maker's number to the 1877 road number is set out in Chapter Five. There is no evidence found that any Canterbury locomotive was named during the provincial period.

\multicolumn{6}{c}{CANTERBURY RAILWAYS LOCOMOTIVE LIST}
Road Numbers	Type	Builder	Maker's Numbers	Year Built	1877 Numbers
1-4	4-4-0ST	Black Hawthorn	278, 279, 281, 282	1873	G 55-58
5-14	0-4-0T	Dubs	647-656	1873	A 60-62, 64-70
15-20	2-6-0	Avonside	1038-1043	1874	J 81-86
21	0-4-0ST	Neilson	1773	1873	C 53
22-23	0-4-0T	Yorkshire	255-256	1875	A 63, A 71
24-28	0-6-0ST	Avonside	1088, 1131, 1132, 1138, 1139	1875-76	F 75-79

HURUNUI - BLUFF SECTION

When the Public Works Department took over the operation of the former Provincial Railways of Otago and Canterbury after the abolition of the Provinces in November 1876, the fledgling Hurunui-Bluff Section consisted of four disjointed segments. However, all the contracts necessary to complete the trunk line were under way with some linking imminent. However, unification was still more than two years from completion.

As soon as the rails of the Oamaru Section of the former Otago Railways were linked to the Canterbury lines through running and interchange of locomotives could occur. Confusion may have arisen from the duplication of running numbers of Canterbury locomotives numbered 1-28 with those of Otago Railways based at Oamaru and numbered 13, 19-21 and 26-28. A system was devised, whether local custom or by official fiat is not clear, to identify locomotives by both class letter and running number thus avoiding possible confusion. Alphabetic classification was introduced to the Hurunui-Bluff Section in May 1877 using the same code as applied in the North Island from 1876. Locomotives known to have been so numbered were Canterbury's G 2, A 7, A 8, A 10 and J 16 and Otago's F 19 and Nº 31 class O engine. *Roswal* may not have carried a number whilst in contractor's service. It was photographed as F 32 *Roswal*, after May 1877, taking the next number above that in use on the combined section. This interim system had only limited use and was soon in abeyance.

The classification list was extended to encompass locomotives owned outright by the former Province of Otago: class M, the Hunslet 0-6-0 tank locomotives at Invercargill; class N, the small Fairlie known as *Lady Mordaunt*, which was soon reclassified to B with the similar *Snake* of Auckland; class P, the Davidson locomotives *Weka* and *Kiwi*; class O was given to the variant of class F (see page 28) and *Robina*, the wharf locomotive was S 52. *Rose* and *Josephine* were included with the large Fairlies in class E.

The Working Railways Department took over the operation of completed railways from the PWD in 1880. Its first Annual Report to Parliament (AJHR 1880 E1) contained at Table N a list of locomotives working on the Hurunui-Bluff Section. This is the earliest official list known. AJHR 1880 E3 table 6 contains similar information for locomotives working on the Dunedin and Invercargill Sections. Thus, by inference, the Canterbury locomotives can be ascertained. (Reference - "The 1880 List").

24 - The Public Works Department Numbering

ABOVE: Canterbury Railways Nº 21, Neilson 1773 of 1873, became C 53 in mid-1877. (S. A. Rockcliff Collection)

BELOW: Another of the few photographs which show Canterbury Railways numbering. Canterbury's F 28, an Avonside locomotive, at Ashburton some time in 1875-77. (S. A. Rockcliff Collection)

The subsequent Railways Department numbering scheme of 1882 varied little from the 1880 List, which by deduction can be shown to be the Public Works Department list of 1877 with alteration caused only by addition or subtraction as locomotives were delivered to or transferred away from the sections.

The first step in the reconstruction of the Public Works Department List of 1877 was to extract from both the 1880 List and the 1881 List the numbers carried by the former provincial locomotives. This renumbering was carried out before the lines at Invercargill, Dunedin and Oamaru were linked, but after the Oamaru and Canterbury lines were joined. Several sequences emerged: Invercargill 3-14; Dunedin 23-27, 34-38, and 40-44; Canterbury 51-86. In each sequence, with one exception, P 54 and P 59, similar locomotives were grouped together. Five engines from the former provincial railways were numbered at 1, 2, 19, 89 and 90. Three provincial locomotives did not appear in the 1880 list: *Rose*, Vulcan 636, Otago Nº 6; the small wharf locomotive at Oamaru, Chaplin 1455, Otago Nº 21; and the class C locomotive transferred to Wellington in 1878, Neilson 1769, Otago Nº 9.

The Canterbury Correspondence Register and the *Southland Times* both recorded that Invercargill locomotives, numbers 1 and 2, were transferred to Christchurch by sea on 1 December 1877 and renumbered M 90 and M 89 shortly afterwards. Renumbering on transfer persisted. Nº 39, assuming that all similar locomotives on a section were grouped together, should be of class O. In the 1880 list there was an O 39 but this engine (Neilson 2409) was not delivered until May 1879. The locomotives numbers 1, 2, and 19 out of sequence were all class O. A feature of the Invercargill district records, as distinct from those of Dunedin, was that in no case is a date into service shown for any locomotive. Since this information is known for O 19 but not for O 1 and O 2 it is presumed that Otago 30 or 32, allocated to O 39, was later numbered O 19. An explanation is that it was on loan and when returned was given a new number in the list. The lowest available number seems to have been issued to both new and returned-to-traffic locomotives.

Rose, after being damaged in an accident at Shag Point on 26 September 1878, did not run again and is not mentioned in the 1880 list. Assuming that sister locomotives were grouped together *Rose* should be next to *Josephine* as E 27, but B 27, the so-called *Lady Mordaunt*, filled this space. The 1918 letters noted that this double Fairlie locomotive was transferred to Christchurch in 1878; Otago authorities would have regarded the number as being available for re-issue to a new engine on the section. It returned to Dunedin in 1879 still with its old number and was issued with the number (B) 27 of the defunct *Rose*. Since the Invercargill portion of the list commenced at Nº 1 and Canterbury's at Nº 51, it is certain that the Dunedin series commenced at Nº 21. Accordingly there were two numbers at the commencement of the Dunedin listing available, one for the class C locomotive transferred to Wellington in 1879 and the other for the *Lady Mordaunt*.

The exception to the rule that similar locomotives were numbered together is found at Oamaru with *Weka* and *Kiwi*, numbered in 1881 P 54 and P 59. *Weka,* shipped to Oamaru in May 1876, was noted in use on the Outram branch in September 1880. *Kiwi* was delivered to Oamaru in October 1876 and noted in the *Lyttelton Times* on the 1 October 1877, as working from Christchurch. Logic indicates that these locomotives should have been numbered 53 and 54 in the scheme, thus placing all of the Oamaru small locomotives together. Once it was realised that the former Canterbury Nº 21 was working in Oamaru - CCR 25 September 1877 and *Kiwi* had changed places the logic remained, the Oamaru small locomotives were indeed together. There is conflicting evidence as to which of the names *Kiwi* and *Weka* belonged to P 54 and P 59.

The 1877 List not only took cognizance of existing provincial locomotives, it also made provision for those on order. At the end of 1877 these were four class D locomotives for Southland (numbers 15-18), six class R Fairlie single-boiler locomotives for Dunedin (numbers 28-33), eight class K 'Yankee Notions', as the *Otago Daily Times* described them, for express trains between Christchurch and Invercargill (numbers 87, 88 and 92-97) and one class L tank engine (Nº 91) ordered for Christchurch. Then, early in 1878, followed an order for eight locomotives for Christchurch from Dubs, five class D (numbers 46-50) and three class O (numbers 98-100). The 1879 orders were in January, six class T 'American Consolidations' (numbers 101-106) and four 'Canterbury J' locomotives (numbers 107-110) and in July a further ten class J locomotives (numbers 115-124).

THE DISTRICT RAILWAYS

The District Railways Act 1877 permitted the setting up of limited liability companies for the purpose of building local railways. Stock and station agency companies imported locomotives to the order of these private concerns.

26 - The Public Works Department Numbering

The following extract from the Annual Report of the Dunedin Chamber of Commerce which was printed in full in the *Otago Daily Times* of 2 July 1879 provides evidence on the supply of locomotives.

> "The locomotive power at the disposal of the Department has hitherto been even more inadequate to meet the requirements of traffic than has the supply of trucks. In this matter the Government appears to have been singularly unfortunate in the manner in which an order for six locomotives sent home as long ago as November 1877 has been executed. Only two of these engines have yet arrived. These came on the "Benares" and if they could have been promptly landed they would have been in use by the time some weeks ago when the complaints of the public were loudest and would have materially assisted the General Manager in the difficulties in which he was placed. The Committee was glad under these circumstances, on urging the Hon. Minister for Public Works to purchase four locomotives which have been imported for private companies, to be informed that he had already taken that step. The Committee understands that three of these engines may be almost immediately ready for use. In addition to the six engines ordered from England a further order was dispatched three months ago to the Baldwin Locomotive Works of Philadelphia for six ten-wheeled consolidation engines similar to those in use on the New South Wales Zig Zag line."

THE NATIONAL MORTGAGE AND AGENCY COMPANY - WAIMATE RAILWAY COMPANY'S LOCOMOTIVE

A paragraph in the 1918 series of letters from elderly railwaymen reads :-

> "The Roderick Dhu was Nº 32 and not 111 as per your list. Nº 111 was certainly a Dubs engine but never had a name, This engine was imported for a private company - I think the Waimea Plains Company but I would not be sure. I have a distinct recollection of this engine being erected in the station yard at Dunedin and after erection being taken over by the Government and run between Dunedin and Clinton, J Forrester being the driver."

To be very fair to this old gentleman he did qualify his thought on the intended company and was certainly correct in his recollection of private locomotives being erected in Dunedin. However, Dubs 1233 was put together at Christchurch.

The Chairman and officers of the Waimate Railway Company gave evidence before the 1880 Railways Commission (AJHR paper E3 pages 62ff) stating: -

> "The company have imported 1500 tons of 52 pound rails and fastenings and one locomotive... through the National Mortgage and Agency Company... (this) was held for a period of six months after delivery in the colony according to agreement... when this time had elapsed the NMA Co. pressed for payment and threatened legal proceedings. The Directors, ascertaining that their debenture would not float through a defect in the District Railways Act, applied to the Government to take over the plant at cost price... The Company disposed of the rolling stock and rails at a low price..."

At reference 1233E, the Order Book of the Glasgow locomotive manufacturer Dubs and Company states that their locomotive Nº 1233 was made to the order of "National Mortgage, New Zealand".

The eight mile line from Waimate to Waihao Downs, built by the Waimate Railway Company, was worked by the NZR at the company's expense from its completion in 1883. F 111 (Dubs 1233) was listed as being in use on the Dunedin Section in the 1880 Railways Statement (AJHR 1880, E3, Table 6).

THE NEW ZEALAND LOAN AND MERCANTILE AGENCY COMPANY'S ORDER

The Order Book of Neilson and Company of Glasgow records an order, Nº E496 on 17 September 1878, for six saddle-tank locomotives, maker's numbers 2409-2414. These were built for the New Zealand Loan and Mercantile Agency Company, whose Dunedin Branch Manager was Henry Driver. On 20 May 1879 half the order was discharged at Port Chalmers from the Albion Company's ship *Westland* which had sailed from Glasgow on 20 January.

Most of the private railways in Otago were the interest of a group of Dunedin capitalists and their prospecti show common directorships with Mr Driver's name appearing on every prospectus discovered. Two were built and equipped with locomotives whilst a third, the Oreti, Waiau and Nightcaps (commonly known as the Otautau and Nightcaps Railway, *Southland Times* 1 June 1879), made considerable progress in its project including placing a tentative order for three locomotives. The Government, realising that a railway to the major Southland coalfield would be an asset, took over the project before any construction was commenced. Its locomotives, being those mentioned in the Dunedin Chamber of Commerce Report as being almost ready for immediate use, were sold to the Government and numbered at the lowest vacant numbers in the list; 20, 21 and 39. The next Albion ship to arrive, the *Otago* on 18 June at Port Chalmers, probably brought the balance of the order. These three locomotives were allocated the next lowest numbers in the list, 112-114, and were disposed of to private companies as shown in the following.

THE DUNTROON AND HAKATARAMEA RAILWAY COMPANY

Neilson's 2413, one of the New Zealand Loan and Mercantile Agency's order, was listed in the 1881 Werry List (Page 1) "F 113 Hakataramea Company's engine". A list of Public Works Department Liabilities (AJHR 1879 paper E3 page 30) notes a balance "Purchase of three locomotives - two Proudfoot, one Hakataramea, £1200"; thus showing that the PWD purchased a locomotive from this company. Proudfoot's locomotives were the two Shanks machines imported for the Western Railways of Southland (page 21). The *Otago Daily Times*, 4 March 1881, noted that on the opening day, 3 March, a train drawn by the company's locomotive ran from Duntroon to the terminus of the line at Kurow. This line was worked by the NZR at the company's expense. The 1880 list of locomotives in use on the Dunedin Section noted the presence of F 113, with a mileage run of 2394 for the year.

THE WAIMEA PLAINS RAILWAY COMPANY

This company had no doubt what it wanted. Announcing the closure of its share list (*Otago Daily Times* 27 June 1878), it stated that it had secured the services of Mr. Higgenson (sic) as its engineer and that it had telegraphed to England for rails and two locomotives that "...will be of the same description as those lately received by the Wellington and Masterton Railway and built by the Avonside Company of Bristol, having 10$^1/_2$ inch cylinders of 18 inch stroke, four wheels coupled three feet in diameter and the leading axle fitted with Windmark's (sic) patent radial axleboxes...". They wanted class L locomotives by Avonside; however, they eventually received two 0-6-0 saddle tanks by Neilson of Glasgow, their numbers 2411 and 2414.

The Waimea Plains Company, reported through the *Otago Daily Times*, 27 August 1879 that it had "...two locomotives which are erected and on the ground ready to commence ballasting operations at both ends of the line..." There is a hint of sharp practice because the *Southland Times* of 18 July noted that "the first of the engines for the Waimea Plains Railway arrived at Gore the other day from Dunedin. It was turned out by a well known English firm..." By no means could the Scottish firm of Neilson be so described, so perhaps a substitution attempt was thwarted. The *Southland Times* further noted on 9 November 1879 that one of the Waimea Company locomotives passed through Invercargill with a train of wagons *en route* for Lumsden to be used for ballasting purposes.

In due course the locomotives came into the Government fold as F 23 and F 24 when the line was purchased in 1886. The allotted numbers ,112 and 114, became available for reissue when the PWD realised that the company intended to work its railway and the locomotives accordingly would not be part of the departmental pool.

THE EXTRA CLASS R FAIRLIE LOCOMOTIVES

Six single-boiler Fairlie locomotives were ordered for the Dunedin Section in November 1877 when numbers 28-33 were issued for them. Eight such machines were delivered. The extra two, the last pair of the order of eighteen, were allocated numbers, as usual, at the lowest vacancies in the list, 22 and 112.

SUMMARY

At this point there is a complete list of locomotives from 1 to 124 for the Hurunui-Bluff Section, broken only by the omission of Nº 114. This number, formerly allocated to one of the Waimea Plains locomotives was not re-issued again until N 114 joined the NZR fleet in 1885. The 1877 Public Works List is completely reconstructed and reconciled with the 1880 Working Railways List. It was retained unaltered, transfers of locomotives away and new locomotives excepted, as the beginning of the Railways Department's first scheme of numbers. It is set out in Chapter Four (pages 33-36); The Hurunui-Bluff Section Locomotive List 1877-1890.

THE O CLASS PROBLEM

Seven manufacturers produced a total of eighty-eight locomotives originally described as "17 ton, 10½ inch cylinder, six-wheel coupled", later universally known as class F, but it was not always so. Motive power was ordered for specific areas. When locomotives arrived they were allocated on the basis of need, resulting in a mixed lot on any section. On the Hurunui-Bluff line a number of these locomotives were known as class 0.

The early members of the type had a problem. Six years after it had first been addressed the plea of the District Locomotive Supervisor Dunedin showed that it had not been solved. "The small mileage made on this section by engines with a rigid wheelbase before the tires are turned indicates the desirability of having bogie engines only. Some of the six-coupled engines have had to be sent to the shops to have tires turned up after running only 3000 miles." (AJHR 1880, E1, p. 107). In that year class O locomotives here were each running an average of 23,300 miles, while those of class F were making only 11,200 miles.

The North Island description was "Class F engines with radial axleboxes". This form appears in both the Head Office Correspondence Registers and the Public Works Statements. The Provincial Railways described them in the long form "17 ton, 10½ inch cylinder, six-wheel coupled" until 1877. In 1878 class F was of this description and class O had the addition "tank engine radial leading axle". Annual PWD statements indicate that five machines remained as class O after 1882; by 1885 this classification was extinct.

A moment's reflection will show that the geometry of radial coupled axles is an impossibility. Engineering literature is full of devices designed to move locomotives around curves with ease and without wear. This volume notes the mechanics only so far as the classification of locomotives is concerned and leaves the engineering for elaboration elsewhere. Charles Rous-Marten, sometime editor of Wellington's *Evening Post* and later editor of the *New Zealand Times* newspapers, gave the essential clue when writing in the (English) *Railway Magazine* of December 1899. He stated "... the six-coupled saddle-tank engines of class O differed from class F solely in the fact of the former being allowed a half an inch of lateral play in the leading axleboxes, whereas in the other case the wheelbase was rigid throughout." Having identified the problem, the first step in solving it was to take details from the Railways Statements 1880 (AJHR E1, Table N and E3, Table 6) of the various batches of locomotive on each section.

ROAD NUMBERS OF CLASS F AND O LOCOMOTIVES ON THE HURUNUI-BLUFF SECTION - 31 MARCH 1880

District	Class	Road Numbers	Builder and Year
Invercargill & Dunedin	O	1, 2, 7-10	Avonside 1875/6
	F	11-14	Neilson 1872, Yorkshire 1874
	O	19, 40-45, 80	Avonside 1875/6
	O	20, 21, 39, 111, 113	Neilson 1878, Dubs 1879
	F	34-38	Black Hawthorn 1873, Neilson 1872/3
Christchurch	O	72-74	Yorkshire 1874
	F	75-79	Avonside 1875/6
	F	98-100	Dubs 1878

It will be seen that the early locomotives, Neilson 1872/3, Black Hawthorn and Yorkshire are classified differently from the Avonsides of 1875/6 and succeeding locomotives and that the Christchurch district had reversed the class letter. Consistently, this district in the interim numbering listed the former Otago Railways locomotive F 19, a Yorkshire locomotive numbered later either O 72 or O 74, also an Avonside, O 31, which became O 80 when later working in Dunedin.

The Avonside locomotives were built to the same drawings as the earlier locomotives but were specified to be fitted with 'Cartazzi Patent' axleboxes on the leading axle. This device, controlled and centred by inclined slides, can be arranged to give lateral movement for coupled axles or radial movement for bogie and truck wheels. Although the classification O was extinct by the time they were delivered, a recent discovery of a Dubs drawing reveals that the Dubs locomotives of 1878-1884 were all equipped with Cartazzi axleboxes.

The answer to the class O problem has three parts:

1. Locomotives correctly classified O: 1, 2, 7-10, 19-21, 39-45, 80, 111 and 113.

2. Locomotives classified F which should have been classified O: 75-79, 98-100.

3. Locomotives classified O which should have been classified F: 72-74.

Yet there is an anomaly. The distinctive Black Hawthorn locomotive, F 34 in 1880, was sometime photographed as O 34. Perhaps it received one of the extra sets of Cartazzi gear ordered with the Avonside locomotives. The disposal of this material has never been traced. However, in January 2001 it was observed that the preserved Yorkshire locomotive of 1874, F 180 *Meg Merrilies*, while under overhaul at the Museum of Transport and Technology (MOTAT) was found to be fitted with Cartazzi slides and gear on the leading axle.

BELOW: Otago Railways Nº 25, Avonside 1062/3 of 1875, at Dunedin about 1878, was transferred to Wanganui in 1886. Written off as E 176 in 1899, the locomotive was still at work at the New Plymouth locomotive depot as late as 1915. (S. A. Rockcliff Collection)

THE SOUTH ISLAND ISOLATED SECTIONS

Some time after the order for the 'Canterbury' class J locomotives 115-124 was placed in April 1879, the locomotive stock of the four isolated sections of railways at Picton, Nelson, Westport and Greymouth was numbered into the PWD South Island List. Before this a simple numeric sequence was in use for these four railways. It is suggested that this was made about June 1877 as the Head Office Register notes "4 June 1877, Greymouth, alterations to numbers of engines" which also allows for a possibility of an earlier sequence or sequences.

The 1881 List noted numbers 11 and 125 at Picton. An old driver's reminiscence records N° 12, *Trout*, and N° 13, *Kingfisher*, at Nelson. The *Nelson Evening Mail*, 22 April 1876, gives a variation, *Kingfish*. It has already been noted that three other of the seven Neilson class D locomotives of 1874 were named in the genus *Pisces*, so *Kingfish* is more likely. Speeches made at the opening of the Brunner Coal Railway and reported in the *Grey River Argus* named the Greymouth locomotives as *Ahaura* and *Pounamu*. C 7 is depicted in a photograph taken at the foot of the Denniston Incline on the Westport Section.

The Railways Department first scheme of numbers of 1882 replaced these two series of numbers.

THE CONTINUATION OF THE SOUTH ISLAND LIST						
1879 Number	Type	Builder	Maker's Number	Name	1877 Number	Notes
PICTON						
125	0-4-0ST	Neilson	1767/73	*Blenheim*	--	Rebuilt to 0-4-2ST. Note 1
--	0-4-0ST	Neilson	1766/73	*Waitohi*	11	
WESTPORT						
--	0-4-0ST	Dubs	801/75	--	--	To New Plymouth 23-1-1879.
126	0-4-0ST	Dubs	804/75	--	--	Rebuilt to 0-4-2ST. Note 2
127	0-4-0ST	Dubs	803/75	--	--	
NELSON						
128	2-4-0T	Neilson	1847/74	*Trout*	12	
129	2-4-0T	Neilson	1849/74	*Kingfish*	13	
GREYMOUTH						
131	0-4-0ST	Neilson	1772/73	*Ahaura*	--	Rebuilt to 0-4-2ST. Note 3
132	0-4-0ST	Dubs	885/75	*Pounamu*	--	

Numbers 12, 13, 131 and 132 are certain, other pairs of numbers may be reversed. 130 was allocated at Nelson for "A third locomotive similar to those now in use (it) is about to be shipped to this section." (AJHR 1879, E1 Appendix M, page 191). This locomotive, D 15 from Hurunui-Bluff, was still D 15 in 1881.

Note 1 "The engines are in good order and have been fitted with cabs and bogies." (AJHR 1879, E3, page 91)

Note 2 "....both engines have been fitted with cabs and bogies...." (AJHR 1879, E3, page 91)

Note 3 Fitted with cabs and bogies about 1880.

CHAPTER FOUR

THE ANSWER TO THE PROBLEM

THE RAILWAYS DEPARTMENT'S FIRST SCHEME OF NUMBERS

In reply to Mr. Werry's complaint, and after a good deal of thought, an instruction emanated from the General Manager's office in Wellington on 18 April 1882. This contained details of a proposal to classify and number locomotives and rolling stock. For brevity only the details of the locomotive numbering are given below.

"The present locomotive class letters will be retained...

Each kind of locomotive stock is to be renumbered as follows: Wellington from 1 upwards to 20; Wanganui and New Plymouth from 21 upward to 40, Wanganui to complete numbering first and then supply New Plymouth with numbers; Napier from 41 up to 50; Auckland, Whangarei, Kawakawa, and Thames to number from 51 upwards; Greymouth, Westport, Picton, Nelson and Hurunui-Bluff each to be numbered independently, from 1 upwards. In renumbering a record must be retained of the old number...."

There was a degree of ambiguity in the instructions for the South Island as it was not clear whether each class or each section should be numbered from 1. The Hurunui-Bluff section retained the status-quo and did not renumber, but the Westport section, having advised the General Manager's office in Wellington in September 1883 that it had numbered its stock C 1, C 2, C 3, and F 4, was instructed in November to renumber the latter to F 1. The Picton and Nelson Sections both advised that they had completed the renumbering operation in March 1883.

In the tables the column 'Former Number' gives details of numbers from earlier series. O.R. and C.R. indicate Otago and Canterbury Railways respectively. Where uncertainty exists alternatives are given. Plain numbers relate to either the South Island Isolated Section numbers or the North Island List as the case may be. Locomotives transferred are shown by the former number, while transfer details are recorded in the 'Notes' column.

BELOW: Invercargill Roundhouse, circa 1882. The distinctive Canterbury (J 121) and Otago numbering styles appear to have persisted for some time after the linking of the two systems. (S. A. Rockliff Collection)

THE NASMYTH WILSON CLASS P and V LOCOMOTIVES

In 1883 Nasmyth Wilson and Company of Manchester contracted to supply ten each of type 2-6-2 and 2-8-0 locomotives, classes N and O respectively. When the first two of class N were received they were found to be ten tons overweight, consequently there was a considerable delay in putting these locomotives into service. In the meantime, with the NZR urgently requiring motive power, six of each type to the same specifications were ordered from the Baldwin Locomotive Works. These were shipped within six months of the placement of the order. The Baldwin 2-6-2 locomotives were always class N. Surviving photographs show that this classification was initially applied to at least three of the English machines. These were soon reclassified V to avoid confusion with those of Baldwin manufacture. NZR diagrams of 1893 show both light and heavy weight configurations for these Nasmyth Wilson locomotives. It is likely that for some time two class letters, U and V, were allocated to the heavy and modified versions. Similarly the English 2-8-0's, ordered as class O, were put into service as class P.

DISTRICT RAILWAYS

The locomotives of three district railways taken over in 1885 and 1886 were numbered on acquisition into the NZR list.

THE WAIMEA PLAINS RAILWAY COMPANY

This line was purchased by the Government in November 1886. The locomotives, whose genesis is set out in Chapter Three, became F 23 and F 24 on the Hurunui-Bluff section.

THE RAKAIA AND ASHBURTON FORKS RAILWAY

Two locomotives built by the Rogers Locomotive Works, Taunton, USA, for the Rakaia and Ashburton Forks Railway Company were discharged from the barque *Mabel* at Lyttelton in August 1879. They became part of the departmental pool of locomotives immediately, working suburban trains between Christchurch and Lyttelton. The *Christchurch Press* of 2 September 1879 noted a wayward *Livingstone* being pulled back onto the line by *Corsair* after thirteen minutes on the ground. The 1880 Parliamentary List and the 1881 Werry List both note these engines as R&AFR numbers 1 and 2. After completion in December 1881 the railway was worked by the NZR and purchased by the Government on 1 April 1885.

Rogers 2510/1878 R&AFR Nº 1 *Livingstone* (the maker's records show the name as *Livingston*) became NZR Q 51.

Rogers 2512/1878 R&AFR Nº 2 *Stanley* became NZR number Q 17.

THE THAMES VALLEY AND ROTORUA RAILWAY COMPANY

The railway between Morrinsville and Lichfield constructed by this company was taken over by the NZR on its completion in June 1886. The Putaruru to Lichfield portion was closed on 1 March 1897.

Evidence put before the 1885 District Railways Commission (AJHR, D5, page 22) stated that the Company owned four locomotives of class F valued at £1325 each, whilst the Statement of Cost of Locomotive Running Auckland Section ,1885 (AJHR ,D1, Return 23) noted "TVRR F 3 only 13 days in steam". Dubs of Glasgow built four locomotives, maker's numbers 1884-1887 under works order 1884E for "New Zealand Agency Company (Thames Valley and Rotorua Railway)". The NZR Boiler Record shows that only one of the four, Dubs 1886, had commenced work by 31 March 1885. This gives an indication that the company numbered them F 1-4 in order of maker's numbers. An old photograph shows that at least one was lettered 'T V R R'. After acquisition by the NZR they became Auckland Section F 65, F 66, F 69 and F 70.

HURUNUI-BLUFF SECTION 1877-1890

Road Number	Class	Type	Builder	Maker's Number	Date in Service	Former Number	Notes
1	M	0-6-0T	Hunslet	141-75	19-12-1875	O.R. 1	Allocated Nº not used, see M 90
1	F	0-6-0ST	Avonside	1095-76	--	O.R. xx	
2	M	0-6-0T	Hunslet	142/75	19-12-1875	O.R. 2	Allocated Nº not used, see M 89
2	F	0-6-0ST	Avonside	1141/76	--	O.R. xx	
3	M	0-6-0T	Hunslet	143/75	--	O.R. 3	
4	M	0-6-0T	Hunslet	144/75	7-1876	O.R. 22	
5	C	0-4-2ST	Neilson	1768/73	1-1874	O.R. 5	
6	A	0-4-0ST	Shanks	--/76	--	--	Sold 1882
6	C	0-4-2ST	Neilson	1770/73	--	--	From Napier 11-1881. Sold 1888
6	D	2-4-0T	Neilson	2564/80	5-1881	D 24	From Wanganui 1886
7	F	0-6-0ST	Avonside	1134/76	--	O.R. xx	
8	F	0-6-0ST	Avonside	1133/76	--	O.R. xx	
9	F	0-6-0ST	Avonside	1137/76	--	O.R. xx	
10	F	0-6-0ST	Avonside	1094/76	--	O.R. xx	
11	F	0-6-0ST	Neilson	1691/72	1-5-1873	O.R. 4	
12	F	0-6-0ST	Yorkshire	241/74	--	O.R. 14-16	
13	F	0-6-0ST	Yorkshire	242/74	--	O.R. 14-16	To Wanganui, F 28, 2-3-1886
13	F	0-6-0ST	Neilson	1692/72	20-12-1873	F 36	From PWD 1886
14	F	0-6-0ST	Yorkshire	243/74	--	O.R. 14-16	To Westport, F 14, 12-1884
14	J	2-6-0	Vulcan	1076/83	17-8-1885	--	
15	D	2-4-0T	Neilson	2309/78	--	--	To Nelson, D 3, 12-1879
15	J	2-6-0	Vulcan	1000/83	3-12-1883	--	
16	D	2-4-0T	Neilson	2306/78	--	--	
17	D	2-4-0T	Neilson	2307/78	--	--	To Picton, D 1, 12-1879
17	Q	2-4-4T	Rogers	2512/78	8-1879	2	From R&AF Railway 1881
18	D	2-4-0T	Neilson	2308/78	--	--	
19	F	0-6-0ST	Avonside	1093/76	27-9-1876	O.R. 30/32	See F 39
20	F	0-6-0ST	Neilson	2412/78	7-8-1879	--	From NZLMACo. 6-1879
21	B	0-4-4-0T	Avonside	1044-5/74	5-4-1875	O.R. 18	Renumbered B 27
21	F	0-6-0ST	Neilson	2410/78	1-9-1879	--	From NZLMACo. 6-1879
22	C	0-4-2ST	Neilson	1769/73	--	O.R. 9	To Wellington 1879, then loaned to a contractor at Picton. Returned to NZR at New Plymouth as C 23 17-9-1884
22	R	0-6-4T	Avonside	1233/79	--	--	
23	E	0-4-4-0T	Avonside	1060-1/75	11-12-1875	O.R. 23	To Wanganui, E 26, 1-11-1886
23	F	0-6-0ST	Neilson	2414/78	--	--	From W. P. Rly. 11-1886. See F 112 and 114
24	E	0-4-4-0T	Avonside,	1064-5/75	5-1-1876	O.R. 24	To Wanganui, E 27, 1-11-1886
24	F	0-6-0ST	Neilson	2411/78	--	--	From W. P. Rly. 11-1886. See F 112 and 114
25	E	0-4-4-0T	Avonside	1062-3/75	13-3-1876	O.R.25	To Wanganui, E 25, 1-11-1886
25	P	2-8-0	Nasmyth Wilson	281/85	2-5-1887	--	
26	E	0-4-4-0T	Vulcan	637-72	10-9-1872	O.R. 7	To Wanganui, E 24, 11-1883
26	J	2-6-0	Vulcan	999/83	4-12-1883	--	
27	E	0-4-4-0T	Vulcan	636/72	14-9-1872	O.R. 6	Not used after accident 20-9-1878
27	B	0-4-4-0T	Avonside	1044-5/74	5-4-1875	B 21	To Wanganui 1885
27	N	2-6-2	Baldwin	7576/85	30-10-1885	--	
28	R	0-6-4T	Avonside	1217/78	23-5-1879	--	
29	R	0-6-4T	Avonside	1218/78	24-5-1879	--	
30	R	0-6-4T	Avonside	1223/78	9-7-1879	--	To Wellington, R 3, 17-4-1884
30	N	2-6-2	Baldwin	7571/85	12-11-1885	--	
31	R	0-6-4T	Avonside	1225/78	--	--	To Greymouth 1881
31	C	0-4-2ST	Neilson	1771/73	--	--	From Napier, 11-1881. To Wellington, C 1, 11-1885

HURUNUI-BLUFF SECTION 1877-1890 (continued)

Road Number	Class	Type	Builder	Maker's Number	Date in Service	Former Number	Notes
31	O	2-8-0	Baldwin	7572/85	12-12-1885	--	
32	R	0-6-4T	Avonside	1229/78	23-8-1879	--	
33	R	0-6-4T	Avonside	1232/79	--	--	
34	F	0-6-0ST	Black Hawthorn	277/73	8-1874	O.R. 12	To Napier, F 48, 5-12-1884
34	N	2-6-2	Baldwin	7575/85	10-11-1885	--	
35	F	0-6-0ST	Yorkshire	248/74	4-1875	O.R. 17	To Napier, F 49, 4-1886
35	V	2-6-2	Nasmyth Wilson	259/85	5-5-1886	--	
36	F	0-6-0ST	Neilson	1692/72	20-12-1873	O.R. 8	To PWD 1879, returned 1886 as F 13
36	N	2-6-2	Baldwin	7579/85	10-11-1885	--	
37	F	0-6-0ST	Neilson	1842/73	7-1874	O.R. 10	To PWD 1879, later PWD #503
37	N	2-6-2	Baldwin	7573/85	9-12-1885	--	
38	F	0-6-0ST	Neilson	1841/73	1-7-1874	O.R. 11	
39	F	0-6-0ST	Avonside	1093/76	27-9-1876	O.R. 30/32	Allocated Nº, not used, see F 19
39	F	0-6-0ST	Neilson	2409/78	5-6-1879	--	From NZLMACo. 6-1879
40	F	0-6-0ST	Avonside	1090/76	4-8-1876	O.R. 29	
41	F	0-6-0ST	Avonside	1140/76	--	O.R. xx	
42	F	0-6-0ST	Avonside	1142/76	9-6-1877	O.R. xx	To Greymouth, F 2, 1-5-1884
42	N	2-6-2	Baldwin	7574/85	9-12-1885	--	
43	F	0-6-0ST	Avonside	1143/76	--	O.R. xx	
44	F	0-6-0ST	Avonside	1091/76	1-9-1876	O.R. 30/32	
45	F	0-6-0ST	Avonside	1144/76	7-9-1877	O.R. xx	
46	D	2-4-0T	Dubs	1168/78	28-1-1879	--	
47	D	2-4-0T	Dubs	1166/78	24-1-1879	--	
48	D	2-4-0T	Dubs	1167/78	29-1-1879	--	
49	D	2-4-0T	Dubs	1165/78	2-1879	--	
50	D	2-4-0T	Dubs	1164/78	4-2-1879	--	
51	D	2-4-0T	Neilson	1848/74	1-1875	O.R. 13	To New Plymouth, D 21, 1881
51	Q	2-4-4T	Rogers	2510/78	8-1879	--	From R.& A.F. Ry. 1881
52	S	0-4-0ST	Hughes	/75	--	O.R. 28	Sold 1886
52	P	2-8-0	Nasmyth Wilson	277/85	28-5-1887	--	
53	C	0-4-2ST	Neilson	1773/73	1-11-1875	C.R. 21	To Westport, C 53, 27-8-1888
54	P	0-6-0ST	Davidson	1/76	5-1876	O.R. 26	sold 1883
54	O	2-8-0	Baldwin	7565/85	12-12-1885	--	
55	G	4-4-0ST	Black Hawthorn	278/73	1-1-1875	C.R. 1-4	
56	G	4-4-0ST	Black Hawthorn	282/73	1-1-1875	C.R. 1-4	
57	G	4-4-0ST	Black Hawthorn	281/73	3-1-1875	C.R. 1-4	
58	G	4-4-0ST	Black Hawthorn	279/73	2-1-1875	C.R. 1-4	
59	P	0-6-0ST	Davidson	3/76	10-1876	O.R. 27	sold 1883
59	J	2-6-0	Vulcan	1002/83	12-1-1884	--	
60	A	0-4-0T	Dubs	655/73	--	C.R. 5-14	To Wellington, A 2, 6-6-1886
60	P	2-8-0	Nasmyth Wilson	279/85	6-7-1887	--	
61	A	0-4-0T	Dubs	650/73	--	C.R. 5-14	To Wanganui, A 23, 1883
61	J	2-6-0	Vulcan	1004/83	10-1-1884	--	
62	A	0-4-0T	Dubs	656/73	1-1-1875	C.R. 5-14	
63	A	0-4-0T	Yorkshire	256/75	--	C.R. 22-23	To Napier, A 41, 6-3-1886
63	V	2-6-2	Nasmyth Wilson	260/85	22-4-1886	--	
64	A	0-4-0T	Dubs	651/73	1-1-1875	C.R. 5-14	
65	A	0-4-0T	Dubs	653/73	12-6-1875	C.R. 5-14	
66	A	0-4-0T	Dubs	648/73	1-2-1875	C.R. 5-14	
67	A	0-4-0T	Dubs	647/73	2-2-1875	C.R. 5-14	
68	A	0-4-0T	Dubs	652/73	1-6-1875	C.R. 5-14	
69	A	0-4-0T	Dubs	654/73	--	C.R. 5-14	To Wellington, A 1, 27-7-1885
69	O	2-8-0	Baldwin	7567/85	21-12-1885	--	
70	A	0-4-0T	Dubs	649/73	--	C.R. 5-14	To Napier, A 41, 1883

HURUNUI-BLUFF SECTION 1877-1890 (continued)

Road Number	Class	Type	Builder	Maker's Number	Date in Service	Former Number	Notes
70	J	2-6-0	Vulcan	1007/83	29-2-1884	--	
71	A	0-4-0T	Yorkshire	255/75	15-12-1875	C.R. 22-23	
72	F	0-6-0ST	Yorkshire	246/74	c.3-1875	O.R. 18/19	
73	F	0-6-0ST	Yorkshire	247/74	c.3-1875	O.R. 20	
74	F	0-6-0ST	Yorkshire	249/74	c.3-1875	O.R 18/19	
75	F	0-6-0ST	Avonside	1088/75	10-9-1876	C.R. 24-28	
76	F	0-6-0ST	Avonside	1132/76	14-12-1876	C.R. 24-28	
77	F	0-6-0ST	Avonside	1131/76	29-12-1876	C.R. 24-28	
78	F	0-6-0ST	Avonside	1138/76	1-4-1877	C.R. 24-28	
79	F	0-6-0ST	Avonside	1139/76	9-4-1877	C.R. 24-28	
80	F	0-6-0ST	Avonside	1085/75	c.9-1876	O.R. 31	
81	J	2-6-0	Avonside	1038/74	31-5-1875	C.R. 15-20	
82	J	2-6-0	Avonside	1040/74	31-8-1875	C.R. 15-20	
83	J	2-6-0	Avonside	1039/74	19-6-1875	C.R. 15-20	
84	J	2-6-0	Avonside	1042/74	2-3-1876	C.R. 15-20	
85	J	2-6-0	Avonside	1041/74	6-3-1876	C.R. 15-20	
86	J	2-6-0	Avonside	1043/74	1-3-1876	C.R. 15-20	
87	K	2-4-2	Rogers	2455/77	9-3-1878	--	*Lincoln*
88	K	2-4-2	Rogers	2454/77	18-3-1878	--	*Washington*
89	M	0-6-0T	Hunslet	142/75	19-12-1875	O.R. 2	
90	M	0-6-0T	Hunslet	141/75	19-12-1875	O.R. 1	
91	L	2-4-0T	Avonside	1199/77	21-6-1878	--	
92	K	2-4-2	Rogers	2468/78	16-12-1878	--	
93	K	2-4-2	Rogers	2469/78	16-12-1878	--	
94	K	2-4-2	Rogers	2470/78	16-12-1878	--	
95	K	2-4-2	Rogers	2471/78	14-11-1878	--	
96	K	2-4-2	Rogers	2473/78	19-11-1878	--	
97	K	2-4-2	Rogers	2474/78	2-11-1878	--	
98	F	0-6-0ST	Dubs	1173/78	--	--	To Greymouth F 3, 12-9-1885
98	O	2-8-0	Baldwin	7566/85	8-1-1886	--	
99	F	0-6-0ST	Dubs	1172/78	--	--	To Nelson F 1, 19-3-1885
99	O	2-8-0	Baldwin	7569/85	11-1-1886	--	
100	F	0-6-0ST	Dubs	1171/78	16-5-1879	--	To Wanganui F 27, 2-5-1885
100	O	2-8-0	Baldwin	7568/85	22-2-1886	--	
101	T	2-8-0	Baldwin	4660/79	2-2-1880	--	
102	T	2-8-0	Baldwin	4661/79	7-2-1880	--	
103	T	2-8-0	Baldwin	4664/79	19-1-1880	--	
104	T	2-8-0	Baldwin	4665/79	9-1-1880	--	
105	T	2-8-0	Baldwin	4666/79	8-2-1880	--	
106	T	2-8-0	Baldwin	4667/79	8-2-1880	--	
107	J	2-6-0	Dubs	1212/79	18-9-1879	--	To Napier J 41, 9-1887
107	P	2-8-0	Nasmyth Wilson	278/85	20-8-1887	--	
108	J	2-6-0	Dubs	1213/79	21-9-1879	--	To Napier J 42, 9-1887
108	D	2-4-0T	Scott	30/87	21-12-1887	--	
109	J	2-6-0	Dubs	1214/79	21-9-1879	--	To Napier J 43, 9-1887
109	D	2-4-0T	Scott	34/87	29-12-1887	--	
110	J	2-6-0	Dubs	1215/79	10-10-1879	--	
111	F	0-6-0ST	Dubs	1233/79	--	--	From NMA Co/Waimate Ry Co
112	F	0-6-0ST	Neilson	241x/78	--	--	To W. P. Ry. See F 23/24
112	R	0-6-4T	Avonside	1234/79	--	--	
113	F	0-6-0ST	Neilson	2413/78	--	--	D & H Ry. Co locomotive
114	F	0-6-0ST	Neilson	241x/78	--	--	To W. P. Ry. See F 23/24
114	V	2-6-2	Nasmyth Wilson	256/85	6-12-1885	--	
115	J	2-6-0	Neilson	2460/79	8-10-1880	--	
116	J	2-6-0	Neilson	2461/79	29-7-1880	--	

HURUNUI-BLUFF SECTION 1877-1890 (continued)

Road Number	Class	Type	Builder	Maker's Number	Date in Service	Former Number	Notes
117	J	2-6-0	Neilson	2462/79	9-7-1880	--	
118	J	2-6-0	Neilson	2463/79	26-7-1880	--	
119	J	2-6-0	Neilson	2464/79	23-6-1880	--	
120	J	2-6-0	Stephenson	2367/79	28-6-1880	--	
121	J	2-6-0	Stephenson	2368/79	28-6-1880	--	
122	J	2-6-0	Stephenson	2369/79	14-6-1880	--	
123	J	2-6-0	Stephenson	2370/79	18-8-1880	--	
124	J	2-6-0	Stephenson	2371/79	10-8-1880	--	
125	V	2-6-2	Nasmyth Wilson	257/85	1-11-1885	--	
126	V	2-6-2	Nasmyth Wilson	261/85	10-11-1885	--	
127	V	2-6-2	Nasmyth Wilson	255/85	3-2-1886	--	
128	V	2-6-2	Nasmyth Wilson	254/85	22-4-1886	--	
129	V	2-6-2	Nasmyth Wilson	258/85	30-9-1886	--	
130	D	2-4-0T	Scott	35/87	10-6-1888	--	
131	D	2-4-0T	Scott	38/87	14-1-1888	--	
132	V	2-6-2	Nasmyth Wilson	253/85	23-6-1888	--	
133	P	2-8-0	Nasmyth Wilson	280/85	31-3-1886	--	
134	P	2-8-0	Nasmyth Wilson	274/85	8-2-1886	--	
135	P	2-8-0	Nasmyth Wilson	275/85	13-2-1886	--	
136	V	2-6-2	Nasmyth Wilson	252/85	10-6-1890	--	
137	D	2-4-0T	Scott	31/87	13-2-1888	--	
138	D	2-4-0T	Scott	32/87	3-2-1888	--	
139	D	2-4-0T	Scott	33/87	19-1-1888	--	
140	D	2-4-0T	Scott	36/87	27-1-1888	--	
141	D	2-4-0T	Scott	37/87	18-2-1888	--	
142	D	2-4-0T	Scott	39/87	7-3-1888	--	

SOUTH ISLAND SECTIONAL NUMBERING 1882-1890

Road Number	Type	Builder	Maker's Number	Date in Service	Former Number	1890 Number	Notes
NELSON SECTION							
D 1	2-4-0T	Neilson	1847/74	4-1875	128	D 143	
D 2	2-4-0T	Neilson	1849/74	6-1875	129	D 144	
D 3	2-4-0T	Neilson	2309/78	--	D 15	D 145	From Hurunui-Bluff 12-1879
F 1	0-6-0ST	Dubs	1172/78	--	F 99	F 146	From Hurunui-Bluff 20-3-1885
PICTON SECTION							
C 1	0-4-2ST	Neilson	1767/73	2-1874	125	C 147	
C 2	0-4-2ST	Neilson	1766/73	2-1874	11	C 148	
D 1	2-4-0T	Neilson	2307/78	--	D 17	D 149	From Hurunui-Bluff 12-1879
GREYMOUTH SECTION							
C 1	0-4-2ST	Dubs	885/75	2-1876	132	--	Sold about 1886
C 2	0-4-2ST	Neilson	1772/73	17-8-1875	131	--	Sold 6-1885
F 1	0-6-0ST	Dubs	1371/80	10-1882	--	F 150	
F 2	0-6-0ST	Avonside	1142/76	9-6-1877	F 42	F 151	From Hurunui-Bluff 1-5-1884
F 3	0-6-0ST	Dubs	1173/78	--	F 98	F 152	From Hurunui-Bluff 12-9-1885
R 1	0-6-4T	Avonside	1225/78	--	R 31	R 153	From Hurunui-Bluff 1881

ABOVE: R 29, Avonside 1218 of 1878, at Balclutha, probably in the 1890s, showing a particularly conspicuous style of numbering. (S. A. Rockcliff Collection)

BELOW: Wellington section S 6, Avonside 1281 of 1880, held up by washouts along the harbourside, probably in 1888. This locomotive became S 217 in 1890 and was sold to the West Australian Government Railways in 1891. (S. A. Rockcliff Collection)

38 - The Answer to the Problem

\multicolumn{8}{c	}{**SOUTH ISLAND SECTIONAL NUMBERING 1882-1890 (continued)**}
Road Number	**Type**	**Builder**	**Maker's Number**	**Date in Service**	**Former Number**	**1890 Number**	**Notes**
\multicolumn{8}{c	}{**WESTPORT SECTION**}
C 1	0-4-2ST	Dubs	804/75	5-8-1876	126	C 158	
C 2	0-4-2ST	Dubs	803/75	5-8-1876	127	--	Sold 10-1886
C 3	0-4-2ST	Dubs	802/75	--	--	--	From Napier 1881, Sold 9-1887
C 53	0-4-2ST	Neilson	1773/73	1-11-1875	C 53	C 53	From Hurunui-Bluff 27-8-1888
F 4	0-6-0ST	Dubs	1370/80	5-2-1883	--	F 154	
F 5	0-6-0ST	Stephenson	2598/86	16-10-1886	--	F 155	
F 6	0-6-0ST	Vulcan	1181/87	17-9-1887	--	F 156	
F 14	0-6-0ST	Yorkshire	243/74		F 14	F 157	From Hurunui-Bluff 12-1884

The two F class locomotives, F 5/155 and F 6/156, were imported by the Westport Harbour Board but delivered to New Zealand Railways in exchange for the two C class locomotives C 2 and C 3

\multicolumn{8}{c	}{**NORTH ISLAND SECTIONAL NUMBERING 1882-1890**}
Road Number	**Type**	**Builder**	**Maker's Number**	**Date in Service**	**Former Number**	**1890 Number**	**Notes**
\multicolumn{8}{c	}{**WELLINGTON SECTION**}
A 1	0-4-0T	Dubs	654/73	--	A 69	A 220	From Hurunui-Bluff 27-7-1885
A 2	0-4-0T	Dubs	655/73	--	A 60	A 193	From Hurunui-Bluff 6-6-1886
C 1	0-4-2ST	Neilson	1771/73	--	C 31	C 194	From Hurunui-Bluff 11-1885
C 1	0-4-0ST	Neilson	1764/73	4-1874	32	--	Sold 31-10-1882
D 1	2-4-0T	Neilson	1846/74	16-11-1874	33	D 195	
D 2	2-4-0T	Neilson	1845/74	16-11-1874	34	D 196	
D 3	2-4-0T	Neilson	1844/74	12-1874	3 (22)	D 197	
D 4	2-4-0T	Neilson	2561/80	16-3-1881	--	D 198	
H 1	0-4-2T	Avonside	1075/75	1-1-1877	35	H 199	
H 2	0-4-2T	Avonside	1074/75	16-10-1878	36	H 200	
H 3	0-4-2T	Avonside	1072/75	17-10-1878	37	H 201	
H 4	0-4-2T	Avonside	1073/75	18-11-1878	38	H 202	
H 5	0-4-2T	Neilson	3469/86	1-11-1886	--	H 203	
H 6	0-4-2T	Neilson	3468/86	9-8-1886	--	H 204	
L 1	2-4-0T	Avonside	1200/77	8-6-1878	39	L 205	
L 2	2-4-0T	Avonside	1201/77	19-6-1878	40	L 206	
L 3	2-4-0T	Avonside	1205/77	17-8-1878	41	L 207	
L 4	2-4-0T	Avonside	1206/77	10-9-1878	42	L 208	
L 21	2-4-0T	Avonside	1207/77	--	30	L 219	From Wanganui 15-4-1888
R 1	0-6-4T	Avonside	1221/78	1-7-1879	--	R 209	
R 2	0-6-4T	Avonside	1226/78	4-3-1880	--	R 210	
R 3	0-6-4T	Avonside	1222/78	7-1879	--	R 273	To Auckland R 53, 3-1883
R 3	0-6-4T	Avonside	1223/78	9-7-1879	R 30	R 211	From Hurunui-Bluff 17-4-1884
S 1	0-6-4T	Avonside	1279/80	13-4-1882	--	S 212	
S 2	0-6-4T	Avonside	1280/80	17-7-1882	--	S 213	
S 3	0-6-4T	Avonside	1284/81	20-7-1883	--	S 214	
S 4	0-6-4T	Avonside	1283/81	18-2-1885	--	S 215	
S 5	0-6-4T	Avonside	1285/81	25-2-1885	--	S 216	
S 6	0-6-4T	Avonside	1281/80	31-7-1886	--	S 217	
S 7	0-6-4T	Avonside	1282/80	21-5-1887	--	S 218	
\multicolumn{8}{c	}{**WANGANUI AND NEW PLYMOUTH SECTION**}
A 21	0-4-0T	Dubs	646/73	4-1875	43	(A 192)	* Sold 12-1889
A 22	0-4-0T	Dubs	645/73	4-1875	44	--	* Sold c1888. see A 215 1890 list
A 23	0-4-0T	Dubs	650/73	--	A 61	A 161	From Hurunui-Bluff 1883. To Auckland A 51. 10-4-1885

The Answer to the Problem - 39

\multicolumn{8}{	c	}{NORTH ISLAND SECTIONAL NUMBERING 1882-1890 (continued)}
Road Number	Type	Builder	Maker's Number	Date in Service	Former Number	1890 Number	Notes
\multicolumn{8}{	c	}{WANGANUI AND NEW PLYMOUTH SECTION continued}
B 27	0-4-4-0T	Avonside	1044-5/74	5-4-1875	B 27	B 165	From Hurunui-Bluff 3-7-1885
C 21	0-4-2ST	Neilson	1765/73	4-1874	45	C 166	*
C 22	0-4-2ST	Dubs	801/75	--	46	C 167	*
C 23	0-4-2ST	Neilson	1769/73	--	C 22 --	C 168	* From contractor 9-1884. Previously Hurunui-Bluff
D 21	2-4-0T	Neilson	1848/74	2-1875	D 51	D 169	*From Hurunui-Bluff, 16-4-1881
D 22	2-4-0T	Neilson	2563/80	21-5-1881	--	D 170	*
D 23	2-4-0T	Neilson	2562/80	28-5-1881	--	D 171	*
D 24	2-4-0T	Neilson	2564/80	5-1881	--	D 6	*To Hurunui-Bluff, D 6, 1886
E 21	0-4-4-0T	Avonside	1070-1/75	7-1876	17/23	E 172	
E 22	0-4-4-0T	Avonside	1068-9/75	5-4-1877	24	E 173	
E 23	0-4-4-0T	Avonside	1066-7/75	7-1876	30	E 174	
E 24	0-4-4-0T	Vulcan	637/72	10-9-1872	E 26	E 175	From Hurunui-Bluff, 11-1883
E 25	0-4-4-0T	Avonside	1062-3/75	13-3-1876	E 25	E 176	From Hurunui-Bluff, 1-11-1886
E 26	0-4-4-0T	Avonside	1060-1/75	11-12-1875	E 23	E 177	From Hurunui-Bluff, 1-11-1886
E 27	0-4-4-0T	Avonside	1064-5/75	5-1-1876	E 24	E 178	From Hurunui-Bluff, 1-11-1886
F 21	0-6-0ST	Yorkshire	245/74	9-1875	25	F 179	
F 22	0-6-0ST	Yorkshire	244/74	9-1875	26	F 180	
F 23	0-6-0ST	Avonside	1084/75	8-1876	27	F 181	Foxton section locomotives before that section was linked to Wanganui.
F 24	0-6-0ST	Avonside	1136/76	3-1877	28	F 182	
F 25	0-6-0ST	Avonside	1135/76	3-1877	29	F 183	
F 26	0-6-0ST	Dubs	1372/80	19-2-1881	--	F 184	
F 27	0-6-0ST	Dubs	1171/78	16-5-1879	F 100	F 185	From Hurunui-Bluff, 2-5-1885
F 28	0-6-0ST	Yorkshire	242/74	--	F 13	F 186	From Hurunui-Bluff, 2-3-1886
L 21	2-4-0T	Avonside	1207/77	--	30	L 219	To Wellington, 15-4-1888
R 21	0-6-4T	Avonside	1224/78	2-6-1879	--	R 187	
R 22	0-6-4T	Avonside	1227/78	28-7-1879	--	R 188	
R 23	0-6-4T	Avonside	1228/78	25-8-1879	--	R 189	
R 24	0-6-4T	Avonside	1230/78	10-9-1879	--	R 190	
R 25	0-6-4T	Avonside	1231/79	15-1-1880	--	R 191	
\multicolumn{8}{	c	}{NAPIER SECTION}
A 41	0-4-0T	Dubs	649/73	--	A 70	--	From Hurunui-Bluff, 1883. Sold 1886
A 41	0-4-0T	Yorkshire	256/75	--	A 63	A 237	From Hurunui-Bluff, 6-3-1886
D 41	2-4-0T	Neilson	2565/80	5-1881	--	D 221	
D 42	2-4-0T	Neilson	2566/80	6-1881	--	D 222	
F 40	0-6-0ST	Stephenson	2595/85	8-1886	--	F 223	
F 41	0-6-0ST	Avonside	1086/75	9-1876	18	F 224	
F 42	0-6-0ST	Avonside	1089/75	9-1876	19	F 225	
F 43	0-6-0ST	Dubs	1169/78	3-1879	46	F 226	
F 44	0-6-0ST	Dubs	1170/78	4-1879	47	F 227	
F 45	0-6-0ST	Dubs	1365/80	4-1882	--	F 228	
F 46	0-6-0ST	Dubs	1369/80	7-1881	F 66	F 229	From Auckland, 11-1883
F 47	0-6-0ST	Dubs	1364/80	7-1881	F 65	F 230	From Auckland, 7-1884
F 48	0-6-0ST	Black Hawthorn	277/73	6-1874	F 34	F 231	From Hurunui-Bluff, 5-12-1884
F 49	0-6-0ST	Yorkshire	248/74	4-1875	F 35	F 232	From Hurunui-Bluff, 4-1886
F 50	0-6-0ST	Stephenson	2593/85	9-8-1886	--	F 233	
J 41	2-6-0	Dubs	1212/79	18-9-1879	J 107	J 234	From Hurunui-Bluff, 9-1887
J 42	2-6-0	Dubs	1213/79	21-9-1879	J 108	J 235	From Hurunui-Bluff, 9-1887
J 43	2-6-0	Dubs	1214/79	21-9-1879	J 109	J 236	From Hurunui-Bluff, 9-1887

* New Plymouth locomotive. See the numbering instruction Page 31. The New Plymouth and Wanganui sections were linked in March 1885.

40 - The Answer to the Problem

ABOVE: One of two Yorkshire class A locomotives, N° 256 of 1875, as Napier A 41. It was sent to Napier in 1886 to replace the previous A 41, a Dubs locomotive which had been sold.
(T. A. McGavin Collection)

BELOW: J 41, Dubs 1212 of 1879, pauses at Te Aute on a trial run from Napier to Waipukurau after being transferred from the South Island in September 1887. (S. A. Rockcliff Collection)

\multicolumn{8}{c}{**NORTH ISLAND SECTIONAL NUMBERING 1882-1890 (continued)**}
Road Number	Type	Builder	Maker's Number	Date in Service	Former Number	1890 Number	Notes
\multicolumn{8}{c}{**AUCKLAND SECTION**}
\multicolumn{8}{c}{Comprising railways at Auckland, Whangarei, Kaipara, Kawakawa and the Thames Valley & Rotorua Railway Co.}
A 51	0-4-0T	Dubs	650/73	--	A 23	A 161	From Wanganui, 10-4-1885
B 51	0-4-4-0T	Avonside	1022-3/74	9-1874	1/10	B 238	
C 51	0-4-2ST	Dubs	800/75	10-1875	15	C 239	
D 51	2-4-0T	Neilson	1843/74	9-1874	16	D 240	
F 51	0-6-0ST	Neilson	1706/72	14-4-1873	2	F 241	
F 52	0-6-0ST	Stephenson	2086/73	12-1873	1	F 242	
F 53	0-6-0ST	Stephenson	2085/73	1-1874	5	F 243	
F 54	0-6-0ST	Stephenson	2087/73	1-1874	6	F 244	
F 55	0-6-0ST	Yorkshire	239/74	11-1874	3	F 164	To Whangarei, 8-1880
F 56	0-6-0ST	Yorkshire	240/74	11-1874	4	F 245	
F 57	0-6-0ST	Vulcan	735/75	9-1875	7	F 246	
F 58	0-6-0ST	Vulcan	737/75	9-1875	8	F 247	
F 59	0-6-0ST	Vulcan	736/75	9-1875	9	F 248	
F 60	0-6-0ST	Dubs	1362/80	7-1881	--	F 249	
F 61	0-6-0ST	Dubs	1363/80	9-1881	--	F 162	To Whangarei, 9-1881
F 62	0-6-0ST	Dubs	1368/80	7-1881	--	F 250	
F 63	0-6-0ST	Dubs	1367/80	7-1881	--	F 163	To Whangarei, 1885
F 64	0-6-0ST	Dubs	1366/80	8-1881	--	F 251	
F 65	0-6-0ST	Dubs	1364/80	7-1881	--	F 230	To Napier F 47, 7-1884
F 66	0-6-0ST	Dubs	1369/80	7-1881	--	F 229	To Napier F 46, 11-1883
F 67	0-6-0ST	Avonside	1092/76	2-1877	--	F 159	Bay of Islands Coal Co.
F 68	0-6-0ST	Avonside	1087/75	2-1877	--	F 160	locomotives.
F 65	0-6-0ST	Dubs	1884/84	4-1885	--	F 252	
F 66	0-6-0ST	Dubs	1885/84	5-1885	--	F 253	Thames Valley and Rotorua
F 69	0-6-0ST	Dubs	1886/84	11-1884	--	F 254	Railway Company locomotives
F 70	0-6-0ST	Dubs	1887/84	5-1885	--	F 255	
F 71	0-6-0ST	Stephenson	2599/86	11-1886	--	F 256	
F 72	0-6-0ST	Stephenson	2600/86	12-1886	--	F 257	
J 51	2-6-0	Vulcan	1001/83	11-1883	--	J 258	
J 52	2-6-0	Vulcan	998/83	12-1883	--	J 259	
J 53	2-6-0	Vulcan	1003/83	11-1883	--	J 260	
J 54	2-6-0	Vulcan	1005/83	12-1883	--	J 261	
J 55	2-6-0	Vulcan	1006/83	1-1884	--	J 262	
J 56	2-6-0	Vulcan	1009/83	1-1884	--	J 263	
L 51	2-4-0T	Avonside	1208/77	7-1878	11	L 264	
L 52	2-4-0T	Avonside	1202/77	7-1878	12	L 265	
L 53	2-4-0T	Avonside	1203/77	7-1878	13	L 266	
L 54	2-4-0T	Avonside	1204/77	7-1878	14	L 267	
P 51	2-8-0	Nasmyth Wilson	272/85	5-1887	--	P 268	
P 52	2-8-0	Nasmyth Wilson	273/85	5-1887	--	P 269	
P 53	2-8-0	Nasmyth Wilson	276/85	2-1887	--	P 270	
R 51	0-6-4T	Avonside	1219/78	7-1879	--	R 271	
R 52	0-6-4T	Avonside	1220/78	7-1879	--	R 272	
R 53	0-6-4T	Avonside	1222/78	7-1879	R 3	R 273	From Wellington, 3-1883

Kawakawa section locomotives A 51, F 67 and F 68.   Kaipara Section engines C 51 and D 51.

F 67 and F 68: The Bay of Islands Coal Company built a 4 feet 8½ inch gauge line and used the former Auckland and Drury Railway locomotives until 1877, when the line was converted to 3 feet 6 inch gauge. These two locomotives commenced work for the company in February 1877. The Government altered the gauge of the railway but the company worked the line until 1884. The locomotives were returned to NZR service, F 67 on 10 January 1884 and F 68 on 7 April 1884. This became the first part of the Kawakawa section.

42 - The Answer to the Problem

ABOVE: The evolution of the NZR standard number plate is not clear as the early instructions and drawings have been lost. Fairlie E 22, always a Wanganui district locomotive, with an early North Island number plate in the 1882 series, became E 173 in 1890. The driver and fireman are both standing in the driver's cab. On a Fairlie double locomotive the firing and driving positions were not duplicated. (A. P. Godber Collection, Alexander Turnbull Library)

BELOW: Auckland C 51, Dubs 800 of 1875. This 1882 style of lettering, with a full point between the class letter and number, replaced the practice of dividing the letter and number by the maker's plate on the Auckland section only. However, on the Napier section (see page 40) the earlier style persisted. (S. A. Rockcliff Collection)

ABOVE: Avonside 1222 of 1878, numbered R 53 on the Auckland section in 1882, became R 273 in the 1890 List. (J. A. T. Terry Collection)

BELOW: A further example of the Auckland style of numbering was carried by J 56, Vulcan 1009 of 1883. (S. A. Rockcliff Collection)

CHAPTER FIVE

THE PURCHASES

The Government purchased the New Zealand Midland Railway Company Ltd. in 1900 and the Wellington and Manawatu Railway Company Ltd. in 1908. These lines became part of the Railways Department's system and the locomotives were renumbered and included in the 1890 list.

\multicolumn{8}{c}{NEW ZEALAND MIDLAND RAILWAY COMPANY LTD}
Road Number	Type	Name	Builder	Maker's Number	Date in Service	NZR Class and Number	Notes
1	4-4-0T	*Reefton*	Nasmyth Wilson	311/87	8-1887	L^A 310	
2	4-4-0T	*Christchurch*	Nasmyth Wilson	315/87	12-1887	L^A 311	
3	4-4-0T	*Nelson*	Nasmyth Wilson	322/87	7-1888	L^A 312	
4	4-4-0T		Nasmyth Wilson	323/87	30-6-1890	L^A 313	
5	4-4-0T		Nasmyth Wilson	312/87	23-11-1892	L^A 314	
6	2-4-0T		Scott	40/90	4-9-1890	D 315	

\multicolumn{8}{c}{WELLINGTON AND MANAWATU RAILWAY COMPANY LTD}
Road Number	Type	Name	Builder	Maker's Number	Date in Service	NZR Class and Number	Notes
1	2-6-2T		Manning Wardle	920/84	11-1884	W^H 447	
2	2-6-2T		Manning Wardle	921/84	11-1884	W^H 448	
3	2-6-2T		Manning Wardle	922/84	--	--	Note 1. Sold
4	2-6-2T		Manning Wardle	923/84	8-1886	W^H 449	
5	2-6-2T		Manning Wardle	924/84	8-1886	--	Note 1. Sold
3	2-8-4T	*Jumbo*	Baldwin	23596/04	7-1904	W^J 466	Note 2
5	2-6-2		Baldwin	19797/01	8-5-1902	N^C 461	
6	2-6-2		Nasmyth Wilson	282/85	by 11-1886	V 450	
7	2-6-2		Nasmyth Wilson	283/85	by 11-1886	V 451	
8	2-6-2		Nasmyth Wilson	284/85	by 11-1886	V 452	
9	2-6-2		Baldwin	12104/91	1-1892	N 453	
10	2-6-2		Baldwin	12106/91	1-1892	N 454	
11	2-8-0		Baldwin	9018/88	9-1888	O^B 455	Formerly N° 9
12	2-8-0		Baldwin	9021/88	9-1888	O^B 456	Formerly N° 10
13	2-8-0	*The Lady*	Baldwin	13908/94	6-8-1894	O^A 457	Note 2
14	2-6-2		Baldwin	13913/94	8-9-1894	N^A 459	
15	2-6-2		Baldwin	15054/96	10-1897	N^A 460	
16	2-8-0		Baldwin	15055/96	20-6-1897	O^C 458	
17	2-8-2		Baldwin	19796/01	10-6-1902	B^C 463	
18	2-6-2		Baldwin	23594/04	9-1904	N^C 462	
19	4-6-0		Baldwin	24086/04	10-11-1904	U^D 464	
20	4-6-0		Baldwin	24087/04	7-12-1904	U^D 465	

Note 1 Wellington and Manawatu Company numbers 3 and 5 were sold to the Timaru Harbour Board in 1901. One was later sold to the Mount Somers Tramway about 1936, the other was scrapped.

Note 2 The names *Jumbo* and *The Lady,* although widely used, were not sanctioned officially.

ABOVE: The New Zealand Midland Railway, taken over by the Government in 1900, named most of its locomotives. NZMR N⁰ 2 *Christchurch* became L^A 311. (Rings photograph, S. A. Rockliff Collection)

BELOW: The Wellington and Manawatu Railway Company's Numbers 6 to 8 were built to the same specification and by the same maker, Nasmyth Wilson, as the NZR class V. WMR N⁰ 6, in company livery at Paekakariki about 1905, became V 450 in the NZR fleet.
(A. P. Godber, Alexander Turnbull Library)

CHAPTER SIX
STEAM LOCOMOTIVE NUMBERING 1890-1971

The 1882 scheme of numbering failed because the block of numbers allocated to each section did not allow for expansion. As early as April 1884 officers at Napier reported that the allocation of numbers for open wagons had been exhausted. In August 1886 the same officers drew attention to the fact that ten F class locomotives had been numbered as instructed, F 41 to F 50, and questioned how the eleventh, then being erected, should be numbered. Head Office decreed that a reverse sequence from 40 to 35 could be used for this class at Napier. Although this was the only case the point was taken. Towards the end of 1887 - no specific date can be given because the document of instruction has not been discovered - preparations were commenced for the final scheme of numbers for steam locomotives. Noted early were F 247 on 30 October 1888, F 186 in April 1889, whilst W 192 emerged from Addington Workshops in December 1889 taking the number of A 192, sold about this time.

Locomotive Superintendent T. F. Rotherham, on 13 January 1890, signed NZR Print 1168 "Numbers and Classes of Locomotives with Names of Builders Etc". "Etc" was the section where a locomotive worked and its old number. Here is the source for the common title "The 1890 List".

Thereafter all steam locomotives were numbered in this list and with few exceptions a locomotive retained its number throughout its working life. In the 1890 list the Hurunui-Bluff locomotives retained their existing numbers and the other sections renumbered in the following ranges: - Nelson 143-146, Picton 147-149, Greymouth 150-153, Westport 154-158, Kawakawa 159-161, Whangarei 162-164, Wanganui 165-192, Wellington 193-220, Napier 221-237 and Auckland 238-273. As the older locomotives were taken out of service their numbers were reallocated to new locomotives.

In the table the "Road Number" is that by which the locomotive was known when working; it was the practice to refer to any locomotive by both its class letter and number. "Type" indicates the wheel arrangement in the Whyte notation (4-6-2 indicates a locomotive having four leading bogie wheels, six-coupled driving wheels, followed by two trailing wheels). Reference to Chapter Eight will reveal details of locomotive builders. "Written Off" indicates the date on which a locomotive was removed from the Department's Stock List; many locomotives had done little or no work for up to five years prior to being written off, but others, notably the Class E Fairlie locomotives, lasted as much as a quarter of a century after official removal from the list. The "Remarks" column gives details, by footnote found at the end of the table, of alterations, renumberings and disposals for further service (sold) or for preservation (preserved). Reference to Chapters Nine and Ten show the continuing existence in these streams of activity.

LOCOMOTIVE REBUILDING

About the end of the nineteenth century some locomotives issued from NZR workshops with new works numbers were said to be rebuilds of earlier units. It is evident from the very considerable alteration that little of the original material was used in these renewals, consequently they are regarded as new locomotives and no mention is made of the 'rebuilding'.

During the 1890s several of the F class locomotives were renewed as class F^A 0-6-0T, but were then found to be deficient in fuel capacity and were subsequently converted to 0-6-2T of class F^B. Upon the conversion of the whole class the classification reverted to F^A. The metamorphosis of the Avonside 2-4-0T into 4-4-2T similarly required four steps in classification; L, L^A, L^B and then finally back to L. It is worth noting that locomotives of the original type long outlasted the renewals and conversions.

The alteration of the class B 4-8-0 tender locomotives into class W^E 4-6-4 tank locomotives involved little more than the addition of side-tanks, bunker and rear bogie, whilst the removal of these items converted the W^{AB} Baltic tanks into A^B Pacifics.

STEAM LOCOMOTIVE NUMBERING 1890-1971

Road Number	Class	Type	Builder	Maker's Number	Date in Service	Written Off	Notes
1	F	0-6-0ST	Avonside	1095/76	--	9-3-1929	
1	D	0-4-0T	Clayton	AW637/29	1930	1936	
2	F	0-6-0ST	Avonside	1141/76	--	2-1954	Sold
3	M	0-6-0T	Hunslet	143/75	--	20-10-1928	Note 1
4	M	0-6-0T	Hunslet	144/75	7-1876	26-9-1924	Note 1
5	C	0-4-2ST	Neilson	1768/73	1-1874	1892	Sold
5	A	0-4-0T	Dubs	647/73	--	1896	Sold (see A 67)
5	F	0-6-0ST	Stephenson	2611/86	--	1-1957	Note 2
6	D	2-4-0T	Neilson	2564/80	5-1881	1917	Sold
7	F	0-6-0ST	Avonside	1134/76	--	9-3-1929	
8	F	0-6-0ST	Avonside	1133/76	--	1-1957	
9	F	0-6-0ST	Avonside	1137/76	--	1897	Note 3
9	FB	0-6-2T	NZR Addington	18/97	--	1943	Note 3. Sold
10	F	0-6-0ST	Avonside	1094/76	--	1893	Note 3
10	FA	0-6-0T	NZR Addington	7/93	--	1919	Note 3. Sold
11	F	0-6-0ST	Neilson	1691/72	1-5-1873	4-7-1932	
12	F	0-6-0ST	Yorkshire	241/74	--	6-1957	Sold
13	F	0-6-0ST	Neilson	1692/72	20-12-1873	10-10-1964	Preserved
14	J	2-6-0	Vulcan	1076/83	17-8-1885	21-8-1933	
15	J	2-6-0	Vulcan	1000/83	3-12-1883	3-1935	
16	D	2-4-0T	Neilson	2306/78	--	9-1918	Sold
17	Q	2-4-4T	Rogers	2512/78	8-1879	31-3-1901	
17	UB	4-6-0	Alco (Brooks)	3925/01	4-12-1901	6-10-1933	
18	D	2-4-0T	Neilson	2308/78	--	1920	Sold
19	F	0-6-0ST	Avonside	1093/76	27-9-1876	1-1957	
20	F	0-6-0ST	Neilson	2412/78	7-8-1879	6-1957	
21	F	0-6-0ST	Neilson	2410/78	1-9-1879	21-7-1932	
22	R	0-6-4T	Avonside	1233/79	--	10-11-1932	
23	F	0-6-0ST	Neilson	2414/78	--	20-3-1931	
24	F	0-6-0ST	Neilson	2411/78	--	23-12-1929	
25	P	2-8-0	Nasmyth Wilson	281/85	2-5-1887	18-12-1928	
26	J	2-6-0	Vulcan	999/83	4-12-1883	24-1-1930	
27	N	2-6-2	Baldwin	7576/85	30-10-1885	6-6-1927	Note 4
28	R	0-6-4T	Avonside	1217/78	23-5-1879	1934	Sold
29	R	0-6-4T	Avonside	1218/78	24-5-1879	3-7-1933	Sold
30	N	2-6-2	Baldwin	7571/85	12-11-1885	27-7-1933	
31	O	2-8-0	Baldwin	7572/85	12-12-1885	27-5-1922	
32	R	0-6-4T	Avonside	1229/78	23-8-1879	9-3-1932	
33	R	0-6-4T	Avonside	1232/79	--	8-1917	Sold
34	N	2-6-2	Baldwin	7575/85	10-11-1885	27-1-1933	
35	V	2-6-2	Nasmyth Wilson	259/85	5-5-1886	6-6-1927	
36	N	2-6-2	Baldwin	7579/85	10-11-1885	1-3-1929	
37	N	2-6-2	Baldwin	7573/85	9-12-1885	11-1926	
38	F	0-6-0ST	Neilson	1841/73	1-7-1874	1-8-1932	
39	F	0-6-0ST	Neilson	2409/78	5-6-1879	6-1957	
40	F	0-6-0ST	Avonside	1090/76	4-8-1876	7-9-1934	Sold
41	F	0-6-0ST	Avonside	1140/76	--	1893	Note 3
41	FA	0-6-0T	NZR Addington	8/93	9-12-1893	18-11-1937	Note 3. Sold
42	N	2-6-2	Baldwin	7574/85	9-12-1885	3-1934	
43	F	0-6-0ST	Avonside	1143/76	--	6-1953	Sold
44	F	0-6-0ST	Avonside	1091/76	1-9-1876	1-1957	
45	F	0-6-0ST	Avonside	1144/76	7-9-1877	15-11-1933	
46	D	2-4-0T	Dubs	1168/78	28-1-1879	1920	Sold
47	D	2-4-0T	Dubs	1166/78	24-1-1879	1917	Sold
48	D	2-4-0T	Dubs	1167/78	29-1-1879	1925	Sold

ABOVE: One of the twelve tank locomotives built by Dubs in 1873 for the Canterbury branch lines was A 62. Timaru, about 1895. (W. W. Stewart Collection)

BELOW: The complete small tank locomotive fleet of classes A, C, D and G, along with many of class F were sold out of service to industrial use. However, D 197 was still in New Zealand Railways service at Petone in 1916. (A. P. Godber, Alexander Turnbull Library)

ABOVE: F 248 at Auckland in 1898 displaying a North Island style of cast number plate with the class letter flanked by stars. (S. A. Rockliff Collection)

BELOW: F 74 very late in life illustrates many updated features including Westinghouse brakes and electric lighting. Bluff, December 1952. (J. M. Creber)

STEAM LOCOMOTIVE NUMBERING 1890-1971 (continued)

Road Number	Class	Type	Builder	Maker's Number	Date in Service	Written Off	Notes
49	D	2-4-0T	Dubs	1165/78	2-1879	1919	Sold
50	D	2-4-0T	Dubs	1164/78	4-2-1879	1900	Sold
50	W^A	2-6-2T	NZR Hillside	47/02	11-1902	8-11-1933	
51	Q	2-4-4T	Rogers	2510/78	8-1879	31-3-1897	
51	U	4-6-0	NZR Addington	20/98	1898	3-1956	
52	P	2-8-0	Nasmyth Wilson	277/85	28-5-1887	9-3-1929	
53	C	0-4-2ST	Neilson	1773/73	1-11-1875	1920	Sold
54	O	2-8-0	Baldwin	7565/85	12-12-1885	27-5-1922	
55	G	4-4-0ST	Black Hawthorn	278/73	1-1-1875	24-7-1915	Sold
55	B^B	4-8-0	Price	83/17	1-1917	7-1965	
56	G	4-4-0ST	Black Hawthorn	282/73	1-1-1875	20-7-1918	Sold
57	G	4-4-0ST	Black Hawthorn	281/73	3-1-1875	23-6-1917	Sold
58	G	4-4-0ST	Black Hawthorn	279/73	2-1-1875	31-3-1919	Sold
59	J	2-6-0	Vulcan	1002/83	12-1-1884	10-1933	
60	P	2-8-0	Nasmyth Wilson	279/85	6-7-1887	31-3-1927	
61	J	2-6-0	Vulcan	1004/83	10-1-1884	6-6-1927	
62	A	0-4-0T	Dubs	656/73	1-1-1875	3-2-1906	Note 5 (see A 196)
62	W^F	2-6-4T	NZR Hillside	84/08	1908	6-1956	
63	V	2-6-2	Nasmyth Wilson	260/85	22-4-1886	31-3-1927	
64	A	0-4-0T	Dubs	651/73	1-1-1875	1890	Sold
64	W^A	2-6-2T	NZR Addington	3/92	3-1892	9-3-1929	
65	A	0-4-0T	Dubs	653/73	12-6-1875	1896	Sold
65	U	4-6-0	NZR Addington	21/98	7-1898	10-1959	
66	A	0-4-0T	Dubs	648/73	1-2-1875	1904	Sold
66	E	2-6-6-0T	NZR Petone	69/05	23-2-1906	1917	
67	A	0-4-0T	Dubs	647/73	2-2-1875	1891	Note 6 Sold
67	W^A	2-6-2T	NZR Addington	4/92	3-1892	11-1941	Sold
68	A	0-4-0T	Dubs	652/73	1-6-1875	1900	Sold
68	W^A	2-6-2T	NZR Hillside	48/03	3-1903	8-1959	Sold
69	O	2-8-0	Baldwin	7567/85	21-12-1885	27-5-1922	
70	J	2-6-0	Vulcan	1007/83	29-2-1884	15-1-1929	
71	A	0-4-0T	Yorkshire	255/75	15-12-1875	1905	Sold
71	A	4-6-2	NZR Addington	70/06	3-7-1906	3-1969	Note 7
72	F	0-6-0ST	Yorkshire	246/74	c3-1875	7-9-1953	Sold
73	F	0-6-0ST	Yorkshire	247/74	c3-1875	9-3-1929	
74	F	0-6-0ST	Yorkshire	249/74	c3-1875	6-1957	
75	F	0-6-0ST	Avonside	1088/75	10-9-1876	1925	Sold
76	F	0-6-0ST	Avonside	1132/76	14-12-1876	19-11-1930	
77	F	0-6-0ST	Avonside	1131/76	29-12-1876	5-7-1932	
78	F	0-6-0ST	Avonside	1138/76	1-4-1877	10-1954	
79	F	0-6-0ST	Avonside	1139/76	9-4-1877	20-3-1931	
80	F	0-6-0ST	Avonside	1085/75	c9-1876	21-11-1931	Sold
81	J	2-6-0	Avonside	1038/74	31-5-1875	22-8-1933	
82	J	2-6-0	Avonside	1040/74	31-8-1875	9-3-1929	
83	J	2-6-0	Avonside	1039/74	19-6-1875	1-1935	
84	J	2-6-0	Avonside	1042/74	2-3-1876	11-3-1931	
85	J	2-6-0	Avonside	1041/74	6-3-1876	18-3-1930	
86	J	2-6-0	Avonside	1043/74	1-3-1876	31-3-1927	
87	K	2-4-2	Rogers	2455/77	9-3-1878	5-1922	
88	K	2-4-2	Rogers	2454/77	18-3-1878	11-1926	Preserved
89	M	0-6-0T	Hunslet	142/75	19-12-1875	26-9-1924	Note 1
90	M	0-6-0T	Hunslet	141/75	19-12-1875	30-10-1928	Note 1
91	L	2-4-0T	Avonside	1199/77	21-6-1878	10-1900	Note 18
91	L	4-4-2T	NZR Hillside	42/00	--	29-7-1932	Note 18
92	K	2-4-2	Rogers	2468/78	16-12-1878	6-6-1927	Preserved

ABOVE: Classes G and L were design modifications to remedy the problems of the over-long coupled wheelbase of the class F. G 55, Blenheim, about 1900. (W. W. Stewart Collection)

BELOW: Sixty-five years old, H 200 was fitted with another new boiler in 1940, and ran for a further sixteen years. Cross Creek, 31 December 1945. (E. J. McClare)

ABOVE: L 219, one of the three original class L transferred to the Public Works Department, working as PWD 509. (J. A. T. Terry Collection)

BELOW: The Hunslet class M 0-6-0T were all rebuilt to 2-4-4T to overcome problems of a long coupled wheelbase and high axle loading. M 90, Napier, 1923. (W. W. Stewart Collection)

Steam Locomotive Numbering 1890-1971 - 53

ABOVE: The most successful Fairlie types were the single boiler locomotives built by Avonside in 1878-1879. Short tank version R 273 exhibits the new standard number plate. R 273, Auckland, about 1898. (E. J. McClare Collection)

BELOW: S 214 portrays the family likeness. Lower Hutt, about 1904.
(A. P. Godber, Alexander Turnbull Library)

STEAM LOCOMOTIVE NUMBERING 1890-1971 (continued)

Road Number	Class	Type	Builder	Maker's Number	Date in Service	Written Off	Notes
93	K	2-4-2	Rogers	2469/78	16-12-1878	5-1922	
94	K	2-4-2	Rogers	2470/78	16-12-1878	11-1926	Preserved
95	K	2-4-2	Rogers	2471/78	14-11-1878	6-6-1927	
95	G	4-6-2	NZR Hillside	307/37	9-1937	5-1956	
96	K	2-4-2	Rogers	2473/78	19-11-1878	5-1922	
96	G	4-6-2	NZR Hillside	308/37	8-1937	11-1955	
97	K	2-4-2	Rogers	2474/78	2-11-1878	11-1926	
97	G	4-6-2	NZR Hillside	309/37	10-1937	11-1955	
98	O	2-8-0	Baldwin	7566/85	8-1-1886	27-5-1922	
98	G	4-6-2+2-6-4	Beyer Peacock	6484/28	5-1929	9-1937	Note 8
98	G	4-6-2	NZR Hillside	310/37	11-1937	5-1956	
99	O	2-8-0	Baldwin	7569/85	11-1-1886	27-5-1922	
99	G	4-6-2+2-6-4	Beyer Peacock	6485/28	6-1929	9-1937	Note 8
99	G	4-6-2	NZR Hillside	311-38	1-1938	5-1956	
100	O	2-8-0	Baldwin	7568/85	22-2-1886	27-5-1922	
100	G	4-6-2+2-6-4	Beyer Peacock	6486/28	7-1929	9-1937	Note 8
100	G	4-6-2	NZR Hillside	312/38	3-1938	5-1956	
101	T	2-8-0	Baldwin	4660/79	2-2-1880	27-5-1922	
102	T	2-8-0	Baldwin	4661/79	7-2-1880	3-1928	
103	T	2-8-0	Baldwin	4664/79	19-1-1880	10-10-1927	
104	T	2-8-0	Baldwin	4665/79	9-1-1880	26-9-1924	
105	T	2-8-0	Baldwin	4666/79	8-2-1880	10-10-1927	
106	T	2-8-0	Baldwin	4667/79	8-2-1880	10-10-1927	
107	P	2-8-0	Nasmyth Wilson	278/85	20-8-1887	6-6-1927	Preserved
108	D	2-4-0T	Scott	30/87	21-12-1887	10-1920	Sold
109	D	2-4-0T	Scott	34/87	29-12-1887	1-1916	Sold
109	B[B]	4-8-0	Price	84/17	3-1917	31-3-1964	
110	J	2-6-0	Dubs	1215/79	10-10-1879	19-10-1930	
111	F	0-6-0ST	Dubs	1233/79	--	18-7-1934	Sold
112	R	0-6-4T	Avonside	1234/79	--	10-11-1932	
113	F	0-6-0ST	Neilson	2413/78	--	3-1941	Sold
114	V	2-6-2	Nasmyth Wilson	256/85	6-12-1885	6-6-1927	
115	J	2-6-0	Neilson	2460/79	8-10-1880	14-12-1932	
116	J	2-6-0	Neilson	2461/79	29-7-1880	4-1934	
117	J	2-6-0	Neilson	2462/79	9-7-1880	7-1934	
118	J	2-6-0	Neilson	2463/79	26-7-1880	24-11-1932	
119	J	2-6-0	Neilson	2464/79	23-6-1880	10-1935	
120	J	2-6-0	Stephenson	2367/79	28-6-1880	10-1935	Note 9
121	J	2-6-0	Stephenson	2368/79	28-6-1880	3-1934	
122	J	2-6-0	Stephenson	2369/79	14-6-1880	9-1935	
123	J	2-6-0	Stephenson	2370/79	18-8-1880	8-1935	
124	J	2-6-0	Stephenson	2371/79	10-8-1880	24-11-1932	Note 9
125	V	2-6-2	Nasmyth Wilson	257/85	1-11-1885	3-1925	
126	V	2-6-2	Nasmyth Wiison	261/85	10-11-1885	6-6-1927	
127	V	2-6-2	Nasmyth Wilson	255/85	3-2-1886	6-6-1927	
128	V	2-6-2	Nasmyth Wilson	254/85	22-4-1886	3-1927	
129	V	2-6-2	Nasmyth Wilson	258/85	30-9-1886	6-6-1927	
130	D	2-4-0T	Scott	35/87	10-6-1888	3-1927	Sold
131	D	2-4-0T	Scott	38/87	14-1-1888	11-1916	Sold
131	W[W]	4-6-4T	NZR Hillside	205/17	21-11-1918	2-1957	
132	V	2-6-2	Nasmyth Wilson	253/85	23-6-1888	3-1925	
133	P	2-8-0	Nasmyth Wilson	280/85	31-3-1886	3-1927	
134	P	2-8-0	Nasmyth Wilson	274/85	8-2-1886	3-1927	
135	P	2-8-0	Nasmyth Wilson	275/85	13-2-1886	10-10-1930	
136	V	2-6-2	Nasmyth Wilson	252/85	10-6-1890	6-6-1927	

STEAM LOCOMOTIVE NUMBERING 1890-1971 (continued)

Road Number	Class	Type	Builder	Maker's Number	Date in Service	Written Off	Notes
137	D	2-4-0T	Scott	31/87	13-2-1888	3-1901	Sold
137	W^A	2-6-2T	NZR Hillside	49/01	7-1901	11-1962	
138	D	2-4-0T	Scott	32/87	3-2-1888	12-1916	Sold
139	D	2-4-0T	Scott	33/87	19-1-1888	10-1919	Sold
140	D	2-4-0T	Scott	36/87	27-1-1888	7-1920	Sold
141	D	2-4-0T	Scott	37/87	18-2-1888	8-1919	Sold
142	D	2-4-0T	Scott	39/87	7-3-1888	10-1920	Sold
143	D	2-4-0T	Neilson	1847/74	4-1875	3-1916	Sold
143	B^B	4-8-0	Price	85/17	4-1917	5-1959	
144	D	2-4-0T	Neilson	1849/74	6-1875	1915	Sold
144	B^B	4-8-0	Price	86/17	7-1917	10-1967	Preserved
145	D	2-4-0T	Neilson	2309/78	--	9-1919	Sold
146	F	0-6-0ST	Dubs	1172/78	--	3-1937	
147	C	0-4-2ST	Neilson	1767/73	2-1874	2-1915	Sold
147	B^B	4-8-0	Price	87/17	8-1917	12-1965	
148	C	0-4-2ST	Neilson	1766/73	2-1874	2-1922	Note 10
148	B^A	4-8-0	NZR Addington	122/11	11-1911	2-6-1964	Note 11
149	D	2-4-0T	Neilson	2307/78	--	1920	Sold
150	F	0-6-0ST	Dubs	1371/80	10-1882	1-1958	Preserved
151	F	0-6-0ST	Avonside	1142/76	9-6-1877	15-11-1933	
152	F	0-6-0ST	Dubs	1173/78	--	2-1954	Sold
153	R	0-6-4T	Avonside	1225/78	--	30-1-1924	
154	F	0-6-0ST	Dubs	1370/80	5-2-1883	10-1929	Sold
155	F	0-6-0ST	Stephenson	2598/86	16-10-1886	22-5-1933	Sold
156	F	0-6-0ST	Vulcan	1181/87	17-9-1887	9-1937	
157	F	0-6-0ST	Yorkshire	243/74	--	1895	Note 3
157	F^A	0-6-0T	NZR Addington	12/95	--	1923	Note 3, Sold
158	C	0-4-2ST	Dubs	804/75	5-8-1876	7-1920	Sold
159	F	0-6-0ST	Avonside	1092/76	2-1877	20-3-1931	
160	F	0-6-0ST	Avonside	1087/75	2-1877	29-3-1928	
161	A	0-4-0T	Dubs	650/73	--	1904	Sold
161	A	4-6-2	NZR Addington	71/06	7-9-1906	10-10-1964	Note 7
162	F	0-6-0ST	Dubs	1363/80	9-1881	20-5-1932	
163	F	0-6-0ST	Dubs	1367/80	7-1881	10-10-1964	Preserved
164	F	0-6-0ST	Yorkshire	239/74	11-1874	24-3-1931	
165	B	0-4-4-0T	Avonside	1044-5/74	5-4-1875	1896	
165	W^A	2-6-2T	NZR Hillside	19/97	3-1898	5-1961	Preserved
166	C	0-4-2ST	Neilson	1765/73	4-1874	3-1892	Sold
166	F	0-6-0ST	Stephenson	2594/85	6-1893	27-7-1909	Note 12, Sold
166	W^G	4-6-4T	NZR Hillside	102/10	4-8-1910	5-1953	
167	C	0-4-2ST	Dubs	801/75	--	1915	Sold
167	B^B	4-8-0	Price	88/17	5-10-1917	12-1965	
168	C	0-4-2ST	Neilson	1769/73	--	5-1919	Sold
169	D	2-4-0T	Neilson	1848/74	1-1875	10-1914	Sold
169	B^B	4-8-0	Price	89/17	6-11-1917	12-1960	
170	D	2-4-0T	Neilson	2563/80	21-5-1881	14-8-1922	Note 13
170	W^G	4-6-4T	NZR Hillside	112/11	28-11-1911	2-1952	
171	D	2-4-0T	Neilson	2562/80	28-5-1881	5-1915	Sold
171	B^B	4-8-0	Price	90/17	20-11-1917	12-1965	
172	E	0-4-4-0T	Avonside	1070-1/75	7-1876	9-12-1899	Note 14
172	U^A	4-6-0	Sharp Stewart	4502/99	23-11-1899	2-1936	
173	E	0-4-4-0T	Avonside	1068-9/75	5-4-1877	4-3-1899	Note 14
173	U^A	4-6-0	Sharp Stewart	4503/99	7-12-1899	7-1934	
174	E	0-4-4-0T	Avonside	1066-7/75	7-1876	9-12-1899	Note 14
174	U^A	4-6-0	Sharp Stewart	4504/99	8-12-1899	9-1935	

ABOVE: Designed as the Canterbury goods engine, several members of class J spent most of their lives in Otago. J 121 was fitted with a new Belpaire firebox boiler in 1909. Invercargill, 1913.
(D. J. Sherriff, E. J. McClare Collection)

BELOW: Reboilered T 102 was transferred to Auckland in 1907 and was later fitted with piston-valve cylinders and Westinghouse brake equipment. Lyttelton, about 1901.
(A. P. Godber Collection, Alexander Turnbull Library)

ABOVE: K 94, a classic Rogers 2-4-2 of 1878, was rebuilt with a Belpaire firebox boiler in 1901. Athol, about 1905. (W. W. Stewart Collection)

BELOW: Two locomotives, supplied by Rogers for the privately built Rakaia and Ashburton Forks Railway, were initially used on suburban trains between Christchurch and Lyttelton. In later life Q 51 worked on Southland branch lines. Invercargill, about 1895. (W. W. Stewart Collection)

STEAM LOCOMOTIVE NUMBERING 1890-1971 (continued)

Road Number	Class	Type	Builder	Maker's Number	Date in Service	Written Off	Notes
175	E	0-4-4-0T	Vulcan	637/72	10-9-1872	4-3-1899	Sold
175	U^A	4-6-0	Sharp Stewart	4506/99	23-12-1899	3-1934	
176	E	0-4-4-0T	Avonside	1062-3/75	13-3-1876	4-3-1899	Note 14
176	U^A	4-6-0	Sharp Stewart	4507/99	23-12-1899	1-1934	
177	E	0-4-4-0T	Avonside	1060-1/75	11-12-1875	4-3-1899	Note 14
177	U^A	4-6-0	Sharp Stewart	4505/99	16-1-1900	3-1937	
178	E	0-4-4-0T	Avonside	1064-5/75	5-1-1876	9-12-1899	Note 14
178	B	4-8-0	Sharp Stewart	4508/99	20-12-1899	--	Note 15
178	A	4-6-2	NZR Addington	72/06	6-5-1907	10-1967	Note 7
179	F	0-6-0ST	Yorkshire	245/74	9-1875	1894	Note 3
179	F^A	0-6-0T	NZR Petone	33/94	--	4-12-1930	Note 3
180	F	0-6-0ST	Yorkshire	244/74	9-1875	1-10-1932	Note 16. Preserved
181	F	0-6-0ST	Avonside	1084/75	8-1876	24-3-1931	
182	F	0-6-0ST	Avonside	1136/76	3-1877	1893	Note 3
182	F^A	0-6-0T	NZR Petone	32/93	6-2-1893	14-12-1928	Note 3
183	F	0-6-0ST	Avonside	1135/76	3-1877	13-4-1932	
184	F	0-6-0ST	Dubs	1372/80	19-2-1881	3-11-1933	Sold
185	F	0-6-0ST	Dubs	1171/78	16-5-1879	11-1933	Sold
186	F	0-6-0ST	Yorkshire	242/74	--	1895	Note 3
186	F^A	0-6-0T	NZR Petone	36/95	25-5-1895	9-2-1929	Note 3
187	R	0-6-4T	Avonside	1224/78	2-6-1879	5-2-1924	
188	R	0-6-4T	Avonside	1227/78	28-7-1879	6-6-1927	
189	R	0-6-4T	Avonside	1228/78	25-8-1879	3-1922	
190	R	0-6-4T	Avonside	1230/78	10-9-1879	3-1922	
191	R	0-6-4T	Avonside	1231/79	15-1-1880	30-1-1924	
192	A	0-4-0T	Dubs	646/73	6-1874	12-1889	Sold
192	W	2-6-2T	NZR Addington	1/89	1-12-1889	7-1959	Preserved
193	A	0-4-0T	Dubs	655/73		1894	Sold
193	U	4-6-0	NZR Addington	16/97	16-7-1897	12-1954	
194	C	0-4-2ST	Neilson	1771/73	--	11-1893	Sold
194	U	4-6-0	NZR Addington	22/99	--	18-5-1954	
195	D	2-4-0T	Neilson	1846/74	16-11-1874	1919	Sold
196	D	2-4-0T	Neilson	1845/74	16-11-1874	1914	Sold
196	A	0-4-0T	Dubs	656/73	1-1-1875	3-1926	Note 5. Preserved
197	D	2-4-0T	Neilson	1844/74	12-1874	1916	Sold
197	B^B	4-8-0	Price	91/18	8-3-1918	12-1962	
198	D	2-4-0T	Neilson	2561/80	16-3-1881	1899	Sold
198	B	4-8-0	Sharp Stewart	4509/99	23-12-1899	--	Note 17
199	H	0-4-2T	Avonside	1075/75	1-1-1877	3-1956	Preserved
200	H	0-4-2T	Avonside	1074/75	16-10-1878	3-1956	
201	H	0-4-2T	Avonside	1072/75	17-10-1878	3-1956	
202	H	0-4-2T	Avonside	1073/75	18-11-1878	3-1956	
203	H	0-4-2T	Neilson	3469/86	1-11-1886	3-1956	
204	H	0-4-2T	Neilson	3468/86	9-8-1886	3-1956	
205	L	2-4-0T	Avonside	1200/77	8-6-1878	8-1897	Note 18
205	L^A	4-4-0T	NZR Petone	38/97	--	6-6-1927	Note 18
206	L	2-4-0T	Avonside	1201/77	19-6-1878	10-1900	Note 18
206	L	4-4-2T	NZR Petone	41/00	1900	3-1922	Note 18
207	L	2-4-0T	Avonside	1205/77	17-8-1878	1901	Sold
207	L	4-4-2T	NZR Petone	50/03	31-3-1903	3-1938	Note 19
208	L	2-4-0T	Avonside	1206/77	10-9-1878	1901	Sold
208	L	4-4-2T	NZR Petone	51/03	1903	1922	
209	R	0-6-4T	Avonside	1221/78	1-7-1879	1927	
210	R	0-6-4T	Avonside	1226/78	4-3-1880	3-1927	
211	R	0-6-4T	Avonside	1223/78	9-7-1879	12-1926	Sold

STEAM LOCOMOTIVE NUMBERING 1890-1971 (continued)

Road Number	Class	Type	Builder	Maker's Number	Date in Service	Written Off	Notes
212	S	0-6-4T	Avonside	1279/80	13-4-1882	3-1927	
213	S	0-6-4T	Avonside	1280/80	17-7-1882	3-1927	
214	S	0-6-4T	Avonside	1284/81	20-7-1883	3-1922	
215	S	0-6-4T	Avonside	1283/81	18-2-1885	8-1891	Sold
215	A	0-4-0T	Dubs	645/73	6-1874	1896	Note 20. Sold
215	U	4-6-0	NZR Addington	23/99	2-1899	3-56	
216	S	0-6-4T	Avonside	1285/81	25-2-1885	8-1891	Sold
216	F	0-6-0ST	Neilson	3751/88	--	20-4-1932	Note 20
217	S	0-6-4T	Avonside	1281/80	31-7-1886	1891	Sold
217	W^A	2-6-2T	NZR Addington	9/93	19-8-1893	5-1961	
218	S	0-6-4T	Avonside	1282/80	21-5-1887	3-1927	
219	L	2-4-0T	Avonside	1207/77	--	1903	Sold
219	L	4-4-2T	NZR Petone	52/03, 162/03	18-7-1903	7-1939	Note 21
220	A	0-4-0T	Dubs	654/73	--	4-1891	Sold
220	W^A	2-6-2T	NZR Addington	14/96	16-2-1897	1946	Sold
221	D	2-4-0T	Neilson	2565/80	5-1881	11-1918	Sold
222	D	2-4-0T	Neilson	2566/80	6-1881	5-1915	Sold
222	B^B	4-8-0	Price	92/18	11-3-1918	4-1966	
223	F	0-6-0ST	Stephenson	2595/85	8-1886	3-2-1932	
224	F	0-6-0ST	Avonside	1086/75	9-1876	18-3-1930	
225	F	0-6-0ST	Avonside	1089/75	9-1876	9-1935	Sold
226	F	0-6-0ST	Dubs	1169/78	3-1879	1892	Note 3
226	F^A	0-6-0T	NZR Petone	30/92	--	12-12-1930	Note 3
227	F	0-6-0ST	Dubs	1170/78	4-1879	20-5-1932	
228	F	0-6-0ST	Dubs	1365/80	4-1882	11-1935	Sold
229	F	0-6-0ST	Dubs	1369/80	7-1881	14-3-1931	
230	F	0-6-0ST	Dubs	1364/80	7-1881	3-2-1932	Sold
231	F	0-6-0ST	Black Hawthorn	277/73	6-1874	11-1931	
232	F	0-6-0ST	Yorkshire	248/74	4-1875	1-1957	
233	F	0-6-0ST	Stephenson	2593/85	9-8-1886	4-1936	Sold
234	J	2-6-0	Dubs	1212/79	18-9-1879	21-11-1933	Note 9
235	J	2-6-0	Dubs	1213/79	21-9-1879	3-9-1931	
236	J	2-6-0	Dubs	1214/79	21-9-1879	3-9-1931	
237	A	0-4-0T	Yorkshire	256/75	--	10-1891	Sold
237	U	4-6-0	NZR Addington	10/94	15-11-1894	12-1954	
238	B	0-4-4-0T	Avonside	1022-3/74	9-1874	1890	
238	W	2-6-2T	NZR Addington	2/91	25-6-1891	8-1959	
239	C	0-4-2ST	Dubs	800/75	10-1875	1890	Sold
239	U	4-6-0	NZR Addington	11/95	26-12-1895	3-1956	
240	D	2-4-0T	Neilson	1843/74	9-1874	1919	Sold
241	F	0-6-0ST	Neilson	1706/72	14-4-1873	3-1927	
242	F	0-6-0ST	Stephenson	2086/73	12-1873	1892	Note 3
242	F^A	0-6-0T	NZR Newmarket	28/92	--	10-10-1930	Note 3
243	F	0-6-0ST	Stephenson	2085/73	1-1874	24-7-1930	Sold
244	F	0-6-0ST	Stephenson	2087/73	1-1874	1895	Note 3
244	F^A	0-6-0T	NZR Newmarket	35/95	--	18-3-1930	Note 3
245	F	0-6-0ST	Yorkshire	240/74	11-1874	4-1935	
246	F	0-6-0ST	Vulcan	735/75	9-1875	18-3-1930	
247	F	0-6-0ST	Vulcan	737/75	9-1875	1892	Note 3
247	F^A	0-6-0T	NZR Newmarket	29/92	--	12-9-1929	Note 3
248	F	0-6-0ST	Vulcan	736/75	9-1875	7-1930	Sold
249	F	0-6-0ST	Dubs	1362/80	7-1881	29-11-1932	
250	F	0-6-0ST	Dubs	1368/80	7-1881	1892	Note 3
250	F^A	0-6-0T	NZR Addington	5/92	--	31-3-1943	Note 3. Sold
251	F	0-6-0ST	Dubs	1366/80	8-1881	1892	Note 3

60 - Steam Locomotive Numbering 1890-1971

ABOVE: The overweight class V locomotives had to be altered before they were permitted to run on NZR tracks. V 126 was the last of the NZR batch built and the second to be placed in service. Dunedin, about 1895. (E. R. Williams, S. A. Rockliff Collection)

BELOW: The first two were used as stationary boilers at Hillside Workshops for a time. V 132, the penultimate in service but the second built, was later equipped with Walschaert valve gear during 1892. V 132, Invercargill, about 1910.
(D. J. Sherriff, A. P. Godber Collection, Alexander Turnbull Library)

ABOVE: N 27 was one of six passenger locomotives ordered from Baldwin in December 1884. The locomotive was equipped with a crosshead feed-water pump and an early Westinghouse air compressor, both soon removed. N 27, newly erected at Addington, November 1885.
(C. Rous-Marten, T. A. McGavin Collection)

BELOW: N 27 was rebuilt in 1895 at Addington with a Belpaire firebox boiler and Vauclain compound cylinders. The locomotive was transferred to the North Island in 1901 and shortly after air brakes were again fitted. N 27, Hawke's Bay district, about 1910.
(A. P. Godber Collection, Alexander Turnbull Library)

ABOVE: The Nasmyth Wilson goods locomotive, ordered to class O specification, went into service as class P. Most of these eight-coupled locomotives ended their lives as shunting engines. P 269, Frankton Junction, 1922. (W. W. Stewart)

BELOW: Six consolidation-type locomotives were ordered from Baldwin in December 1884 to class O specification. All six were at work fourteen months later. O 99, Dunedin, about 1897.
(E. R. Williams, S. A. Rockliff Collection)

ABOVE: The first 'homespun' design was a 2-6-2 tank locomotive, W 192. NZR Nº 1 of 1889 had its official portrait taken at Addington Workshops prior to its transfer to Wellington in March 1890. (E. J. McClare Collection)

BELOW: Seventy years later it was written off. When photographed W 192 still had almost twelve years of life left in NZR service. Greymouth, 11 December 1947. (E. J. McClare)

STEAM LOCOMOTIVE NUMBERING 1890-1971 (continued)

Road Number	Class	Type	Builder	Maker's Number	Date in Service	Written Off	Notes
251	F^A	0-6-0T	NZR Addington	6/92	--	3-1939	Sold. Note 3
252	F	0-6-0ST	Dubs	1884/84	4-1885	24-3-1931	
253	F	0-6-0ST	Dubs	1885/84	5-1885	26-10-1933	
254	F	0-6-0ST	Dubs	1886/84	11-1884	2-1944	
255	F	0-6-0ST	Dubs	1887/84	5-1885	9-1934	
256	F	0-6-0ST	Stephenson	2599/86	11-1886	5-1953	
257	F	0-6-0ST	Stephenson	2600/86	12-1886	30-6-1953	
258	J	2-6-0	Vulcan	1001/83	11-1883	11-5-1932	
259	J	2-6-0	Vulcan	998/83	12-1883	3-1929	
260	J	2-6-0	Vulcan	1003/83	11-1883	14-12-1928	
261	J	2-6-0	Vulcan	1005/83	12-1883	14-12-1928	
262	J	2-6-0	Vulcan	1006/83	1-1884	21-11-1933	Note 9
263	J	2-6-0	Vulcan	1009/83	1-1884	14-12-1928	
264	L	2-4-0T	Avonside	1208/77	7-1878	1900	Note 18
264	L	4-4-2T	NZR Newmarket	40/00	1900	3-1922	Note 18
265	L	2-4-0T	Avonside	1202/77	7-1878	1894	Note 18
265	L^A	4-4-0T	NZR Newmarket	34/94	1894	24-10-1929	Note 18
266	L	2-4-0T	Avonside	1203/77	7-1878	1899	Note 18
266	L	4-4-2T	NZR Newmarket	39/99	6-9-1899	3-1922	Note 18
267	L	2-4-0T	Avonside	1204/77	7-1878	10-1893	Note 18
267	L^A	4-4-0T	NZR Newmarket	31/93	--	3-1922	Note 18
268	P	2-8-0	Nasmyth Wilson	272/85	5-1887	3-1922	
269	P	2-8-0	Nasmyth Wilson	273/85	5-1887	3-1927	
270	P	2-8-0	Nasmyth Wilson	276/85	2-1887	3-1922	
271	R	0-6-4T	Avonside	1219/78	7-1879	3-1936	
272	R	0-6-4T	Avonside	1220/78	7-1879	3-1928	
273	R	0-6-4T	Avonside	1222/78	7-1879	2-1927	
274	U	4-6-0	NZR Addington	17/97	7-1897	3-1956	
275	W^A	2-6-2T	NZR Addington	15/96	24-12-1896	8-1939	
276	F^A	0-6-0T	NZR Newmarket	37/96	--	24-3-1931	Note 3
277	F	0-6-0ST	Stephenson	2597/86	3-1898	1-1957	Note 22
278	U^B	4-6-0	Baldwin	16042/98	14-12-1898	14-9-1934	
279	U^B	4-6-0	Baldwin	16043/98	17-12-1898	24-3-1933	
280	U^B	4-6-0	Baldwin	16044/98	10-12-1898	1-9-1936	
281	U^B	4-6-0	Baldwin	16045/98	5-12-1898	6-1936	
282	U^B	4-6-0	Baldwin	16046/98	4-12-1898	4-1934	
283	U^B	4-6-0	Baldwin	16047/98	17-12-1898	8-12-1933	
284	U^B	4-6-0	Baldwin	16048/98	6-12-1898	9-1934	
285	U^B	4-6-0	Baldwin	16049/98	23-11-1898	5-1934	
286	U^B	4-6-0	Baldwin	16050/98	16-12-1898	4-1935	
287	U^B	4-6-0	Baldwin	16051/98	11-12-1898	14-1-1933	
288	W^A	2-6-2T	NZR Hillside	27/99	31-3-1899	3-12-1932	
289	W^A	2-6-2T	NZR Hillside	25/99	31-10-1899	11-1962	
290	W^B	2-6-2T	Baldwin	16173/98	17-1-1899	29-1-1929	
291	W^B	2-6-2T	Baldwin	16171/98	20-1-1899	12-1931	
292	W^B	2-6-2T	Baldwin	16172/98	1-1899	1-1957	
293	W^B	2-6-2T	Baldwin	16174/98	21-9-1899	3-12-1932	
294	W^B	2-6-2T	Baldwin	16170/98	8-2-1899	5-1935	
295	W^B	2-6-2T	Baldwin	16168/98	2-1899	14-10-1929	
296	W^B	2-6-2T	Baldwin	16169/98	3-1899	3-8-1931	
297	W^B	2-6-2T	Baldwin	16166/98	28-2-1899	6-10-1932	
298	W^B	2-6-2T	Baldwin	16167/98	4-1899	9-1955	
299	W^B	2-6-2T	Baldwin	16175/98	26-5-1899	1-1957	Preserved
300	W^B	2-6-2T	Baldwin	16176/98	17-2-1899	10-1955	
301	W^B	2-6-2T	Baldwin	16177/98	21-4-1899	6-6-1927	

STEAM LOCOMOTIVE NUMBERING 1890-1971 (continued)

Road Number	Class	Type	Builder	Maker's Number	Date in Service	Written Off	Notes
302	B	4-8-0	NZR Addington	24/99	4-5-1899	2-12-1960	
303	B	4-8-0	NZR Addington	26/01	15-5-1901	12-1967	Note 11
304	B	4-8-0	NZR Addington	43/02	31-3-1902	12-1967	Notes 11 & 41
305	B	4-8-0	NZR Addington	53/02	9-2-1903	23-5-1964	
306	B	4-8-0	NZR Addington	54/03	31-3-1903	4-11-1961	Note 11
307	B	4-8-0	NZR Addington	55/03	5-1903	6-1965	Note 11
308	B	4-8-0	Sharp Stewart	4511/99	15-1-1900	10-1963	Note 41
309	B	4-8-0	Sharp Stewart	4510/99	1-1900	--	Note 23
310	L[A]	4-4-0T	Nasmyth Wilson	311/87	8-1887	8-12-1924	NZMR 1.
311	L[A]	4-4-0T	Nasmyth Wilson	315/87	12-1887	19-3-1920	NZMR 2. Sold
312	L[A]	4-4-0T	Nasmyth Wilson	322/87	7-1888	31-3-1928	NZMR 3.
313	L[A]	4-4-0T	Nasmyth Wiison	323/87	30-6-1890	8-11-1924	NZMR 4.
314	L[A]	4-4-0T	Nasmyth Wilson	312/87	23-11-1892	30-1-1926	NZMR 5. Sold
315	D	2-4-0T	Scott	40/90	4-9-1890	1901	NZMR 6. Sold
315	F[B]	0-6-2T	NZR Addington	44/02	1902	1936	Note 3
316	W[D]	2-6-4T	Baldwin	18543/01	14-6-1901	3-4-1934	Sold
317	W[D]	2-6-4T	Baldwin	18544/01	29-6-1901	12-1934	Sold
318	W[D]	2-6-4T	Baldwin	18545/01	9-7-1901	2-10-1933	
319	W[D]	2-6-4T	Baldwin	18546/01	15-6-1901	9-1934	
320	W[D]	2-6-4T	Baldwin	18547/01	2-6-1901	2-1936	
321	W[D]	2-6-4T	Baldwin	18548/01	8-6-1901	7-1934	
322	W[D]	2-6-4T	Baldwin	18549/01	30-5-1901	7-8-1933	
323	W[D]	2-6-4T	Baldwin	18550/01	24-5-1901	15-6-1933	
324	W[D]	2-6-4T	Baldwin	18551/01	30-7-1901	7-8-1933	
325	W[D]	2-6-4T	Baldwin	18552/01	30-7-1901	18-10-1933	
326	W[D]	2-6-4T	Baldwin	18553/01	15-6-1901	7-8-1933	
327	W[D]	2-6-4T	Baldwin	18554/01	8-6-1901	5-1936	
328	U[B]	4-6-0	Baldwin	18574/01	17-6-1901	3-1935	
329	U[B]	4-6-0	Baldwin	18575/01	11-6-1901	1-1957	
330	U[B]	4-6-0	Baldwin	18576/01	3-6-1901	1-1957	
331	U[B]	4-6-0	Baldwin	18577/01	17-6-1901	3-1955	
332	U[B]	4-6-0	Baldwin	18578/01	20-6-1901	3-1955	
333	U[B]	4-6-0	Baldwin	18579/01	7-6-1901	3-1935	
334	U[B]	4-6-0	Baldwin	18580/01	29-6-1901	3-1935	
335	U[B]	4-6-0	Baldwin	18581/01	20-6-1901	6-1953	
336	U[B]	4-6-0	Baldwin	18582/01	13-6-1901	3-1955	
337	U[B]	4-6-0	Baldwin	18583/01	6-6-1901	3-1955	
338	Q	4-6-2	Baldwin	19202/01	9-3-1902	28-2-1948	
339	Q	4-6-2	Baldwin	19203/01	5-3-1902	5-1-1957	
340	Q	4-6-2	Baldwin	19204/01	11-3-1902	8-11-1941	
341	Q	4-6-2	Baldwin	19205/01	6-3-1902	24-5-1941	
342	Q	4-6-2	Baldwin	19206/01	11-3-1902	28-2-1948	
343	Q	4-6-2	Baldwin	19207/01	7-3-1902	7-12-1957	
344	Q	4-6-2	Baldwin	19248/01	7-3-1902	21-6-1941	
345	Q	4-6-2	Baldwin	19249/01	5-3-1902	28-2-1948	
346	Q	4-6-2	Baldwin	19250/01	11-3-1902	22-6-1957	
347	Q	4-6-2	Baldwin	19251/01	25-12-1902	5-3-1955	
348	Q	4-6-2	Baldwin	19252/01	16-9-1902	28-2-1948	
349	Q	4-6-2	Baldwin	19253/01	24-12-1901	28-2-1948	
350	Q	4-6-2	Baldwin	19254/01	17-9-1902	24-7-1948	
351	N	2-6-2	Baldwin	19270/01	20-11-1901	31-3-1927	
352	N	2-6-2	Baldwin	19271/01	18-11-1901	27-8-1929	
353	N	2-6-2	Baldwin	19272/01	22-11-1901	31-3-1927	
354	N	2-6-2	Baldwin	19273/01	22-11-1901	31-3-1927	
355	W[D]	2-6-4T	Baldwin	19259/01	25-12-1901	4-1934	

ABOVE: F^A 186 was built as class F in 1874. Its first reincarnation as an 0-6-0T at Petone in 1895 included a new boiler, new cylinders with outside Walschaert valve gear and new water tanks. F^A 186, Cross Creek, about 1899. (A. P. Godber Collection, Alexander Turnbull Library)

BELOW: The last rebuild as class F^B included a larger bunker, cab and trailing bogie. When all of the rebuilt locomotives and six new machines had been made to this type they were reclassified as F^A. F^A 157 was altered to the 0-6-2T configuration at Hillside in 1903. Oamaru, about 1920.
(S. A. Rockliff Collection)

ABOVE: Seven of the class L^A locomotives were renewed from the Avonside class L 2-4-0T of 1877. L^A 267, remanufactured at Newmarket Workshops in 1893 as a 4-4-0T, was further altered to a 4-4-2T in 1900. Probably only the number plates survived into the renewal. (W. W. Stewart Collection)

BELOW: New Zealand Midland Railway locomotive N° 4 became L^A 313 when the company was vested in the NZR in 1900. Greymouth, about 1923.
(A. P. Godber Collection, Alexander Turnbull Library)

STEAM LOCOMOTIVE NUMBERING 1890-1971 (continued)

Road Number	Class	Type	Builder	Maker's Number	Date in Service	Written Off	Notes
356	W^D	2-6-4T	Baldwin	19260/01	11-2-1902	23-12-1932	Sold
357	W^D	2-6-4T	Baldwin	19261/01	21-12-1901	3-1935	Sold
358	W^D	2-6-4T	Baldwin	19262/01	22-1-1902	8-1934	
359	W^D	2-6-4T	Baldwin	19263/01	1-2-1902	3-1936	
360	W^D	2-6-4T	Baldwin	19264/01	5-12-1901	3-1936	
361	U^C	4-6-0	Sharp Stewart	4745/01	16-8-1901	1-1957	
362	U^C	4-6-0	Sharp Stewart	4746/01	7-8-1901	10-1958	
363	U^C	4-6-0	Sharp Stewart	4747/01	28-9-1901	8-1936	
364	U^C	4-6-0	Sharp Stewart	4748/01	28-9-1901	2-1957	
365	U^C	4-6-0	Sharp Stewart	4749/01	7-10-1901	10-1959	
366	U^C	4-6-0	Sharp Stewart	4750/01	10-10-1901	8-1936	
367	U^C	4-6-0	Sharp Stewart	4751/01	12-10-1901	10-1955	
368	U^C	4-6-0	Sharp Stewart	4752/01	18-10-1901	12-1934	
369	U^C	4-6-0	Sharp Stewart	4753/01	21-10-1901	1-1957	
370	U^C	4-6-0	Sharp Stewart	4754/01	24-10-1901	1-1957	
371	U^B	4-6-0	Alco (Richmond)	3275/01	29-2-1902	20-9-1933	
372	F^B	0-6-2T	NZR Addington	45/02	16-8-1902	3-1936	Notes 3 & 24
373	F^B	0-6-2T	NZR Addington	46/02	5-11-1902	7-1936	Note 3
374	F^B	0-6-2T	NZR Addington	52/02	22-1-1903	1936	Note 3
375	F^B	0-6-2T	NZR Addington	56/03	29-7-1903	3-1936	Note 3
375	W^E	4-6-4T	NZR Hillside	--	--	3-1969	Note 23
376	F^B	0-6-2T	NZR Addington	57/03	28-8-1903	20-3-1931	Note 3
376	W^E	4-6-4T	NZR Addington	--	--	29-2-1964	Note 17
377	W^E	4-6-4T	NZR Hillside	--	--	9-1966	Note 15
378	U	4-6-0	NZR Addington	58/03	5-11-1903	3-1956	
379	W^F	2-6-4T	NZR Addington	59/04	9-6-1904	10-10-1964	
380	W^F	2-6-4T	NZR Addington	60/04	23-7-04	9-1966	
381	W^F	2-6-4T	NZR Addington	61/04	13-9-1904	1939	Sold
382	W^F	2-6-4T	NZR Addington	62/04	29-9-1904	10-10-1964	
383	W^F	2-6-4T	NZR Addington	63/04	16-12-1904	12-1967	
384	W^F	2-6-4T	NZR Addington	64/05	17-2-1905	12-1958	
385	W^F	2-6-4T	NZR Addington	65/05	4-4-1905	1939	Sold
386	W^F	2-6-4T	NZR Addington	66/05	22-9-1905	10-1958	Preserved
387	W^F	2-6-4T	NZR Addington	67/05	14-8-1905	10-10-1964	
388	W^F	2-6-4T	NZR Addington	68/05	25-9-1905	6-1965	
389	W^F	2-6-4T	Price	1/04	1-9-1904	10-1960	
390	W^F	2-6-4T	Price	2/04	27-9-1904	10-1963	
391	W^F	2-6-4T	Price	3/04	11-11-1904	9-1966	
392	W^F	2-6-4T	Price	4/04	29-11-1904	1944	Sold
393	W^F	2-6-4T	Price	5/04	20-12-1904	3-1967	Preserved
394	W^F	2-6-4T	Price	6/04	9-2-1905	10-10-1964	
395	W^F	2-6-4T	Price	7/04	21-3-1905	2-1956	
396	W^F	2-6-4T	Price	8/04	18-4-1905	11-1957	
397	W^F	2-6-4T	Price	9/05	30-5-1905	6-1956	
398	W^F	2-6-4T	Price	10/05	29-6-1905	5-1954	Note 25
399	A	4-6-2	NZR Addington	73/06	27-3-1907	2-1959	Note 7
400	W^F	2-6-4T	NZR Hillside	74/07	1-7-1907	5-1954	
401	W^F	2-6-4T	NZR Hillside	75/07	5-7-1907	11-1966	
402	W^F	2-6-4T	NZR Hillside	76/07	18-9-1907	10-10-1964	
403	W^F	2-6-4T	NZR Hillside	77/07	4-10-1907	7-1969	
404	W^F	2-6-4T	NZR Hillside	78/07	10-12-1907	6-1956	
405	W^F	2-6-4T	NZR Hillside	79/07	30-12-1907	1944	Sold
406	A	4-6-2	NZR Addington	80/07	20-12-1907	3-1968	Note 7
407	A	4-6-2	NZR Addington	81/08	12-3-1908	10-1962	Note 7
408	A	4-6-2	NZR Addington	82/08	31-3-1908	7-1961	Note 7

STEAM LOCOMOTIVE NUMBERING 1890-1971 (continued)							
Road Number	Class	Type	Builder	Maker's Number	Date in Service	Written Off	Notes
409	A	4-6-2	NZR Addington	83/08	20-7-1907	10-1959	Note 26
410	A	4-6-2	Price	13/07	6-12-1907	8-1960	Note 7
411	A	4-6-2	Price	14/08	14-2-1908	8-1966	Note 7
412	A	4-6-2	Price	15/08	30-2-1908	7-1961	Note 7
413	A	4-6-2	Price	16/08	28-5-1908	23-5-1964	Note 7
414	A	4-6-2	Price	17/08	30-6-1908	23-5-1964	Note 7
415	A	4-6-2	Price	18/08	1-8-1908	7-1962	Note 7
416	A	4-6-2	Price	19/08	16-9-1908	10-1967	Note 7
417	A	4-6-2	Price	20/08	23-9-1908	23-5-1964	Note 7
418	A	4-6-2	Price	21/08	27-11-1908	3-1965	Note 7
419	A	4-6-2	Price	22/08	21-12-1908	7-1961	Note 7
420	A	4-6-2	Price	23/08	12-2-1909	11-1961	Note 7
421	A	4-6-2	Price	24/09	15-3-1909	3-1965	Note 7
422	A	4-6-2	Price	25/09	16-4-1909	20-6-1964	Note 7
423	A	4-6-2	Price	26/09	15-5-1909	7-1969	Note 7. Preserved
424	A	4-6-2	Price	27/09	18-6-1909	3-1969	Note 7
425	A	4-6-2	Price	28/08	16-7-1909	3-1965	Note 7
426	A	4-6-2	Price	29/09	27-8-1909	3-1969	Note 7
427	A	4-6-2	Price	30/09	20-8-1909	10-10-1964	Note 7
428	A	4-6-2	Price	31/09	6-11-1909	7-1969	Note 7. Preserved
429	A	4-6-2	Price	32/09	29-11-1909	9-1959	Note 7
430	W^F	2-6-4T	NZR Hillside	85/08	26-10-1908	9-1966	
431	W^F	2-6-4T	NZR Hillside	86/08	3-11-1908	1944	Sold
432	W^F	2-6-4T	NZR Hillside	87/08	30-12-1908	4-1959	
433	W^F	2-6-4T	NZR Hillside	88/08	3-2-1909	3-1968	
434	W^F	2-6-4T	NZR Hillside	89/08	27-2-1909	1944	Sold
435	W^F	2-6-4T	NZR Hillside	90/08	26-3-1909	2-1961	
436	W^F	2-6-4T	NZR Hillside	91/09	31-3-1909	1939	Sold
437	W^F	2-6-4T	NZR Hillside	92/09	15-5-1909	1939	Sold
438	W^F	2-6-4T	NZR Hillside	93/09	22-5-1909	10-10-1964	
439	X	4-8-2	NZR Addington	94/08	9-1-1909	2-3-1957	Note 27
440	X	4-8-2	NZR Addington	95/08	25-3-1909	2-3-1957	Note 27
441	X	4-8-2	NZR Addington	96/09	10-5-1909	2-3-1957	
442	X	4-8-2	NZR Addington	97/09	10-7-1909	4-3-1944	Note 27. Sold
443	X	4-8-2	NZR Addington	98/09	1-12-1909	2-3-1957	Note 27
444	X	4-8-2	NZR Addington	99/09	3-2-1910	2-3-1957	Note 27
445	X	4-8-2	NZR Addington	100/09	24-5-1910	26-5-1949	
446	X	4-8-2	NZR Addington	101/09	30-4-1910	6-12-1946	Note 27. Sold
447	W^H	2-6-2T	Manning Wardle	920/84	11-1884	12-11-1927	WMR 1. Sold
448	W^H	2-6-2T	Manning Wardle	921/84	11-1884	11-12-1926	WMR 2. Sold
449	W^H	2-6-2T	Manning Wardle	923/84	8-1886	15-8-1914	WMR 4. Sold
449	W^W	4-6-4T	NZR Hillside	206/17	4-1918	2-1956	
450	V	2-6-2	Nasmyth Wilson	282/85	by 11-1886	31-3-1926	WMR 6
451	V	2-6-2	Nasmyth Wilson	283/85	by 11-1886	19-11-1923	WMR 7
452	V	2-6-2	Nasmyth Wilson	284/85	by 11-1886	19-11-1923	WMR 8
453	N	2-6-2	Baldwin	12104/91	1-1892	13-11-1926	WMR 9
454	N	2-6-2	Baldwin	12106/91	1-1892	7-3-1928	WMR 10
455	O^B	2-8-0	Baldwin	9018/88	9-1888	24-3-1931	WMR 11
456	O^B	2-8-0	Baldwin	9021/88	9-1888	21-9-1929	WMR 12
457	O^A	2-8-0	Baldwin	13908/94	6-8-1894	12-12-1929	WMR 13
458	O^C	2-8-0	Baldwin	15055/96	20-6-1897	30-7-1930	WMR 16
459	N^A	2-6-2	Baldwin	13913/94	8-9-1894	31-3-1929	WMR 14
460	N^A	2-6-2	Baldwin	15054/96	10-1897	1-7-1929	WMR 15
461	N^C	2-6-2	Baldwin	19797/01	8-5-1902	20-3-1931	WMR 5
462	N^C	2-6-2	Baldwin	23594/04	9-1904	10-9-1928	WMR 18

70 - Steam Locomotive Numbering 1890-1971

ABOVE: Addington Workshops commenced building class W^A locomotives in 1892. W^A 220, new in 1897, commenced work at Palmerston North and was transferred to Gisborne in 1910. Petone, just after overhaul, 1910. (W. W. Stewart Collection)

BELOW: The Greymouth trio, equipped to work on the Rewanui and Blackball Inclines, were all different. W^A 217 featured a longer cab and early style iron rod cowcatchers modified with lift-up flaps to clear the Fell centre braking rail on the inclines. Greymouth, 20 November 1956. (J. M. Creber)

ABOVE: W^A 289 was unique with the paired air reservoirs on the cab roof and air compressor mounted on the driver's side of the smokebox. The cowcatchers were the later iron strap type similarly fitted with lift-up clearance flaps. Greymouth, 25 July 1960.   (B. D. Whebell)

BELOW: W^A 137, one of the last three of the class built new with piston-valve cylinders, exhibited its individual details including an elongated front sand dome and modified strap cowcatchers. Greymouth, 1 December 1952.   (K. T. Cullen)

72 - Steam Locomotive Numbering 1890-1971

ABOVE: Originally conceived as a 4-4-0, the new passenger locomotive evolved into a 4-6-0. U 237, the first of the class, had a single-window cab; the second, U 239 had a double-window cab, while the remainder were built with continuous high running boards. U 237, new at Addington Workshops, 1894. (G W. Emerson Collection)

BELOW: In its last days U 237 exhibited many changes from new. Equipped for shunting it had a tender cab and rear cowcatcher. It had also received a round-top superheater boiler, piston-valve cylinders, Westinghouse brake gear and electric lighting. Invercargill, 1949. (E. J. McClare)

STEAM LOCOMOTIVE NUMBERING 1890-1971 (continued)

Road Number	Class	Type	Builder	Maker's Number	Date in Service	Written Off	Notes
463	B^C	2-8-2	Baldwin	19796/01	10-6-1902	31-3-1927	WMR 17
464	U^D	4-6-0	Baldwin	24086/04	10-11-1904	1-7-1929	WMR 19
465	U^D	4-6-0	Baldwin	24087/04	7-12-1904	24-3-1931	WMR 20
466	W^J	2-8-4T	Baldwin	23596/04	7-1904	6-6-1927	WMR 3
467	W^F	2-6-4T	Price	11/06	28-5-1906	31-3-1964	Note 28
468	W^F	2-6-4T	Price	12/06	26-6-1906	6-1965	Note 28
469	A	4-6-2	Price	33/10	18-10-1910	7-1961	Note 7
470	A	4-6-2	Price	34/10	29-11-1910	12-1965	Note 7
471	A	4-6-2	Price	35/11	31-1-1911	4-1962	Note 7
472	A	4-6-2	Price	36/11	13-3-1911	9-1966	Note 7
473	A	4-6-2	Price	37/11	25-4-1911	2-1959	Note 7
474	A	4-6-2	Price	38/11	2-6-1911	8-1966	Note 7
475	A	4-6-2	Price	39/11	14-7-1911	5-1963	Note 7
476	A	4-6-2	Price	40/11	22-8-1911	7-1961	Note 7
477	A	4-6-2	Price	41/11	9-10-1911	3-1962	Note 7
478	A	4-6-2	Price	42/11	7-11-1911	3-1965	Note 7
479	W^G	4-6-4T	NZR Hillside	103/10	13-9-1910	31-3-1964	Note 29
480	W^G	4-6-4T	NZR Hillside	104/10	18-10-1910	6-1969	Note 29. Preserved
481	W^G	4-6-4T	NZR Hillside	105/10	20-10-1910	5-1959	Note 29
482	W^G	4-6-4T	NZR Hillside	106/10	3-11-1910	2-1957	Note 29
483	W^G	4-6-4T	NZR Hillside	107/10	12-12-1910	2-1956	
484	W^G	4-6-4T	NZR Hillside	108/10	12-12-1910	2-1956	
485	W^G	4-6-4T	NZR Hillside	109/11	23-3-1911	2-1952	
486	W^G	4-6-4T	NZR Hillside	110/11	13-4-1911	29-1-1964	Note 29
487	W^G	4-6-4T	NZR Hillside	111/11	13-4-1911	6-1953	
488	W^G	4-6-4T	NZR Hillside	113/11	20-12-1911	29-2-1964	Note 29
489	W^G	4-6-4T	NZR Hillside	114/12	8-6-1912	3-1957	Note 29
490	W^G	4-6-4T	NZR Hillside	115/12	18-6-1912	8-1959	Note 29
491	W^G	4-6-4T	NZR Hillside	116/12	15-6-1912	8-1955	Note 29. Preserved
492	W^G	4-6-4T	NZR Hillside	117/12	21-8-1912	2-1956	Note 29
493	W^G	4-6-4T	NZR Hillside	118/12	7-9-1912	3-1957	Note 29
494	W^G	4-6-4T	NZR Hillside	119/12	10-9-1912	3-1957	Note 29
495	W^G	4-6-4T	NZR Hillside	120/12	21-10-1912	2-1956	Note 29
496	W^G	4-6-4T	NZR Hillside	121/12	2-11-1912	2-1956	Note 29
497	B^A	4-8-0	NZR Addington	123/11	20-12-1911	23-5-1964	
498	B^A	4-8-0	NZR Addington	124/12	25-3-1912	9-1966	Note 11
499	B^A	4-8-0	NZR Addington	125/12	6-4-1912	10-10-1964	Note 11
500	B^A	4-8-0	NZR Addington	126/12	13-6-1912	12-1965	
501-550							Note 30
542	Y	0-6-0T	Hunslet	1444/23	19-10-1923	17-8-1957	Note 31. Sold
543	Y	0-6-0T	Hunslet	1443/23	20-11-1923	1-2-1958	Note 31
544	Y	0-6-0T	Hunslet	1445/23	20-12-1923	17-8-1957	Note 31
551	B^A	4-8-0	NZR Addington	127/12	2-10-1912	8-1968	
552	B^A	4-8-0	NZR Addington	128/12	12-12-1912	6-1969	Note 11. Preserved
553	B^A	4-8-0	NZR Addington	129/13	18-2-1913	10-1967	Note 11
554	B^A	4-8-0	NZR Addington	130/13	9-4-1913	5-1963	
555	B^A	4-8-0	NZR Addington	131/13	14-5-1913	6-1957	
556	W^W	4-6-4T	NZR Hillside	132/13	29-5-1913	2-1963	
557	W^W	4-6-4T	NZR Hillside	133/13	1-7-1913	8-1958	
558	W^W	4-6-4T	NZR Hillside	134/13	10-7-1913	3-1957	
559	W^W	4-6-4T	NZR Hillside	135/13	10-8-1913	3-1957	
560	W^W	4-6-4T	NZR Hillside	136/13	19-8-1913	8-1961	
561	W^W	4-6-4T	NZR Hillside	137/13	11-10-1913	2-1963	
562	W^W	4-6-4T	NZR Hillside	138/13	31-10-1913	--	Note 32

74 - Steam Locomotive Numbering 1890-1971

ABOVE: B 302, the new goods train locomotive, was painted in a special works grey livery for its official photograph. Addington, May 1899. (W. W. Stewart Collection)

BELOW: B 302 exhibits many alterations since new, including Westinghouse air brakes, raised running boards and a sand dome. Dunedin, about 1910. (W. W. Stewart Collection)

ABOVE: Equipped for shunting with a tender cab and rear cowcatcher, B 303 shows other changes. A round-top superheated boiler has been fitted. The superheater header is the casting on the side of the smokebox. B 303, Dunedin 1930. (W. W. Stewart Collection)

BELOW: In 1928 work commenced on improving the South Island 4-8-0 fleet. Over a twenty year period nine of this type were fitted with wide-firebox boilers. B 303 received its new boiler in October 1948. B 303, Reefton, 17 November 1955. (J. M. Creber)

76 - Steam Locomotive Numbering 1890-1971

ABOVE: The Baldwin Locomotive Works received substantial orders from NZR in 1898 and 1901. The 'American W^A' delivered in 1899 were soon reclassified to W^B. Eight worked until about 1930 and the remaining four hauled coal trains at Westport until the mid-1950s. W^B 292 and W^B 299 were both dumped in the Mokihinui River in 1960 from where they were recovered for preservation purposes almost thirty years later. W^B 299, Westport, 23 November 1951. (J. M. Creber)

BELOW: Eighteen similar locomotives with a larger bunker, a four-wheeled trailing bogie and a higher working boiler pressure, arrived in 1901. W^D 327, the last to run in NZR service, was employed on the Wellington car shunt in 1935. (W. W. Stewart)

ABOVE: In 1895 three-quarters of the NZR fleet were tank locomotives. This proportion altered over the next ten years with the arrival of sixty-seven machines equipped with tenders; some built locally and others in America and Scotland. Sharp Stewart of Glasgow supplied six 4-6-0 passenger locomotives in 1899. The 'English (sic) U' was reclassified to U^A in 1902. U^A 176, although fitted with a superheated boiler, retained its slide-valves and a low running plate until the end of its life. U^A 176, Invercargill, 1926. (W. W. Stewart Collection)

BELOW: The Victorian era locomotive re-equipping was completed with the arrival of ten more 4-6-0s from Sharp Stewart in 1901. U^C 369 was fitted with a superheater equipped boiler in 1929. A late era U^C 369 shows a number of detail differences to the as-built locomotive as illustrated on page 135. Reefton, 24 November 1952. (K. T. Cullen)

STEAM LOCOMOTIVE NUMBERING 1890-1971 (continued)

Road Number	Class	Type	Builder	Maker's Number	Date in Service	Written Off	Notes
563	W^W	4-6-4T	NZR Hillside	139/13	23-12-1913	2-1956	
564	W^W	4-6-4T	NZR Hillside	140/13	23-12-1913	2-1963	
565	W^W	4-6-4T	NZR Hillside	141/13	16-1-1914	2-1957	
566	W^W	4-6-4T	NZR Hillside	142/14	7-1914	2-1957	
567	W^W	4-6-4T	NZR Hillside	143/14	1-8-1914	3-1957	
568	W^W	4-6-4T	NZR Hillside	144/14	1-9-1914	3-1957	
569	W^W	4-6-4T	NZR Hillside	145/14	12-9-1914	31-3-1964	
570	W^W	4-6-4T	NZR Hillside	146/14	7-10-1914	2-1957	
571	W^W	4-6-4T	NZR Hillside	147/14	4-11-1914	7-1969	Note 33. Preserved
572	W^W	4-6-4T	NZR Hillside	148/14	19-11-1914	3-1957	
573	W^W	4-6-4T	NZR Hillside	149/14	10-12-1914	9-1966	Note 33
574	W^W	4-6-4T	NZR Hillside	150/14	19-12-1914	7-1969	Note 33
575	W^W	4-6-4T	NZR Hillside	151/14	12-1-1915	5-1968	Note 33
576	D	2-4-0T	Neilson	2563/80	21-5-1881	14-8-1922	Note 13. Sold
577	C	0-4-2ST	Neilson	1766/73	10-7-1874	2-1922	Note 10. Sold
578	A	4-6-2	Price	43/12	2-7-1912	2-1963	Note 7
579	A	4-6-2	Price	44/12	6-8-1912	8-1958	Note 7
580	A	4-6-2	Price	45/12	27-9-1912	12-1967	Note 7
581	A	4-6-2	Price	46/12	1-11-1912	20-6-1964	Note 7
582	A	4-6-2	Price	47/12	3-12-1912	7-1961	Note 7
583	A	4-6-2	Price	48/13	14-2-1913	10-1954	Note 7
584	A	4-6-2	Price	49/13	25-3-1913	2-1957	Note 7
585	A	4-6-2	Price	50/13	16-5-1913	3-1957	Note 7
586	A	4-6-2	Price	51/13	20-6-1913	2-1957	Note 7
587	A	4-6-2	Price	52/13	13-8-1913	10-1954	Note 7
588	X	4-8-2	NZR Addington	152/13	14-10-1913	2-3-1957	Note 27
589	X	4-8-2	NZR Addington	153/13	11-11-1913	6-1949	
590	X	4-8-2	NZR Addington	154/14	27-1-1914	2-3-1957	
591	X	4-8-2	NZR Addington	155/14	17-3-1914	2-3-1957	Note 27
592	X	4-8-2	NZR Addington	156/14	22-6-1914	2-3-1957	Note 27
593	X	4-8-2	NZR Addington	157/14	3-9-1914	2-3-1957	Note 27
594	X	4-8-2	NZR Addington	158/14	31-10-1914	2-3-1957	Note 27
595	X	4-8-2	NZR Addington	159/14	3-12-1914	2-3-1957	
596	X	4-8-2	NZR Addington	160/14	26-1-1915	2-3-1957	Note 27
597	X	4-8-2	NZR Addington	161/15	1-4-1915	2-3-1957	
598	A	4-6-2	Price	53/13	31-10-1913	10-1968	Note 7
599	A	4-6-2	Price	54/13	28-11-1913	10-1959	Note 7
600	A	4-6-2	Price	55/14	19-2-1914	12-1957	Note 7
601	A	4-6-2	Price	56/14	16-3-1914	6-1961	Note 7
602	A	4-6-2	Price	57/14	28-4-1914	6-1969	Note 7
603	A	4-6-2	Price	58/14	30-5-1914	3-1957	Note 7
604	A	4-6-2	Price	59/14	10-7-1914	2-1957	Note 7
605	A	4-6-2	Price	60/14	12-8-1914	12-1957	Note 7
606	A	4-6-2	Price	61/14	26-8-1914	2-1957	Note 7
607	A	4-6-2	Price	62/14	10-10-1914	2-1957	Note 7
608	A^B	4-6-2	NZR Addington	163/15	10-1915	10-1967	Preserved
609	A^B	4-6-2	NZR Addington	164/15	12-12-1915	25-4-1964	
610	A^B	4-6-2	NZR Addington	165/15	1-1916	8-1968	
611	A^B	4-6-2	NZR Addington	166/16	3-1916	8-1960	
612	A^B	4-6-2	NZR Addington	167/16	5-1916	10-1967	
613	A^B	4-6-2	NZR Addington	168/16	6-1916	10-1967	
614	A^B	4-6-2	NZR Addington	183/17	5-1917	29-2-1964	
615	A^B	4-6-2	NZR Addington	170/16	8-1916	4-1966	
616	A^B	4-6-2	NZR Addington	171/16	9-1916	9-1967	
617	A^B	4-6-2	NZR Addington	172/16	10-1916	3-1969	

STEAM LOCOMOTIVE NUMBERING 1890-1971 (continued)

Road Number	Class	Type	Builder	Maker's Number	Date in Service	Written Off	Notes
618	B^B	4-8-0	Price	63/15	2-1915	5-1966	
619	B^B	4-8-0	Price	64/15	3-1915	5-1959	
620	B^B	4-8-0	Price	65/15	4-1915	7-1965	
621	B^B	4-8-0	Price	66/15	5-1915	9-1959	
622	B^B	4-8-0	Price	67/15	6-1915	5-1959	
623	B^B	4-8-0	Price	68/15	7-1915	8-1959	
624	B^B	4-8-0	Price	69/15	8-1915	6-1957	
625	B^B	4-8-0	Price	70/15	8-1915	9-1962	
626	B^B	4-8-0	Price	71/15	9-1915	8-1968	
627	B^B	4-8-0	Price	72/15	11-1915	4-1966	
628	B^B	4-8-0	Price	73/15	12-1915	2-1963	
629	B^B	4-8-0	Price	74/15	12-1915	4-1966	
630	B^B	4-8-0	Price	75/16	2-1916	10-1967	
631	B^B	4-8-0	Price	76/16	5-1916	9-1966	
632	B^B	4-8-0	Price	77/16	5-1916	8-1959	
633	B^B	4-8-0	Price	78/16	6-1916	8-1968	
634	B^B	4-8-0	Price	79/16	6-1916	10-1963	
635	B^B	4-8-0	Price	80/16	9-1916	12-1965	
636	B^B	4-8-0	Price	81/16	9-1916	5-1966	
637	B^B	4-8-0	Price	82/16	11-1916	10-1963	
638	W^W	4-6-4T	NZR Hillside	173/15	5-1915	3-1957	
639	W^W	4-6-4T	NZR Hillside	174/15	6-1915	2-1957	
640	W^W	4-6-4T	NZR Hillside	175/15	7-1915	2-1957	
641	W^W	4-6-4T	NZR Hillside	176/15	8-1915	3-1957	
642	W^W	4-6-4T	NZR Hillside	177/15	8-1915	2-1957	
643	W^W	4-6-4T	NZR Hillside	178/15	9-1915	11-1958	
644	W^W	4-6-4T	NZR Hillside	179/15	10-1915	7-1969	Note 33. Preserved
645	W^W	4-6-4T	NZR Hillside	180/15	10-1915	3-1957	
646	W^W	4-6-4T	NZR Hillside	181/15	11-1915	2-1956	
647	W^W	4-6-4T	NZR Hillside	182/15	12-1915	3-1957	
648	A^A	4-6-2	Baldwin	41826/14	6-1915	22-12-1955	
649	A^A	4-6-2	Baldwin	41827/14	6-1915	2-1957	
650	A^A	4-6-2	Baldwin	41828/14	6-1915	2-1957	
651	A^A	4-6-2	Baldwin	41829/14	6-1915	2-1957	
652	A^A	4-6-2	Baldwin	41830/14	6-1915	22-12-1955	
653	A^A	4-6-2	Baldwin	41831/14	6-1915	22-12-1955	
654	A^A	4-6-2	Baldwin	41832/14	6-1915	22-12-1955	
655	A^A	4-6-2	Baldwin	41833/14	6-1915	22-12-1955	
656	A^A	4-6-2	Baldwin	41834/14	6-1915	2-1957	
657	A^A	4-6-2	Baldwin	41835/14	6-1915	22-12-1955	
658	A^B	4-6-2	NZR Addington	169/16	8-1916	10-1968	
659	A^B	4-6-2	NZR Addington	184/17	7-1917	29-2-1964	
660	A^B	4-6-2	NZR Addington	185/17	8-1917	8-1968	
661	A^B	4-6-2	NZR Addington	186/17	9-1917	31-3-1964	
662	A^B	4-6-2	NZR Addington	187/17	11-1917	10-1967	
663	A^B	4-6-2	NZR Addington	188/17	12-1917	7-1969	Preserved
664	A^B	4-6-2	NZR Addington	189/17	2-1918	11-1963	
665	A^B	4-6-2	NZR Addington	190/18	3-1918	4-1963	
666							Note 34
667							Note 34
667	W^W	4-6-4T	NZR Hillside	138/13		3-1957	Note 32
668	W^W	4-6-4T	NZR Hillside	193/16	7-1916	3-1957	
669	W^W	4-6-4T	NZR Hillside	194/16	8-1916	6-1965	Note 33
670	W^W	4-6-4T	NZR Hillside	195/16	9-1916	2-1956	
671	W^W	4-6-4T	NZR Hillside	196/16	10-1916	31-3-1964	

ABOVE: The classic nineteenth century American 4-6-0, equipped with slide valves and inside Stephenson valve gear, known as the 'American U', later became class U^B. This first series, also known as the 'flat-valve U^B', were all out of use by 1936. U^B 282 and one other were dumped on the Oamaru foreshore. U^B 282, location unknown, about 1900. (G. W. Emerson Collection)

BELOW: The NZR specified that the second series should be fitted with piston-valves and outside Walschaert valve gear. U^B 330, late in its life, shows many of the alterations made when compared with the new U^B 329 on page 135. U^B 330, Greymouth, 21 November 1955. (J. M. Creber)

ABOVE: The Orphans. NZR also placed orders for trial locomotives with the American Locomotive Company. U^B 17, built at the Brooks Locomotive Works, was the heaviest and most handsome of the NZR 4-6-0 types. U^B 17, Linwood, 1923. (W. W. Stewart)

BELOW: The second sample was the smaller U^B 371, delivered from the Richmond Locomotive and Machine Works. U^B 371, Linwood, 1923. (W. W. Stewart)

ABOVE: Q 344 brand new at Addington. The tender and cab are lined, and the road number is painted on the sand dome. An oil headlight was also fitted. These locomotives were initially equipped with piston tail rods, later removed. (W. W. Stewart Collection)

New Zealand Railways most significant contribution to locomotive design was made in February 1901 when the Baldwin Locomotive Works was instructed to build twelve, later increased to thirteen six-coupled locomotives. A significant feature was the use of a trailing truck to support the weight of a wide overhanging firebox, thus making the NZR class Q the world's first true Pacific, as this 4-6-2 type locomotive became known. Two were in service by Christmas 1901, nine more by the following March while the last pair commenced running from Auckland in September 1902.

BELOW: Q 343, showing early changes made: NZR flanged funnel, Westinghouse compressor relocated to the smokebox, acetylene generator and headlight and a ballast block placed over the leading bogie. Q 343, Frankton, August 1922. (W. W. Stewart)

ABOVE: Q 350, newly fitted with an A^B-type boiler and a flower pot funnel. The air compressor had returned to its original position in front of the firebox. Auckland, February 1928. (W. W. Stewart)

BELOW: In the mid-1930s nine of the class, including Q 346, acquired larger tenders that were sourced from parts of surplus tenders. A late modification were the stay rods bent to give clearance to the ash hopper doors at the base of the smokebox. Q 346, Invercargill, January 1953.
(J. A. T. Terry)

84 - Steam Locomotive Numbering 1890-1971

ABOVE: The 1901 orders were completed with the delivery of four 2-6-2 locomotives from the Baldwin Locomotive Works. These were similar to the 1885 class N but had piston-valves and a steel cab. N 353, Newmarket, 1902. (W. W. Stewart Collection)

BELOW: L 207, a 4-4-2T built new at Petone in 1903, was the final stage of development of the old Avonside 2-4-0T of 1877. Compare with L 219/PWD 509, page 52 for the original form; and L^A 267, page 67, for the intermediate state. L 207, Auckland, 1940. (E. J. McClare)

STEAM LOCOMOTIVE NUMBERING 1890-1971 (continued)

Road Number	Class	Type	Builder	Maker's Number	Date in Service	Written Off	Notes
672	W^W	4-6-4T	NZR Hillside	197/16	11-1916	12-1967	Note 33
673	W^W	4-6-4T	NZR Hillside	198/16	12-1916	2-1957	
674	W^W	4-6-4T	NZR Hillside	199/16	1-1917	2-1956	
675	W^W	4-6-4T	NZR Hillside	200/16	2-1917	3-1957	
676	W^W	4-6-4T	NZR Hillside	201/16	3-1917	3-1957	
677	W^W	4-6-4T	NZR Hillside	202/17	3-1917	2-1957	
678	W^W	4-6-4T	NZR Hillside	209/19	5-1919	7-1969	Note 33
679	W^W	4-6-4T	NZR Hillside	210/19	5-1919	6-1969	Note 33
680	W^W	4-6-4T	NZR Hillside	211/19	6-1919	7-1969	Note 33
681	W^W	4-6-4T	NZR Hillside	212/19	12-1919	2-1956	
682	W^W	4-6-4T	NZR Hillside	203/17	10-1917	2-1957	
683	W^W	4-6-4T	NZR Hillside	204/17	11-1917	10-1968	Note 33
684	W^W	4-6-4T	NZR Hillside	207/17	3-1918	12-1967	Note 33
685	W^W	4-6-4T	NZR Hillside	208/17	5-1918	2-1956	
686	W^S	4-6-4T	NZR Addington	213/17	7-1917	4-1963	Note 35
687	W^{AB}	4-6-4T	NZR Addington	214/18	4-1918	1-1966	
688	A^B	4-6-2	NZR Addington	191/21	10-1921	5-1968	
689	A^B	4-6-2	NZR Addington	192/21	1-1922	4-1967	
690	A^B	4-6-2	NZR Addington	215/22	3-1922	3-1969	
691	A^B	4-6-2	NZR Addington	216/22	6-1922	7-1968	
692	A^B	4-6-2	NZR Addington	217/22	8-1922	10-1968	
693	A^B	4-6-2	NZR Addington	218/22	11-1922	3-1969	
694	A^B	4-6-2	NZR Addington	219/22	12-1922	3-1969	
695	A^B	4-6-2	NZR Addington	220/23	2-1923	4-1966	
696	A^B	4-6-2	NZR Addington	221/23	4-1923	20-6-1964	
697	A^B	4-6-2	NZR Addington	222/23	5-1923	20-6-1964	
698	A^B	4-6-2	Price	93/22	5-1922	10-1959	
699	A^B	4-6-2	Price	94/22	8-1922	3-1968	Preserved
700	A^B	4-6-2	Price	95/22	9-1922	1-1966	
701	A^B	4-6-2	Price	96/22	12-1922	7-1968	
702	A^B	4-6-2	Price	97/23	5-1923	3-1965	
703	A^B	4-6-2	Price	98/23	7-1923	9-1966	
704	A^B	4-6-2	Price	99/23	9-1923	6-1969	
705	A^B	4-6-2	Price	100/23	10-1923	3-1969	
706	A^B	4-6-2	Price	101/23	11-1923	7-1969	
707	A^B	4-6-2	Price	102/24	6-1924	3-1969	
708	A^B	4-6-2	Price	103/24	7-1924	11-1966	
709	A^B	4-6-2	Price	104/24	8-1924	11-1966	
710	A^B	4-6-2	Price	105/24	10-1924	10-1963	
711	A^B	4-6-2	Price	106/24	12-1924	11-1966	
712	A^B	4-6-2	Price	107/25	2-1925	7-1965	
713	A^B	4-6-2	Price	108/25	3-1925	7-1968	
714	A^B	4-6-2	Price	109/25	6-1925	9-1966	
715	A^B	4-6-2	Price	110/25	8-1925	5-1968	
716	A^B	4-6-2	Price	111/25	10-1925	3-1964	
717	A^B	4-6-2	Price	112/25	12-1925	10-1967	
718	A^B	4-6-2	North British	22848/21	1-1922	3-1969	
719	A^B	4-6-2	North British	22849/21	1-1922	7-1968	
720	A^B	4-6-2	North British	22853/21	1-1922	8-1968	
721	A^B	4-6-2	North British	22856/21	2-1922	3-1969	
722	A^B	4-6-2	North British	22857/21	2-1922	11-1966	
723	A^B	4-6-2	North British	22860/21	3-1922	10-1968	
724	A^B	4-6-2	North British	22869/21	4-1922	3-1969	
725	A^B	4-6-2	North British	22873/21	4-1922	3-1969	
726	A^B	4-6-2	North British	22875/21	5-1922	10-1968	

ABOVE: Designed in 1902 and built over a twenty-five year period, the modest and elegant class W^F tank locomotive worked over most of the NZR system. W^F 386 was the only member of the Addington batch to work in the North Island. Shown at Petone in 1905, after transfer from the South Island. (A. P. Godber, Alexander Turnbull Library)

BELOW: W^F 843, one of the last batch built, was overhauled at her birthplace, A & G Price of Thames, in July 1958. The protruding smokebox ash hopper doors are the outward sign of a Waikato-type spark arrestor having been fitted. Otahuhu, 29 July 1958. (E. J. McClare)

Steam Locomotive Numbering 1890-1971 - 87

ABOVE: Built at Hillside in 1912, W^G 491 was working the Auckland car shunt in 1938, still in essentially original condition. (W. W. Stewart)

BELOW: Four class W^G and twelve similar W^W tank locomotives were rebuilt between 1950 and 1960 with a deep firebox boiler to extend their working life. Included in the former group was W^G 488, which received a 'high' boiler and reclassification to W^W in 1951. W^W 488, Taumarunui, 19 August 1953. (J. M. Creber)

ABOVE: A need for shunting locomotives resulted in the conversion of four class J 2-6-0 tender locomotives into 2-6-2 tank locomotives. Vulcan-built J 262, altered at Newmarket in 1917, became a W^A bearing the same road number. W^A 262, Auckland, about 1930. (W. W. Stewart)

BELOW: W^E 375 was converted from B 309, a 4-8-0 tender locomotive, in November 1943; forty-one years after the other two examples. W^E 375 stands ready to work a coal train on the Rewanui Incline not long after conversion. Greymouth, 21 October 1944. (E. J. McClare)

STEAM LOCOMOTIVE NUMBERING 1890-1971 (continued)

Road Number	Class	Type	Builder	Maker's Number	Date in Service	Written Off	Notes
727	A^B	4-6-2	North British	22876/21	5-1922	7-1968	
728	A^B	4-6-2	North British	22877/21	5-1922	8-1968	
729	A^B	4-6-2	North British	22881/22	7-1922	10-1968	
730	A^B	4-6-2	North British	22883/22	8-1922	3-1969	
731	A^B	4-6-2	North British	22884/22	9-1922	3-1969	
732	A^B	4-6-2	North British	22878/22			Note 36
732	A^B	4-6-2	North British	23043/23	10-1923	3-1969	
733	A^B	4-6-2	North British	22838/21	11-1921	4-1966	
734	A^B	4-6-2	North British	22845/21	12-1921	2-1965	
735	A^B	4-6-2	North British	22844/21	12-1921	3-1968	
736	A^B	4-6-2	North British	22841/21	12-1921	3-1966	
737	A^B	4-6-2	North British	22847/21	1-1922	3-1969	
738	A^B	4-6-2	North British	22852/21	1-1922	1-1965	
739	A^B	4-6-2	North British	22855/21	2-1922	7-1965	
740	A^B	4-6-2	North British	22859/21	2-1922	10-1967	
741	A^B	4-6-2	North British	22868/21	2-1922	2-1965	
742	A^B	4-6-2	North British	22872/21	4-1922	2-1965	
743	A^B	4-6-2	North British	22871/21	4-1922	6-1969	
744	A^B	4-6-2	North British	22874/21	5-1922	3-1964	
745	A^B	4-6-2	North British	22880/22	7-1922	1-1957	Preserved
746	A^B	4-6-2	North British	22885/22	8-1922	3-1969	
747	A^B	4-6-2	North British	22836/21	12-1921	10-1963	
748	A^B	4-6-2	North British	22837/21	11-1921	9-1966	
749	A^B	4-6-2	North British	22839/21	1-1922	10-1959	
750	A^B	4-6-2	North British	22840/21	1-1922	6-1964	
751	A^B	4-6-2	North British	22842/21	12-1921	10-1967	
752	A^B	4-6-2	North British	22843/21	12-1921	2-1964	
753	A^B	4-6-2	North British	22846/21	1-1922	10-1968	
754	A^B	4-6-2	North British	22850/21	2-1922	3-1969	
755	A^B	4-6-2	North British	22851/21	2-1922	3-1968	
756	A^B	4-6-2	North British	22854/21	3-1922	8-1962	
757	A^B	4-6-2	North British	22858/21	3-1922	3-1964	
758	A^B	4-6-2	North British	22866/21	3-1922	9-1966	
759	A^B	4-6-2	North British	22867/21	4-1922	1-1965	
760	A^B	4-6-2	North British	22870/21	4-1922	3-1964	
761	A^B	4-6-2	North British	22882/22	8-1922	6-1965	
762	A^B	4-6-2	North British	22879/22			Note 36
762	A^B	4-6-2	North British	23039/23	9-1923	10-1967	
763	W^{AB}	4-6-4T	NZR Hillside	223/23	5-1923	4-1963	
764	W^S	4-6-4T	NZR Hillside	224/23	7-1923	7-1963	Note 37
765	W^S	4-6-4T	NZR Hillside	225/23	8-1923	4-1963	Note 37
766	W^S	4-6-4T	NZR Hillside	226/23	9-1923	5-1964	Note 37
767	W^S	4-6-4T	NZR Hillside	227/23	11-1923	4-1963	Note 37
768	W^S	4-6-4T	NZR Hillside	228/23	1-1924	4-1963	Note 37
769	W^S	4-6-4T	NZR Hillside	229/24	5-1924	4-1963	Note 37
770	W^S	4-6-4T	NZR Hillside	230/24	5-1924	9-1962	Note 37
771	W^S	4-6-4T	NZR Hillside	231/24	7-1924	9-1962	Note 37
772	W^{AB}	4-6-4T	NZR Hillside	232/24	7-1924	9-1962	
773	A^B	4-6-2	North British	23040/23	9-1923	10-1968	
774	A^B	4-6-2	North British	23041/23	9-1923	10-1959	
775	A^B	4-6-2	North British	23042/23	9-1923	10-1958	
776	A^B	4-6-2	NZR Addington	233/25	5-1925	4-1966	
777	A^B	4-6-2	NZR Addington	234/25	6-1925	3-1969	
778	A^B	4-6-2	NZR Addington	235/25	9-1925	7-1969	Note 38. Sold
779	A^B	4-6-2	NZR Addington	236/25	12-1925	7-1968	

90 - Steam Locomotive Numbering 1890-1971

ABOVE: The Edwardian elegance of NZR's own Pacific design is seen in this view of brand new four-cylinder compound A 178, on display at the 1906 Christchurch Exhibition.
(Christchurch Press Collection, Alexander Turnbull Library)

BELOW: From 1941 all of the compound A were converted to two-cylinder simple propulsion. A feature exclusive to the South Island A was the fitting of a ballast block over the leading bogie. A 178, Invercargill, December 1950. (J. M. Creber)

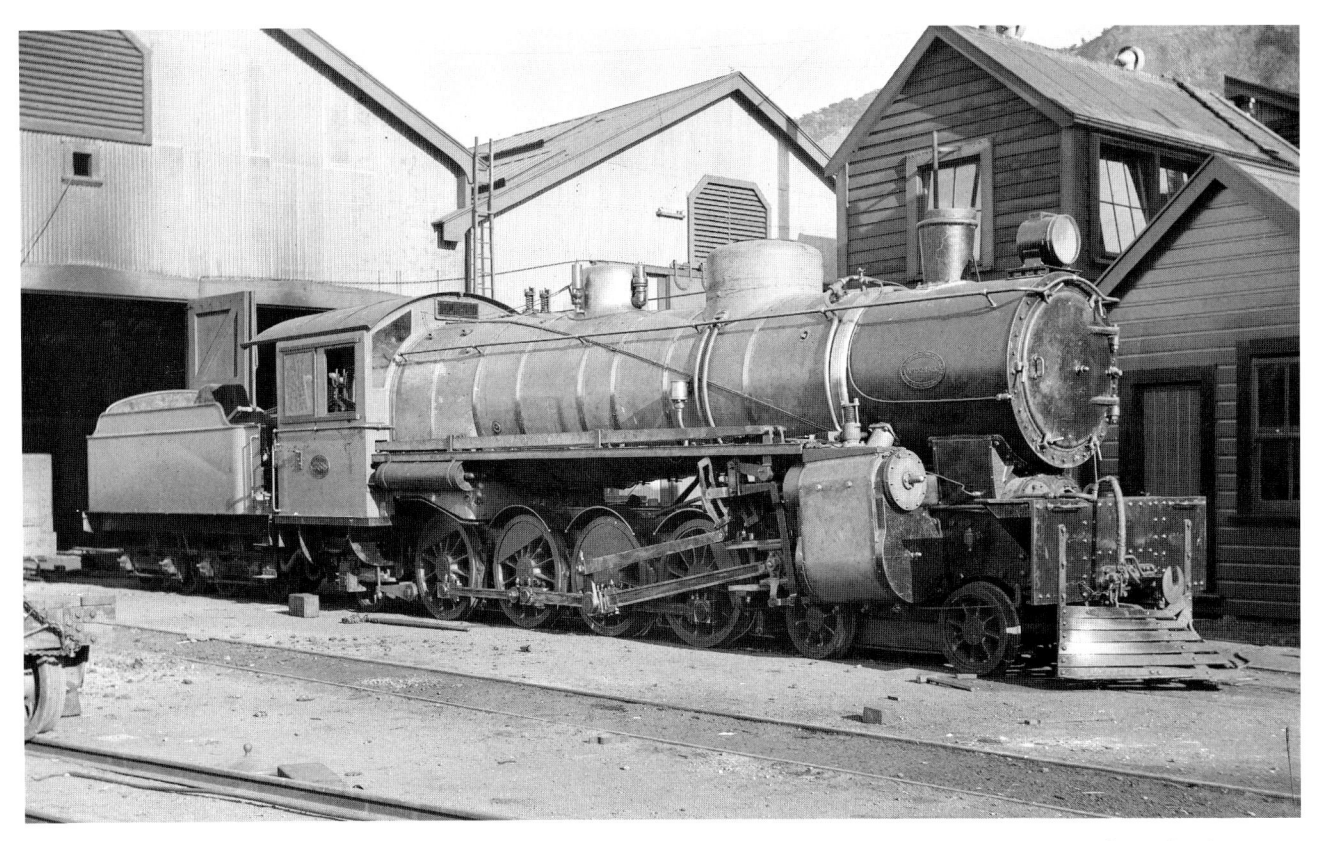

ABOVE: The world's first 'Mountain' type, built at Addington Workshops in 1908, entered service in January 1909. A wide firebox 4-8-2, the class X were the goods locomotive version of the compound four-cylinder class A. A later example was X 588, newly erected in works grey livery. Petone, 1913. (A. P. Godber, Alexander Turnbull Library)

BELOW: Twelve of the compound X locomotives were converted to simple propulsion between 1943 and 1951. One of these was X 591 which was altered in December 1950. X 591 nearing retirement, Marton, 1955. (L. J. Hostick)

STEAM LOCOMOTIVE NUMBERING 1890-1971 (continued)

Road Number	Class	Type	Builder	Maker's Number	Date in Service	Written Off	Notes
780	A^B	4-6-2	NZR Addington	237/26	2-1926	3-1969	
781	A^B	4-6-2	NZR Addington	238/26	3-1926	8-1968	
782	A^B	4-6-2	NZR Addington	239/26	5-1926	7-1969	
783	A^B	4-6-2	NZR Addington	240/26	7-1926	11-1966	
784	A^B	4-6-2	NZR Addington	241/26	9-1926	3-1969	
785	A^B	4-6-2	NZR Addington	242/26	10-1926	2-1963	
786	W^{AB}	4-6-4T	NZR Hillside	243/25	7-1926	10-1968	Note 39
787	W^{AB}	4-6-4T	NZR Hillside	244/25	8-1926	4-1966	Note 39
788	W^{AB}	4-6-4T	NZR Hillside	245/25	9-1926	3-1969	Note 39
789	W^{AB}	4-6-4T	NZR Hillside	246/25	10-1926	3-1969	Note 39
790	W^{AB}	4-6-4T	NZR Hillside	247/25	12-1926	2-1966	Note 39
791	W^{AB}	4-6-4T	NZR Hillside	248/26	12-1926	10-1967	Note 39
792	W^{AB}	4-6-4T	NZR Hillside	249/26	3-1927	7-1969	Note 39
793	W^{AB}	4-6-4T	NZR Hillside	250/26	3-1927	3-1969	Note 39
794	W^{AB}	4-6-4T	NZR Hillside	251/27	5-1927	31-8-1955	Sold.
795	W^{AB}	4-6-4T	NZR Hillside	252/27	5-1927	7-1969	Notes 38 & 39. Sold
796	W^{AB}	4-6-4T	Price	113/26	9-1926	9-1962	
797	W^{AB}	4-6-4T	Price	114/26	9-1926	5-1963	
798	W^{AB}	4-6-4T	Price	115/26	11-1926	3-1969	Note 39
799	W^S	4-6-4T	Price	116/26	12-1926	9-1962	Note 37
800	W^S	4-6-4T	Price	117/26	2-1927	5-1967	Note 37. Preserved
801	W^S	4-6-4T	Price	118/27	3-1927	1-1966	Note 37
802	W^S	4-6-4T	Price	119/27	4-1927	1-1966	Note 37
803	W^S	4-6-4T	Price	120/27	7-1927	7-1968	Notes 37 & 39
804	A^B	4-6-2	North British	23173/25	6-1925	4-1966	
805	A^B	4-6-2	North British	23174/25	7-1925	7-1968	
806	A^B	4-6-2	North British	23175/25	7-1925	3-1969	
807	A^B	4-6-2	North British	23176/25	7-1925	3-1969	
808	A^B	4-6-2	North British	23183/25	7-1925	9-1967	
809	A^B	4-6-2	North British	23184/25	7-1925	4-1966	
810	A^B	4-6-2	North British	23185/25	7-1925	10-1967	
811	A^B	4-6-2	North British	23186/25	7-1925	7-1969	
812	A^B	4-6-2	North British	23182/25	7-1925	10-1967	
813	A^B	4-6-2	North British	23187/25	7-1925	3-1969	
814	A^B	4-6-2	North British	23177/25	6-1925	3-1964	
815	A^B	4-6-2	North British	23178/25	6-1925	11-1963	
816	A^B	4-6-2	North British	23179/25	6-1925	6-1969	
817	A^B	4-6-2	North British	23180/25	6-1925	11-1966	
818	A^B	4-6-2	North British	23191/25	8-1925	10-1963	
819	A^B	4-6-2	North British	23192/25	8-1925	11-1966	
820	A^B	4-6-2	North British	23193/25	7-1925	3-1969	
821	A^B	4-6-2	North British	23194/25	7-1925	3-1969	
822	A^B	4-6-2	North British	23195/25	7-1925	3-1969	
823	A^B	4-6-2	North British	23196/25	7-1925	7-1969	
824	A^B	4-6-2	North British	23197/25	8-1925	1-1966	
825	A^B	4-6-2	North British	23198/25	8-1925	10-1967	
826	A^B	4-6-2	North British	23203/25	9-1925	10-1967	
827	A^B	4-6-2	North British	23204/25	9-1925	5-1964	
828	A^B	4-6-2	North British	23207/25	8-1925	8-1966	
829	A^B	4-6-2	North British	23181/25	6-1925	5-1968	
830	A^B	4-6-2	North British	23188/25	7-1925	10-1959	
831	A^B	4-6-2	North British	23189/25	7-1925	3-1969	
832	A^B	4-6-2	North British	23190/25	7-1925	12-1967	Preserved
833	A^B	4-6-2	North British	23199/25	7-1925	4-1966	
834	A^B	4-6-2	North British	23200/25	7-1925	9-1966	

ABOVE: When the Wellington and Manawatu Railway was taken over in 1908 twenty locomotives were added to NZR stock. Manning Wardle supplied the Manawatu Company with its first five locomotives. Numbers 3 and 5 were sold by the Company in 1901, while 1, 2 and 4 went to the NZR. W^H 449 (formerly WMR N^O 4), Wellington, about 1912. (A. P. Godber, Alexander Turnbull Library)

BELOW: In 1904 the Company purchased from Baldwin a large 2-8-4 tank locomotive specifically for banking heavy trains out of Wellington. Affectionately known as *Jumbo*, it was the only example of this wheel arrangement in the country. NZR W^J 466 (formerly WMR N^O 3), Thorndon, Wellington, about 1910. (A. P. Godber, Alexander Turnbull Library)

ABOVE: The Baldwin Locomotive Works supplied a total of fourteen locomotives to the company. N 453 (formerly WMR N° 9), built in 1891 to the NZR class N specification, as overhauled at Petone in 1909. (A. P. Godber, Alexander Turnbull Library)

BELOW: The last of the Company's main line locomotives were a pair of large Baldwin 4-6-0's, numbers 19 and 20. At 4 feet 10 inches the class U^D had the largest diameter driving wheels in the country. U^D 464 (formerly WMR N° 19), following an overhaul at Petone, about 1915.
(A. P. Godber, Alexander Turnbull Library)

ABOVE: NZR O^C 458 (formerly WMR N° 16) was a typical American Vauclain-system compound 2-8-0. Paekakariki, about 1910. (A. P. Godber, Alexander Turnbull Library)

BELOW: B^C 463, N° 17 in the Company's roster, was the only 2-8-2 to run in New Zealand. Over its short life of twenty-five years, less than seven were with the Wellington and Manawatu Railway Company. Paekakariki, about 1910. (A. P. Godber, Alexander Turnbull Library)

STEAM LOCOMOTIVE NUMBERING 1890-1971 (continued)

Road Number	Class	Type	Builder	Maker's Number	Date in Service	Written Off	Notes
835	A^B	4-6-2	North British	23201/25	7-1925	2-1964	
836	A^B	4-6-2	North British	23202/25	8-1925	9-1963	
837	A^B	4-6-2	North British	23205/25	8-1925	8-1965	
838	A^B	4-6-2	North British	23206/25	8-1925	9-1966	
839	F	0-6-0ST	Stephenson	2594/85		1930	Note 40. Sold
840	F	0-6-0ST	Vulcan	1180/87		6-6-1927	Note 40. Sold
841	F	0-6-0ST	Stephenson	2596/86		1930	Note 40. Sold
842	W^F	2-6-2T	Price	121/28		12-1965	
843	W^F	2-6-2T	Price	122/28		4-1964	
844	W^F	2-6-2T	Price	123/28		10-1964	
845	C	2-6-2	NZR Hillside	253/30	10-1930	4-1967	
846	C	2-6-2	NZR Hillside	254/30	11-1930	5-1968	
847	C	2-6-2	NZR Hillside	255/30	12-1930	10-1968	Preserved
848	C	2-6-2	NZR Hillside	256/31	1-1931	9-1963	
849	C	2-6-2	NZR Hillside	257/31	2-1931	1-1965	
850	C	2-6-2	NZR Hillside	258/31	3-1931	9-1966	
851	C	2-6-2	NZR Hutt	259/30	11-1930	10-1966	
852	C	2-6-2	NZR Hutt	260/30	12-1930	11-1963	
853	C	2-6-2	NZR Hutt	261/30	12-1930	11-1963	
854	C	2-6-2	NZR Hutt	262/30	1-1931	11-1963	
855	C	2-6-2	NZR Hutt	263/31	2-1931	11-1963	
856	C	2-6-2	NZR Hutt	264/31	3-1931	2-1964	
857	C	2-6-2	NZR Hutt	265/31	4-1931	10-1966	
858	C	2-6-2	NZR Hutt	266/31	5-1931	7-1963	
859	C	2-6-2	NZR Hutt	267/31	5-1931	11-1963	
860	C	2-6-2	NZR Hutt	268/31	6-1931	2-1964	
861	C	2-6-2	NZR Hutt	269/31	7-1931	7-1963	
862	C	2-6-2	NZR Hutt	270/31	7-1931	11-1963	
863	C	2-6-2	NZR Hillside	271/31	7-1931	9-1963	
864	C	2-6-2	NZR Hillside	272/31	8-1931	5-1968	Preserved
865	C	2-6-2	NZR Hillside	273/31	8-1931	10-1967	
866	C	2-6-2	NZR Hillside	274/31	9-1931	6-1964	
867	C	2-6-2	NZR Hillside	275/31	10-1931	4-1966	
868	C	2-6-2	NZR Hillside	276/31	11-1931	6-1965	
900	K	4-8-4	NZR Hutt	277/32	11-1932	5-1965	Notes 45 & 47. Pres.
901	K	4-8-4	NZR Hutt	278/32	12-1932	7-1964	Note 45
902	K	4-8-4	NZR Hutt	279/33	2-1933	7-1964	Note 45
903	K	4-8-4	NZR Hutt	280/33	3-1933	7-1964	Note 45
904	K	4-8-4	NZR Hutt	281/33	3-1933	7-1964	Note 45
905	K	4-8-4	NZR Hutt	282/33	6-1933	2-1965	Notes 45 & 47
906	K	4-8-4	NZR Hutt	283/33	7-1933	7-1964	Note 45
907	K	4-8-4	NZR Hutt	284/33	8-1933	7-1964	Note 45
908	K	4-8-4	NZR Hutt	285/33	9-1933	7-1964	Notes 45 & 47
909	K	4-8-4	NZR Hutt	286/33	10-1933	7-1964	Note 45
910	K	4-8-4	NZR Hutt	287/34	3-1934	7-1964	Note 45
911	K	4-8-4	NZR Hutt	288/34	3-1934	12-1967	Notes 45 & 47. Pres.
912	K	4-8-4	NZR Hutt	289/34	6-1934	4-1966	Note 45
913	K	4-8-4	NZR Hutt	290/34	7-1934	7-1964	Note 45
914	K	4-8-4	NZR Hutt	291/34	8-1934	3-1965	Note 45
915	K	4-8-4	NZR Hutt	292/34	10-1934	7-1964	Note 45
916	K	4-8-4	NZR Hutt	293/34	12-1934	7-1964	Note 45
917	K	4-8-4	NZR Hutt	294/34	3-1935	7-1964	Notes 45 & 47. Pres.
918	K	4-8-4	NZR Hutt	295/35	5-1935	7-1964	Note 45
919	K	4-8-4	NZR Hutt	296/35	7-1935	2-1965	Notes 42 & 45
920	K	4-8-4	NZR Hutt	297/35	11-1935	7-1964	Note 45

STEAM LOCOMOTIVE NUMBERING 1890-1971 (continued)

Road Number	Class	Type	Builder	Maker's Number	Date in Service	Written Off	Notes
921	K	4-8-4	NZR Hutt	298/35	12-1935	7-1964	Notes 45 & 47
922	K	4-8-4	NZR Hutt	299/35	2-1936	7-1964	Notes 45 & 47
923	K	4-8-4	NZR Hutt	300/36	4-1936	7-1964	Note 45
924	K	4-8-4	NZR Hutt	301/36	6-1936	7-1964	Notes 45 & 47
925	K	4-8-4	NZR Hutt	302/36	7-1936	7-1964	Note 45
926	K	4-8-4	NZR Hutt	303/36	9-1936	9-1965	Note 45
927	K	4-8-4	NZR Hutt	304/36	10-1936	7-1964	Notes 45 & 47
928	K	4-8-4	NZR Hutt	305/36	11-1936	7-1964	Note 45
929	K	4-8-4	NZR Hutt	306/36	12-1936	7-1964	Notes 45 & 47
930	K^A	4-8-4	NZR Hutt	313/40	3-1940	10-1966	Notes 43, 44, 45
931	K^A	4-8-4	NZR Hutt	314/40	5-1940	4-1966	Notes 43, 44, 45
932	K^A	4-8-4	NZR Hutt	315/40	5-1940	5-1967	Notes 43, 44, 45
933	K^A	4-8-4	NZR Hutt	316/40	7-1940	10-1966	Notes 43, 44, 45, 47
934	K^A	4-8-4	NZR Hutt	317/41	8-1941	10-1966	Notes 43, 44, 45
935	K^A	4-8-4	NZR Hutt	318/41	10-1941	12-1967	Notes 43, 44, 45. Pres.
936	K^A	4-8-4	NZR Hutt	319/42	2-1942	1-1966	Notes 43, 44, 45
937	K^A	4-8-4	NZR Hutt	320/43	11-1943	11-1967	Notes 43, 44, 45
938	K^A	4-8-4	NZR Hutt	321/43	12-1943	7-1964	Notes 43, 44, 45
939	K^A	4-8-4	NZR Hutt	322/44	3-1944	1-1965	Notes 43, 44, 45
940	K^A	4-8-4	NZR Hillside	323/40	9-1940	12-1965	Notes 43, 44, 45
941	K^A	4-8-4	NZR Hillside	324/40	10-1940	12-1967	Notes 43, 44, 45
942	K^A	4-8-4	NZR Hillside	325/40	11-1940	8-1967	Notes 43, 44, 45. Pres.
943	K^A	4-8-4	NZR Hillside	326/41	2-1941	5-1967	Notes 43, 44, 45, 47
944	K^A	4-8-4	NZR Hillside	327/41	5-1941	12-1965	Notes 43, 44, 45
945	K^A	4-8-4	NZR Hutt	328/39	7-1939	12-1967	Notes 43, 44, 45. Pres.
946	K^A	4-8-4	NZR Hutt	329/39	8-1939	1-1965	Notes 43, 44, 45, 47
947	K^A	4-8-4	NZR Hutt	330/39	8-1939	5-1966	Notes 43, 44, 45
948	K^A	4-8-4	NZR Hutt	331/39	8-1939	5-1966	Notes 43, 44, 45, 47
949	K^A	4-8-4	NZR Hutt	332/39	10-1939	3-1955	Notes 43, 44, 45
950	K^A	4-8-4	NZR Hutt	333/39	11-1939	12-1965	Notes 43, 44, 45, 47
951	K^A	4-8-4	NZR Hutt	334/39	11-1939	3-1965	Notes 43, 44, 45
952	K^A	4-8-4	NZR Hutt	335/39	12-1939	10-1966	Notes 43, 44, 45, 47
953	K^A	4-8-4	NZR Hutt	336/44	7-1944	5-1967	Notes 43, 44, 45
954	K^A	4-8-4	NZR Hutt	337/44	10-1944	9-1966	Notes 43, 44, 45
955	K^A	4-8-4	NZR Hutt	338/44	12-1944	5-1967	Notes 44, 45
956	K^A	4-8-4	NZR Hutt	339/45	5-1945	10-1966	Notes 44, 45
957	K^A	4-8-4	NZR Hutt	340/46	4-1946	10-1966	Notes 44, 45, 47
958	K^A	4-8-4	NZR Hutt	341/50	15-3-1950	2-1967	Notes 44, 45, 46, 47
959	K^A	4-8-4	NZR Hutt	342/50	29-3-1950	10-1966	Notes 44, 45, 46, 47
960	K^A	4-8-4	NZR Hillside	343/39	3-1939	9-1966	Notes 43, 44, 45
961	K^A	4-8-4	NZR Hillside	344/40	4-1940	9-1966	Notes 43, 44, 45
962	K^A	4-8-4	NZR Hillside	345/40	4-1940	9-1966	Notes 43, 44, 45, 47
963	K^A	4-8-4	NZR Hillside	346/40	8-1940	10-1966	Notes 43, 44, 45
964	K^A	4-8-4	NZR Hillside	347/41	6-1941	10-1966	Notes 43, 44, 45
965	K^B	4-8-4	NZR Hillside	348/39	6-1939	3-1969	Note 43
966	K^B	4-8-4	NZR Hillside	349/39	8-1939	10-1967	Note 43
967	K^B	4-8-4	NZR Hillside	350/39	9-1939	10-1968	Note 43
968	K^B	4-8-4	NZR Hillside	351/39	10-1939	3-1969	Note 43. Preserved
969	K^B	4-8-4	NZR Hillside	352/39	12-1939	10-1967	Note 43
970	K^B	4-8-4	NZR Hillside	353/39	1-1940	3-1969	Note 43
1200	J	4-8-2	North British	24523/39	10-1939	7-1964	Notes 48 & 49
1201	J	4-8-2	North British	24524/39	10-1939	7-1969	Note 48
1202	J	4-8-2	North British	24525/39	10-1939	4-1966	Notes 47, 48
1203	J	4-8-2	North British	24526/39	11-1939	10-1964	Notes 47, 48, 49
1204	J	4-8-2	North British	24527/39	11-1939	1-1966	Note 48

98 - Steam Locomotive Numbering 1890-1971

ABOVE: Ten 4-8-0 heavy tender engines for goods trains emerged from Addington workshops between 1911 and 1913. Classified B^A, they were a modified version of class B. The wedge headstock, possibly a form of snowplough, was removed about 1918. B^A 499, new at Christchurch, 1912.
(A. P. Godber, Alexander Turnbull Library)

BELOW: B^A 148 was fitted with a wide-firebox boiler in June 1948. Dunedin, 1958. (G. W. Emerson)

Steam Locomotive Numbering 1890-1971 - 99

ABOVE: A & G Price contracted in February 1914 to supply thirty heavy goods locomotives for North Island duties. These became class B^B upon entering service. B^B 619 new at Petone, 1915.
(A. P. Godber, Alexander Turnbull Library)

BELOW: The advent of the new and powerful class K locomotives relegated all of the North Island 4-8-0's to shunting and branch line use. Modifications for this service included a shunting tender and an extra sand dome. B^B 55, Frankton, July 1955. (J. M. Creber)

ABOVE: Imported for but unsuccessful when used on lightly-patronised branch line trains, D 1 was equally ineffective as the workshops shunter at Otahuhu. New on the traverser, emerging from the Hutt Workshops, 27 January 1930. (A. P. Godber, Alexander Turnbull Library)

BELOW: E 66, a Mallet-system Vauclain-compound 2-6-6-0T, built specially for working on the Rimutaka Incline, was modified at Petone Workshops in April 1912, when alterations were made to the rear exhaust system. Photographer A. P. Godber is seen in the cab.
(A. P. Godber, Alexander Turnbull Library)

ABOVE: Newly commissioned A^A 650 was one of ten Pacifics ordered from the Baldwin Locomotive Works in November 1914. Petone, July 1915. (A. P. Godber, Alexander Turnbull Library)

BELOW: A^A 653, fitted with an A^B-type boiler in 1942, was ready to work N° 108 passenger, the workshops staff train. Otahuhu, 20 September 1946. (E. J. McClare)

102 - Steam Locomotive Numbering 1890-1971

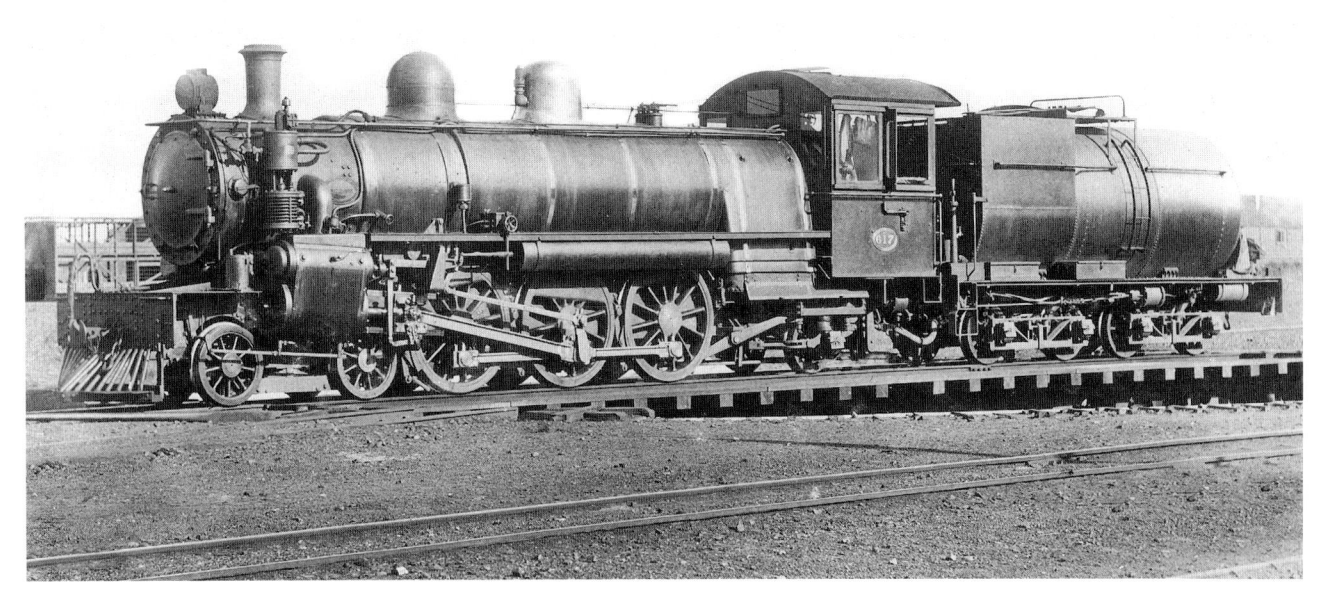

ABOVE: The most numerous type of steam locomotive on the New Zealand Railways was the class A^B. An early South Island member of the class in original condition, A^B 617 was fitted with a short cab, flanged funnel, acetylene generator and headlight. In service the class exhibited many variations in detail over the years. A^B 617, Dunedin, 1917. (W. W. Stewart Collection)

BELOW: The tank engine version of the class A^B were the similar W^S and W^{AB} machines. W^S 771, in as-built condition was fitted with the original pattern trailing bogie and 'fore and aft' sand domes. The locomotive also displayed a fine example of the cleaner's art. Auckland, 1931. (W. W. Stewart)

Steam Locomotive Numbering 1890-1971 - 103

ABOVE: The South Island allocated W^{AB} locomotives ran primarily between Dunedin and Oamaru. In March 1946 W^{AB} 791 displayed their main line features; ballast block, sand-domes up front, exhaust steam injector, delta trailing bogie and the absence of a rear cowcatcher. (E. J. McClare)

BELOW: The last stage of the W^S/W^{AB} story was the rebuilding of eleven of these weight-restricted machines to the useful general purpose class A^B. These rebuilt locomotives were fitted with a Hodges pattern roller-bearing trailing truck and a larger class G tender. W^{AB} 788 became A^B 788 in 1948. Oamaru, December 1952. (J. M. Creber)

STEAM LOCOMOTIVE NUMBERING 1890-1971 (continued)

Road Number	Class	Type	Builder	Maker's Number	Date in Service	Written Off	Notes
1205	J	4-8-2	North British	24528/39	11-1939	10-1967	Notes 48 & 49
1206	J	4-8-2	North British	24529/39	11-1939	5-1965	Notes 47, 48, 49
1207	J	4-8-2	North British	24530/39	11-1939	4-1966	Notes 47 & 48
1208	J	4-8-2	North British	24531/39	11-1939	7-1969	Note 48
1209	J	4-8-2	North British	24532/39	11-1939	7-1969	Note 48
1210	J	4-8-2	North British	24533/39	12-1939	3-1969	Note 48
1211	J	4-8-2	North British	24534/39	12-1939	16-11-1971	Notes 47 & 48. Pres.
1212	J	4-8-2	North British	24535/39	12-1939	7-1969	Notes 47 & 48
1213	J	4-8-2	North British	24536/39	12-1939	12-1967	Notes 48 & 49
1214	J	4-8-2	North British	24537/39	12-1939	1-1965	Notes 47 & 48
1215	J	4-8-2	North British	24538/39	1-1940	1-1965	Note 48
1216	J	4-8-2	North British	24539/39	1-1940	7-1969	Note 48
1217	J	4-8-2	North British	24540/39	1-1940	3-1969	Note 48
1218	J	4-8-2	North British	24541/39	1-1940	4-1967	Notes 48 & 49
1219	J	4-8-2	North British	24542/39	1-1940	4-1966	Note 48
1220	J	4-8-2	North British	24543/39	2-1940	1-1966	Note 48
1221	J	4-8-2	North British	24544/39	2-1940	5-1966	Note 48
1222	J	4-8-2	North British	24545/39	2-1940	1-1965	Note 48
1223	J	4-8-2	North British	24546/39	2-1940	1-1966	Note 48
1224	J	4-8-2	North British	24547/39	2-1940	8-1967	Notes 48 & 49
1225	J	4-8-2	North British	24548/39	2-1940	1-1966	Note 48
1226	J	4-8-2	North British	24549/39	2-1940	7-1969	Note 48
1227	J	4-8-2	North British	24550/39	2-1940	3-1969	Note 48
1228	J	4-8-2	North British	24551/39	3-1940	3-1968	Notes 48 & 49
1229	J	4-8-2	North British	24552/39	3-1940	1-1965	Notes 48 & 49
1230	J	4-8-2	North British	24553/39	3-1940	10-1964	Notes 48 & 49
1231	J	4-8-2	North British	24554/39	3-1940	7-1969	Notes 47 & 48
1232	J	4-8-2	North British	24555/39	3-1940	7-1969	Note 48
1233	J	4-8-2	North British	24556/39	3-1940	12-1967	Notes 48 & 49
1234	J	4-8-2	North British	24557/39	3-1940	16-11-1971	Notes 47 & 48. Pres.
1235	J	4-8-2	North British	24558/39	3-1940	9-1967	Note 48
1236	J	4-8-2	North British	24559/39	3-1940	16-11-1971	Notes 47 & 48. Pres.
1237	J	4-8-2	North British	24560/39	3-1940	3-1969	Note 48
1238	J	4-8-2	North British	24561/39	3-1940	2-1967	Notes 47 & 48
1239	J	4-8-2	North British	24562/39	3-1940	3-1968	Notes 48 & 49
1240	JA	4-8-2	NZR Hillside	363/46	4-1947	16-11-1971	Preserved
1241	JA	4-8-2	NZR Hillside	364/46	3-1947	8-1968	
1242	JA	4-8-2	NZR Hillside	365/46	12-1946	6-1969	
1243	JA	4-8-2	NZR Hillside	366/46	3-1947	8-1968	
1244	JA	4-8-2	NZR Hillside	367/46	5-1947	3-1969	
1245	JA	4-8-2	NZR Hillside	368/46	8-1947	6-1969	
1246	JA	4-8-2	NZR Hillside	369/46	11-1947	5-1971	
1247	JA	4-8-2	NZR Hillside	370/47	1-1948	11-1969	
1248	JA	4-8-2	NZR Hillside	371/48	3-1948	13-7-1971	
1249	JA	4-8-2	NZR Hillside	372/48	7-1948	3-1968	
1250	JA	4-8-2	NZR Hillside	373/49	6-1949	16-11-1971	Preserved
1251	JA	4-8-2	NZR Hillside	374/49	7-1949	16-8-1971	
1252	JA	4-8-2	NZR Hillside	375/49	9-1949	16-8-1971	
1253	JA	4-8-2	NZR Hillside	376/49	11-1949	16-11-1971	
1254	JA	4-8-2	NZR Hillside	377/49	1-1950	6-1969	
1255	JA	4-8-2	NZR Hillside	378/50	3-1950	6-1969	
1256	JA	4-8-2	NZR Hillside	379/51	7-1951	16.11-1971	Note 50
1257	JA	4-8-2	NZR Hillside	380/51	10-1951	16-8-1971	Note 50
1258	JA	4-8-2	NZR Hillside	381/51	12-1951	16-11-1971	Note 50
1259	JA	4-8-2	NZR Hillside	382/52	6-1952	6-1969	Note 50

STEAM LOCOMOTIVE NUMBERING 1890-1971 (continued)

Road Number	Class	Type	Builder	Maker's Number	Date in Service	Written Off	Notes
1260	JA	4-8-2	NZR Hillside	383/52	11-1952	16-8-1971	Preserved
1261	JA	4-8-2	NZR Hillside	384/53	3-1953	16-11-1971	
1262	JA	4-8-2	NZR Hillside	385/53	11-1953	7-1969	
1263	JA	4-8-2	NZR Hillside	386/53	1-1954	7-1969	
1264	JA	4-8-2	NZR Hillside	387/54	7-1954	6-1969	
1265	JA	4-8-2	NZR Hillside	388/50	5-1950	6-1969	Note 50.
1266	JA	4-8-2	NZR Hillside	389/50	7-1950	6-1969	Note 50.
1267	JA	4-8-2	NZR Hillside	390/50	9-1950	16-11-1971	Note 50. Preserved
1268	JA	4-8-2	NZR Hillside	391/50	11-1950	8-1968	Note 50.
1269	JA	4-8-2	NZR Hillside	392/54	1-1955	6-1969	
1270	JA	4-8-2	NZR Hillside	393/55	12-1955	6-1969	
1271	JA	4-8-2	NZR Hillside	394/56	4-1956	16-11-1971	Preserved
1272	JA	4-8-2	NZR Hillside	395/56	8-1956	3-1968	
1273	JA	4-8-2	NZR Hillside	396/56	10-1956	7-1969	
1274	JA	4-8-2	NZR Hillside	397/56	12-1956	16-11-1971	Preserved
1275	JA	4-8-2	North British	27104/51	19-7-1952	3-1968	Preserved
1276	JA	4-8-2	North British	27105/51	19-7-1952	3-1968	
1277	JA	4-8-2	North British	27106/51	16-8-1952	5-1966	
1278	JA	4-8-2	North British	27107/51	19-7-1952	3-1968	
1279	JA	4-8-2	North British	27108/51	16-8-1952	7-1964	
1280	JA	4-8-2	North British	27109/51	13-9-1952	5-1967	
1281	JA	4-8-2	North British	27110/51	13-9-1952	9-1966	
1282	JA	4-8-2	North British	27111/51	13-9-1952	11-1967	
1283	JA	4-8-2	North British	27112/51	21-6-1952	3-1968	
1284	JA	4-8-2	North British	27113/51	21-6-1952	8-1967	
1285	JA	4-8-2	North British	27114/51	11-10-1952	10-1967	
1286	JA	4-8-2	North British	27115/51	11-10-1952	11-1967	
1287	JA	4-8-2	North British	27116/51	8-11-1952	10-1966	
1288	JA	4-8-2	North British	27117/51	8-11-1952	9-1966	
1289	JA	4-8-2	North British	27118/51	11-10-1952	2-1966	
1290	JA	4-8-2	North British	27119/51	6-12-1952	10-1966	

BELOW: An impressive line-up of North British oil-fired 4-8-2 locomotives at the Auckland loco depot, 9 May 1965. JAs 1275, 1284, 1276, 1281, 1280 and 1277. (R. B. Croker)

ABOVE: G 98, a new double Pacific Beyer-Garratt type in works grey livery. Hutt Workshops, May 1929. (A. P. Godber, Alexander Turnbull Library)

BELOW: The engine units of the unsuccessful Garratts had twenty years of useful life left when mated with modified A^B-type boilers and tenders. G 96, just out of Hillside Workshops after conversion, shows off the front sheet metal cover over the Gresley derived motion levers. Dunedin locomotive depot, 8 September 1937. (S. A. Rockliff)

ABOVE: The class C 2-6-2 tender shunting locomotive of 1930, equipped with many modern devices, proved inadequate for heavy shunting duties, having insufficient weight on the driving wheels. C 851, Auckland, August 1952. (J. M. Creber)

BELOW: Why? The last type of steam locomotive acquired by the NZR, in 1938 and 1945, skipped eight vacant class letters when later classified. The three locomotives retained their Public Works Department numbers and were eventually given their Y classification in March 1952. Number 544, Huntly, January 1951. (W. W. Stewart)

108 - Steam Locomotive Numbering 1890-1971

NOTES TO THE 'STEAM LOCOMOTIVE NUMBERING 1890-1971' TABLE

Note 1 The class M 0-6-0T locomotives were altered to 2-4-4T wheel arrangement at Addington Workshops :M 3 in 1889, M 4 in 1888, M 89 and M 90 in 1890.

Note 2 F 5 was purchased from the Westport Harbour Board in May 1897.

Note 3 From 1892 twelve class F locomotives were rebuilt to 0-6-0 side tank configuration with larger cylinders, outside valve motion and larger boilers; these were classified F^A and retained their original road numbers. F^A 276 was built new to this form. In 1897 F 9, rebuilt to the new design but with a larger bunker and trailing truck, was classified F^B. From 1900 the 0-6-0 side tank locomotives were similarly altered and reclassified. When the last one, F^A 244, was altered to the F^B pattern in 1905 the classification reverted to F^A for all of them. The six new engines fitted with piston valves, F^A 315 and 372-6, were classified F^B from new until 1905.

Road Number	Built as F^A 0-6-0T	Built as F^B 0-6-2T	Works	Converted to F^B 0-6-2T	Works
F^B 9	--	1897	Addington	--	
F^A 10	1893	--	Addington	1903	Hillside
F^A 41	1893	--	Addington	1903	Hillside
F^A 157	1895	--	Addington	1903	Hillside
F^A 179	1894	--	Petone	1904	Petone
F^A 182	1893	--	Petone	1904	Petone
F^A 186	1895	--	Petone	1903	Petone
F^A 226	1892	--	Petone	1903	Petone
F^A 242	1892	--	Newmarket	1904	Newmarket
F^A 244	1895	--	Newmarket	1905	Newmarket
F^A 247	1892	--	Newmarket	1904	Newmarket
F^A 250	1892	--	Addington	1900	Westport
F^A 251	1892	--	Addington	1903	Hillside
F^A 276	1896	--	Newmarket	1904	Newmarket

Note 4 N 27 was rebuilt to a compound engine on the Vauclain system at Addington workshops in 1895, maker's number 13. Some authorities allege that this number was expunged from the records. However, the "Loco 56" Engine Record Card refers to the boiler by this number until the general renumbering of boilers in 1925.

Note 5 A 62 was transferred to the Maintenance Branch in 1906 and used at a number of locations. It was laid up about 1925 and placed on display at Otahuhu Workshops about the time these were opened in January 1929. The number A 196 was probably issued soon after its transfer to the Maintenance Branch.

Note 6 A 67 was sold in 1891. It was taken back into NZR service in the following year as A 5.

Note 7 The class A Pacifics were built as balanced four-cylinder compounds. They were converted to two-cylinder simple-expansion locomotives between 1941 and 1949.

	Date Converted		Date Converted		Date Converted		Date Converted
A 71	4-12-1942	A 418	6-12-1945	A 471	16-2-1944	A 584	12-10-1944
A 161	22-12-1942	A 419	22-12-1941	A 472	31-3-1942	A 585	2-3-1943
A 178	2-12-1943	A 420	16-8-1944	A 473	9-2-1944	A 586	25-5-1945
A 399	15-11-1946	A 421	6-1947	A 474	22-5-1942	A 587	11-3-1942
A 406	28-5-1943	A 422	29-9-1942	A 475	14-7-1942	A 598	23-11-1943
A 407	25-6-1943	A 423	20-2-1942	A 476	8-8-1941	A 599	11-12-1944
A 408	13-9-1946	A 424	3-1949	A 477	4-1947	A 600	7-5-1943
A 410	7-11-1941	A 425	13-7-1945	A 478	9-1948	A 601	23-7-1943
A 411	2-1949	A 426	7-1948	A 578	15-10-1943	A 602	28-10-1943
A 412	3-1948	A 427	3-1949	A 579	5-5-1944	A 603	4-1948
A 413	3-1948	A 428	9-2-1943	A 580	19-2-1945	A 604	15-6-1944
A 414	29-4-1944	A 429	11-1947	A 581	8-3-1942	A 605	3-1949
A 415	17-12-1943	A 469	12-1947	A 582	21-3-1941	A 606	10-3-1943
A 416	3-1948	A 470	2-4-1943	A 583	6-8-1945	A 607	9-11-1945
A 417	9-7-1943						

Note 8 G 98, G 99 and G 100 were of the Beyer-Garratt type. Although these locomotives were written off in 9-1937 they had not been used for some time prior to that date. The engine portions, fitted with A^B type boilers, became the G class Pacifics G 95 - G 100.

Note 9 Four class J locomotives were converted to 2-6-2T and reclassified W^A.

Road Number	Converted at	Date Converted	Road Number	Converted at	Date Converted
120	Hillside	9-1917	234	Petone	1-1918
124	Newmarket	11-1918	262	Newmarket	3-1917

Note 10 C 148 was renumbered C 577 in 1912.

Note 11 Nine 4-8-0 type locomotives were fitted with wide-firebox boilers. The classification was not altered.

Road Number	Date Converted	Road Number	Date Converted	Road Number	Date Converted
B^A 148	6-1948	B 306	3-1930	B^A 499	11-1949
B 303	10-1948	B 307	1-1935	B^A 552	1-1929
B 304	7-1931	B^A 498	10-1929	B^A 553	5-1948

Note 12 F 166 was bought from the Westport Harbour Board, 6-1893.

Note 13 D 170 was renumbered D 576 in 1912.

Note 14 The class E Fairlies although written off in 1899 were still in use after this date. E 177 was broken up 8-1902, E 173 was broken up in 1904. E 172, E 174 and E 176 were in use until 1915 and were sold for scrap 6-1925. E 178 was in service until 1918.

Note 15 B 178 was converted to class W^E 4-6-4T and renumbered W^E 377 in 1902.

Note 16 F 180 was in use as the East Town (Wanganui) works shunter until 1965.

Note 17 B 198 was converted to class W^E 4-6-4T in 1902 and renumbered W^E 376 in 1942.

Note 18 Of the ten Avonside 2-4-0T of class L, three, 207, 208 and 219 were sold and replaced by new locomotives; three were renewed as 4-4-0T of class L^A and later altered to 4-4-2T; 205-1897/1901, 265-1894/1902 and 267-1893/1900. The remainder were renewed as 4-4-2T of class L^A; 91, 206 and 264 in 1900, and 266 in 1899. The classification of the 4-4-2T locomotives was altered to L in 1903.

Note 19 L 207 was Otahuhu works shunter during 1939-40 and was in use at Whangarei until 4-1942.

Note 20 A 215 and F 216 were purchased from the Kaihu Valley Railway Company 1-1-1893. A 215, formerly Wanganui section A 22, was sold to the company in 1888. F 216 was imported by the company.

Note 21 NZR maker's number 52 was also issued to F^A 374, which retained it. The duplication was corrected in 1913 by the issue of maker's number 162 to L 219. L 219 was the Hutt works shunter from 1939 to 1954.

Note 22 F 277 was purchased new by the contractor to the Greymouth Harbour Board, Messrs Hungerford and Mackay, who sold it to NZR 3-1898.

Note 23 B 309 was converted to class W^E 4-6-4T and renumbered W^E 375 in 1943.

Note 24 F^A 372 was still working at Picton in 1944.

Note 25 W^F 398 was the Hutt works shunter from 1954 to 5-1958.

ABOVE: Newly arrived at Auckland in December 1932, K 900 exhibited features new to the NZR, such as a pressed steel smokebox door and smoke deflectors around the funnel. (W. W. Stewart)

BELOW: K 900 had a K^A style funnel fitted when photographed at Frankton on 10 March 1963. Earlier alterations included the distinctive recessed headlight mounting as well as the installation of a cross-compound air compressor and conversion to oil-firing. (J. M. Creber)

Steam Locomotive Numbering 1890-1971 - 111

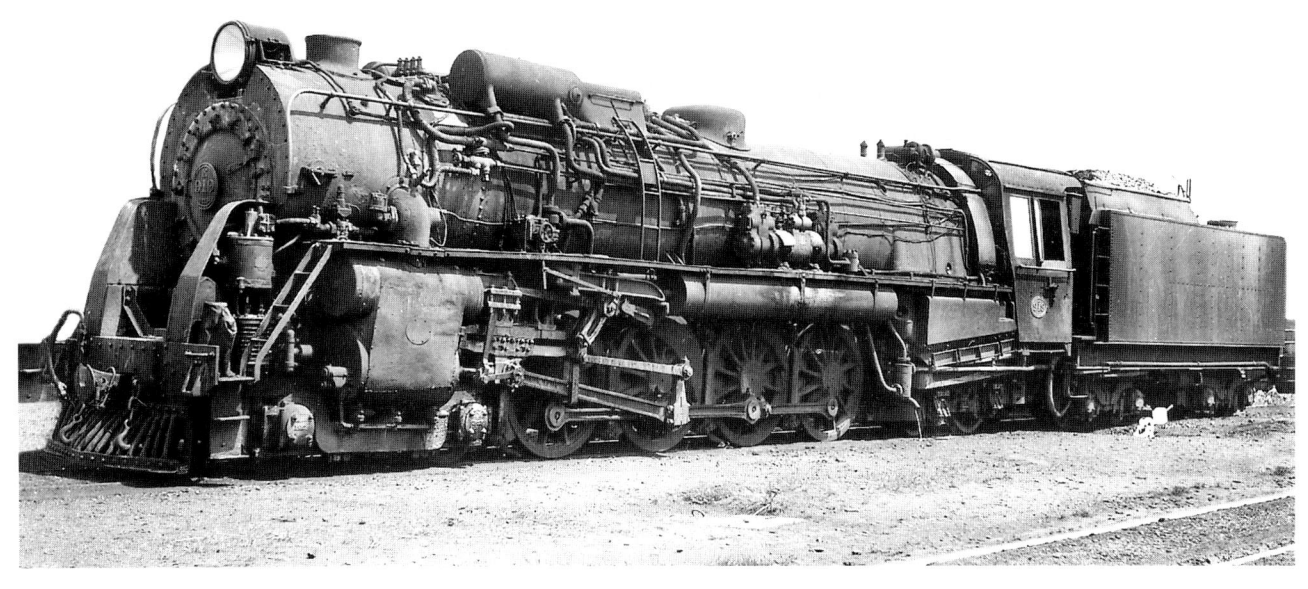

ABOVE: When new K 919 was fitted with ACFI feedwater heater equipment. Although successful in service the appearance of the locomotive attracted adverse comment. Palmerston North, December 1945. (E. J. McClare)

BELOW: As a result, thirty class K^A and six K^B similarly equipped had the componentry and pipework concealed by streamlined casings over the smokebox and panels elsewhere. K^A 935, with all the frills, had these components removed in 1951. Paekakariki, December 1943. (E. J. McClare)

ABOVE: The last two K^A locomotives were a long time coming. Entering service four years after the last of their sisters, these two had all the modern features, being fitted for oil firing, and with cross-compound air compressors, exhaust steam injectors and Baker valve gear from the J^A building programme. K^A 958 at Frankton Junction, February 1962. (J. A. T. Terry)

BELOW: The main difference between the K^A and K^B classes was the fitting of a booster - an auxiliary steam engine on the cab bogie. K^B 970 stands at the Dunedin locomotive depot on 24 August 1948 after overhaul at Hillside Workshops when the streamline casing was removed. 970 was the first of the class to appear unadorned. The front number plate had yet to be fitted. (S. A. Rockliff)

Note 26 A 409 was built as a two-cylinder simple-expansion locomotive for comparison with the class A compounds. It was classified A^B between 1915 and 1930.

Note 27 The class X locomotives were built as four-cylinder compounds on the de Glehn system. Twelve were altered to four-cylinder simple-expansion locomotives:

Date Converted		Date Converted		Date Converted		Date Converted	
X 439	6-1949	X 443	7-1947	X 588	5-1951	X 593	6-1950
X 440	7-1948	X 444	12-1949	X 591	12-1950	X 594	5-1945
X 442	6-1943	X 446	12-1946	X 592	10-1950	X 596	12-1949

Note 28 W^F 467 and W^F 468 were purchased from the Public Works Department in 1908; these had been previously PWD 501 and 502.

Note 29 Ten of the class W^G locomotives were fitted with larger cylinders and reclassified W^W: 489, 490, 492 and 496 in 1940, 491 and 495 in 1941, 481, 482, 493 and 494 in 1942. Four more, fitted with a new design of boiler and other modifications, were also reclassified W^W: 479 in 1952, 480 in 1951, 486 in 1950, and 488 in 1951.

Note 30 The block of numbers 501 to 550 was allocated to the Public Works Department for its locomotives. The Railways Department agreed not to use these numbers.

Note 31 Class Y locomotives were purchased from the PWD; 543 on 11-10-1938. the others on 3-8-1945 and were allocated to the Maintenance Branch. They were brought on to the records as additional locomotive stock on 28-4-1951 and classified Y in March 1952.

Note 32 W^W 562 was renumbered W^W 667 in 1938. This locomotive was badly damaged in an accident in 1937. In the course of repair it received new frames and other modifications, becoming similar to the second batch of locomotives of this class. It was renumbered in sequence with the modified locomotives.

Note 33 The following class W^W locomotives were fitted with larger boilers and other modifications. No alteration was made to the classification.

Date Converted		Date Converted		Date Converted		Date Converted	
W^W 571	7-1956	W^W 575	8-1952	W^W 672	1-1960	W^W 680	3-1955
W^W 573	9-1956	W^W 644	7-1953	W^W 678	8-1959	W^W 683	12-1953
W^W 574	5-1953	W^W 669	11-1952	W^W 679	4-1960	W^W 684	9-1954

Note 34 Two class A^B locomotives were ordered and would have been numbered 666 and 667. The material was used in the construction of the 4-6-4T locomotives 686 and 687.

Note 35 W^S 686 was altered to the W^{AB} type 9-12-1932 and reclassified W^{AB} 12-11-1936.

Note 36 Two class A^B locomotives, allocated numbers 732 and 762, were lost in the wreck of *TSS Wiltshire* at Great Barrier Island on 31-5-1922.

Note 37 The class W^S locomotives were modified with fabricated Delta trailing bogies and reclassified W^{AB}.

Date Converted		Date Converted		Date Converted		Date Converted	
764	7-1932	768	3-1933	771	5-1933	801	7-1934
765	12-1933	769	9-1932	799	7-1933	802	5-1932
766	11-1933	770	8-1932	800	5-1932	803	9-1934
767	8-1934						

Note 38 A^B 778 and A^B 795 were returned to service as special stock on 22 December 1971 for the *Kingston Flyer* train running between Lumsden and Kingston and in the later seasons out of Invercargill. This service ceased on 31 January 1982 and the locomotives were then leased in December 1982 to Kingston Flyer Ltd. and operated between Kingston and Fairlight. Tranz Rail took over the operation in May 1997 and continued to operate the service until 30 April 2002 when the business was sold to Invest South Limited and subsequently leased to Kingston Flyer Steam Train Ltd. Both locomotives continue in service for the new operator.

114 - Steam Locomotive Numbering 1890-1971

ABOVE: J 1212 in original fully streamlined condition except that the speed recorder has been disconnected. Frankton locomotive depot, 1940. (A. R. Schmidt, J. M. Creber Collection)

Forty modern and powerful locomotives were delivered from the North British Locomotive Company in 1939 and 1940. Class J was ordered with the capability of running over secondary lines laid with 53-56 lb per yard (23kg per metre) rails. Initially, these highly efficient machines were less than popular. Locomotive crews complained that fumes were conveyed into the cab through the streamline casing. Maintenance staff had to remove covers to get at various working components. Consequently the streamlining was 'lost', often piecemeal. An instruction to remove all of the streamlining was issued in April 1948 with this work being completed by 1953. J 1212 demonstrates the metamorphosis from the original streamlined form to the final class J^A likeness.

BELOW: The first stage of destreamlining gave the class J a distinctive look with the conical headlight mounted on the smokebox front the most noticeable feature. Frankton, August 1948. (L. J. Hostick)

ABOVE: Now completely destreamlined, J 1212 displayed the features of the class as running in the 1950s and 60s. Auckland locomotive depot, 9 March 1958. (D. J. Sims)

BELOW: Prior to transfer to the South Island in November 1963, a cross-compound air compressor was installed in December 1958, while the J^A pattern funnel and sand dome date from an earlier 1955 overhaul. A North British J^A boiler was fitted during an overhaul at Hillside in 1964 (note the diamond shaped maker's plate on the smokebox). Oamaru locomotive depot, 15 April 1967.
(G. M. Cosgrove, C. J. Howell Collection)

ABOVE: The final member of thirty-five similar machines built over a ten year period, and the last steam locomotive built for New Zealand Railways, J^A 1274 steamed out of Hillside Workshops, 6 December 1956. (G. W. Emerson)

BELOW: Sixteen similar locomotives, but fitted for oil firing, were ordered from the North British Locomotive Company in 1950 and were all in service by December 1952. J^A 1283, newly arrived at Auckland locomotive depot, August 1952. (J. M. Creber)

Note 39 Eleven class W^{AB} tank locomotives were converted to type A^B tender locomotives

Road Number	Date Converted	Road Number	Date Converted	Road Number	Date Converted
786	19-9-1947	790	3-9-1957	795	17-12-1947
787	22-10-1947	791	19-11-1947	798	21-11-1957
788	23-1-1948	792	27-6-1947	803	14-12-1957
789	22-8-1947	793	26-2-1948		

Note 40 F 839-F 841, formerly Westport Harbour Board F 237-239, were taken over from the Marine Department, Westport in 5-1922. They were renumbered by NZR in 5-1927.

Note 41 The correct maker's number of B 304 should be 43 of 1901. However, the number used on the locomotive history card for this engine and the Addington maker's plate carried on the rear of the tender showed 27 of 1901. The matter was further confused when this tender was coupled to B 308 in later years.

Note 42 K 919 was fitted with the French ACFI feedwater heating system to test its suitability on the NZR.

Note 43 Following successful tests conducted with K 919, K^A 930-954, 960-964 and K^B 965-970 were fitted with ACFI feedwater heaters shrouded by a casing over the smokebox and panels along the boiler top and running boards. The equipment and shrouding were removed as the locomotives were overhauled after 1948.

Note 44 The responsibility for construction of the class K^A locomotives was divided; twenty-five K^A 930-939 and 945-959 to Hutt Workshops and ten, K^A 940-944 and 960-964, allocated to Hillside Shops. The Vulcan Foundry, Newton-le-Willows, England supplied parts for fifteen locomotives ostensibly K^A 930-944, comprising most of the chassis components, tender bogies, boiler foundation rings and much steelplate cut to size. The General Casting Corporation of Eddystone, Pennsylvania, USA supplied trailing bogie and rear end framing for all of the 4-8-4 locomotives. The boiler plates for fifteen boilers were flanged at Hutt, then delivered to Hillside which made the boilers. Although the imported components were ordered for specific locomotives, these and the Hillside boilers were used indiscriminately in the K^A building programme. Hillside essentially manufactured and finished ten class K^A locomotives with the final erection carried out at Hutt.

Note 45 All class K and K^A locomotives were modified to burn oil fuel.

	Date Converted		Date Converted		Date Converted		Date Converted
900	28-3-1950	916	25-11-1949	932	5-12-1947	948	28-7-1947
901	9-12-1948	917	21-12-1949	933	19-12-1947	949	3-5-1947
902	24-11-1948	918	18-8-1950	934	30-7-1947	950	30-5-1947
903	28-11-1947	919	19-5-1947	935	29-9-1948	951	13-9-1947
904	16-12-1948	920	6-11-1947	936	6-6-1947	952	10-10-1947
905	1-10-1948	921	11-12-1947	937	6-8-1947	953	18-11-1947
906	13-10-1949	922	14-10-1949	938	29-8-1947	954	15-8-1947
907	5-9-1947	923	9-12-1949	939	15-7-1947	955	9-9-1947
908	15-6-1950	924	9-9-1949	940	17-3-1949	956	7-7-1947
909	12-11-1948	925	15-11-1946	941	29-10-1948	957	13-6-1947
910	5-12-1947	926	10-11-1949	942	26-11-1948	958-959	from new
911	10-9-1948	927	31-10-1946	943	13-3-1949	960	6-10-1947
912	19-8-1949	928	7-10-1949	944	18-12-1947	961	11-3-1948
913	4-11-1949	929	22-11-1947	945	3-12-1947	962	12-10-1948
914	24-4-1947	930	16-12-1947	946	26-9-1947	963	20-8-1948
915	15-10-1948	931	13-4-1948	947	21-6-1947	964	5-11-1948

Locomotives 902, 904, 906, 913, 916, 917, 923, 935, 937, 938, 939, 940, 943, 944, 945, 957, 960, 962 and 964 were converted at Otahuhu Workshops, Auckland; the remainder at Hutt Shops.

Note 46 K^A 958 and 959 were fitted with Baker valve motion from new.

118 - Steam Locomotive Numbering 1890-1971

Note 47 Some class J, K and K^A locomotives were fitted with Westinghouse cross-compound air compressors.

Road Number	Date Fitted	Road Number	Date Fitted	Road Number	Date Fitted
K 900	28-3-1950	K^A 933	10-8-1950	J 1202	18-8-1950
K 905	23-3-1955	K^A 943	18-12-1958	J 1203	27-5-1950
K 908	15-6-1950	K^A 946	31-5-1962	J 1206	21-7-1950
K 911	10-12.57	K^A 948	27-5-1950	J 1207	6-3-1959
K 917	4-3-1955	K^A 950	6-3-1959	J 1211	23-5-1959
K 921	21-7-1950	K^A 952	31-3-1950	J 1212	17-12-1958
K 922	26-9-1956	K^A 957	28-4-1950	J 1214	16-6-1950
K 924	15-12-1955	K^A 958	From new	J 1231	13-2-1959
K 927	30-6-1950	K^A 959	From new	J 1234	27-3-1950
K 929	23-7-1955	K^A 962	23-3-1959	J 1236	20-8-1948
				J 1238	31-3-1950

Note 48 Class J locomotives were built with torpedo-shaped smokebox fronts and a streamlined casing along the boiler top. These casings were removed, often piecemeal, between 1948 and 1953.

Note 49 Twelve Class J locomotives were converted to oil firing and were reclassified J^B in March 1952.

Road Number	Date Converted	Road Number	Date Converted	Road Number	Date Converted
1200	14-10-1949	1213	22-9-1949	1229	13-10-1949
1203	27-5-1950	1218	17-9-1949	1230	14-9-1949
1205	1-9-1949	1224	14-12-1949	1233	7-9-1949
1206	21-8-1950	1228	16-12-1948	1239	25-8-1949

Locomotives 1230, 1233 and 1239 were converted at Hillside Workshops, the remainder at Hutt Shops.

Note 50 J^A 1265-1268, allocated maker's numbers 388-391, ran with plates 379-382 which properly belonged to J^A 1256-1259. The latter locomotives did not have maker's plates fitted.

BELOW: The first locomotive built in the New Zealand Railways' workshops was W 192, seen at Greymouth with the other member of the class, W 238. A practice prevalent in Canterbury and Westland in the 1950s was the painting of the road number on the smokebox door. W 192 has survived into preservation. (G. W. Emerson)

CHAPTER SEVEN

LOCOMOTIVE NAMES

The authority to name locomotives was contained in the Engineer-in Chief's memorandum of 6 January 1874. It was not a new practice, since the second locomotive of the Auckland and Drury Railway is known to have had a nameplate, although the name cannot be deciphered in the photograph, both of the Dunedin and Port Chalmers Railway locomotives had names, and the first of the Dunedin and Clutha Railway locomotives was recorded as *Clutha*. Later this became, in conformity with the instruction, *Edie Ochiltree*.

As with the early schemes of numbers a full list of names has not survived; thus it is necessary to reconstruct, relying on photographs and secondary sources. The Dunedin Engines list of April 1876 with its pencilled additions is trustworthy because it is supported by photographs, news reports, and engine drivers' reminiscences. These reminiscences are also useful but may contain errors; Jack Sargent's list of ten Auckland locomotives, given to the late W. W. Stewart some eighty years ago, authenticated by five newspaper reports and four photographs, is known to transpose the identities of two engines. Newspaper reports of accidents and mishaps identifying locomotives by name are reliable. However, journalists' flights of fancy, engendered by the spirit of the occasion, must be disregarded even though they do have amusement value, as witness the story of the naming of the G class locomotive *Pride of Prebbleton* found in the *Christchurch Press* of 24 September 1874, or the Napier fantasy related at page 11.

Some reported names are no more than nicknames, as surviving photographs indicating an absence of a name do not support the newspaper listings of locomotives being "called, known as, christened or baptised". Some christenings, however, were carried over into later industrial service. The reported speeches given at the opening of the Brunner Coal Railway quote locomotive names *Ahaura* and *Pounamu*; the Greymouth Harbour Board inherited and always knew Dubs 1772 as *Ahaura*.

It appears, generally, that a section which named its locomotives named all of them. However, there are exceptions; Wellington named only the Fell locomotives, *Belmont*, and retained the name *Eel* when it was transferred from Napier; Invercargill named only the class M locomotives, plus the "known as" *Rat* and *Possum*. No names are recorded from Westport, whilst in Canterbury there were no named locomotives during the provincial period.

The policy of applying names ceased early in 1877. The appellations were allowed to lapse as locomotives were overhauled and repainted. The last names recorded by the *Otago Daily Times* were *Weka* in September 1880, *Corsair* in January of the same year, and *Saladin* a year earlier. Strangely, the Canterbury section, devoid of names earlier, retained those of four; two K and two Q locomotives which had been named in the builder's factories - *Lincoln*, *Washington*, *Stanley* and *Livingstone*.

Thereafter NZR motive power was not named with one exception. A[B] 608 was given the commemorative *Passchendaele* nameplates in 1925, as a memorial to the railwaymen killed in the First World War. These were removed in 1943 and briefly replaced when the locomotive was displayed at the Railways Centennial Exhibition in 1963. The original nameplates were put on display at Dunedin and Christchurch railway stations.

Towards the end of the steam era three of the F class locomotives were overhauled and repainted for special excursion services. In 1958, F 13, the former *Edie Ochiltree*, acquired *Peveril*, the name of a former Dunedin stablemate. *Ivanhoe*, the name of an Auckland locomotive, was bestowed on F 163 at the time of the Railways Centennial Exhibition in 1963, while F 180 assumed its old name *Meg Merrilies* in 1960.

At various times unofficial names have been given to their charges by enginemen. An example of this was W[W] 680 which carried the name *Sapper* at Westport in the last days of steam. Other locomotives known by nicknames throughout their lives were E 66 *Pearson's Dream*, L 206 *Mrs Peterkin*, while U[B] 17 and U[B] 371 were always *The Brooks* and *The Richmond* after their makers. O[A] 457 (WMR N[o] 13) was *The Lady* both in company and later NZR service.

In the table of names the column headed "Provenance" details the source of the locomotive name; 1 - being a positive record from a photograph, 2 - a name shown in an official list, 3 - a name recorded in a newspaper incident report, 4 - railwaymens' reminiscences, 5 - christenings carried on into later industrial service, 6 - christenings, "known as" or "called" in news reports. An asterisk indicates that a name cannot be discerned on surviving photographs.

120 - Locomotive Names

ABOVE: *MacCallum Mhor*, F 9 in the Auckland livery style of 1874, became F 59 in 1882 and F 248 in the 1890 list. The top-hatted gentleman is Mr. Withers, painter. (W. W. Stewart Collection)

BELOW: *Snake*, Auckland Section Nº 1 and B 10, later B 51 and B 238, had several claims to fame. It employed the first British use of Walschaert valve gear and was one of the only six locomotives fitted with a cast nameplate. (A. P. Godber Collection, Alexander Turnbull Library)

ABOVE: *Mount Egmont*, soon after arrival, had the sandbox enlarged and the cab extended. The outside Stephenson valve gear, elsewhere found in New Zealand only on the Mills class A locomotives, is clearly visible. Wellington, H 37, later H 3 and H 201, about 1880.
(New Zealand Railways Publicity, T. A. McGavin Collection)

BELOW: *Mazeppa* retained its Otago livery after transfer to Christchurch in December 1878. M 89, Christchurch 1879. (W. W. Stewart Collection)

LOCOMOTIVE NAMES

Name	Section	Section or Maker's Number	Isolated Section Number	1890 Number	Provenance
Ada	Auckland	1	F 52	F 242	1
Ahaura	Greymouth	--	C 131/C 2	--	5
Albatross	Kaipara & Wanganui	17 & 23	E 21	E 172	6 *
Belmont	Wellington	32	--	--	1
Black Dwarf	Wanganui/Foxton	28 or 29	F 24 or F 25	F 182 or F 183	3
Blenheim	Picton	--	11 or 125	C 147 or C 148	1
Bluff	Bluff & Invercargill	2 or 3	--	--	6
Bothwell	Otago	31	--	F 80	3 *
Christchurch	NZ Midland Rly	2	--	L^A 311	1
Clutha	Otago	8	--	F 13	6
Corsair	Otago	1	--	M 90	1
Dandie Dinmont	Otago	12	--	F 231	2
Diana Vernon	Napier	18 or 19	F 41 or F 42	F 224 or F 225	6
Dougal	Wanganui/Foxton	28 or 29	F 24 or F 25	F 182 or F 183	3
Driver	Auckland & Drury Rly	MW162	--	--	--
Eel	Napier & Wellington	3 (22)	D 3	D 197	3
Edie Ochiltree	Otago	8	--	F 13	2
Ferret	New Plymouth	44	A 22	A 215	3, 5
Flora McIvor	Auckland	5	F 53	F 243	3, 4
Fox	New Plymouth	43	A 21	(A 192)	1, 3
Guy Mannering	Wanganui/Foxton	25	F 21	F 179	6
Hastings	Napier	1 or 2	C ?	--	6
Helen McGregor	Wanganui/Foxton	27	F 23	F 181	1
Ivanhoe	Auckland	2	F 51	F 241	3, 4
Ivanhoe	Otago	12	--	F 231	6 *
Jeanie Deans	Auckland	8	F 58	F 247	3, 4
Josephine	DPCR No 2, Otago	7	--	E 175	2
Kingfish(er)	Nelson	13	128 or 129	D 144	3, 4
Kaihu	Kaipara	15	C 51	C 239	6
Kangaroo	Otago & Greymouth	--	--	--	5
Kiwi	Otago	27	--	--	3
Lady Barkly	Oreti Railway	1	--	--	1, 3
Lady Mordaunt	Otago	18	--	B 165	4 *
Lady of the Lake	Auckland	3	F 55	F164	4
Lincoln	Hurunui-Bluff	--	--	K 87	1
Livingstone	Rakaia & Ashb'n Forks	1	--	Q 51	3 *
Lord of the Isles	Auckland	4	F 56	F 245	3, 4
Madge Wildfire	Auckland	7	F 57	F 246	3, 4
Manfred	Otago	22	--	M 4	--
Marmion	Auckland	6	F 54	F 244	2, 3, 4
Mazeppa	Otago	2	--	M 89	1
Meg Merrilies	Wanganui/Foxton	26	F 22	F 180	4
Moana	Wellington	31	C 21	C 166	5
Mont Cenis	Wellington	35	H 1	H 199	1
Mount Cook	Wellington	36	H 2	H 200	1,3
Mount Egmont	Wellington	37	H 3	H 201	1
Mount Tongariro	Wellington	38	H 4	H 202	
Mouse	Hurunui-Bluff	--	--	A 6	
MacCallum Mhor	Auckland	9	F 59	F 248	1
Nelson	NZ Midland Rly	3	--	L^A 312	1
Nigel	Otago	29	--	F40	1, 4
Opossum	Foxton	--	--	--	6
Passchendaele	NZR	--	--	A^B 608	1
Pelican	Wanganui	24	E 22	E 173	3
Peveril	Otago	17	--	F 232	2, 3

| **LOCOMOTIVE NAMES (continued)** ||||||
Name	Section	Section or Maker's Number	Isolated Section Number	1890 Number	Provenance
Pilgrim	Canterbury (Broad Ga.)	1	--	--	6 *
Pioneer	Canterbury (Narrow Ga.)	Dubs A	--	--	6 *
Pirate	Otago	30	--	F 44 or F 19	3, 4
Possum	Otago	13	--	D 169	3 *
Pounamu	Greymouth	--	C 132/C 1	--	5
Rat	Otago	5	--	C 5	6
Reefton	NZ Midland Rly	1	--	L^A 310	1
Robina	Otago	26	--	S 52	3
Rob Roy	Otago	10	--	F 37	1
Roderick Dhu	Otago	32	--	F 44 or F 19	4
Rose	DPCR Nº1, Otago	6	--	--	1, 2
Roswal	Otago	--	--	F 72 or F 74	1
Saladin	Otago	20	--	F 73	1
Skunk	Foxton	--	--	--	
Snake	Auckland	1 later 10	B 51	B 238	1
Schnapper	Kaipara	16	D 51	D 240	1, 6
Stanley	Rakaia & Ashb'n Forks	2	--	Q 17	
Talisman	Otago	19	--	F 72 or F 74	3 *
Trout	Nelson	12	128 or 129	D 143	1
Waitohi	Picton	--	11 or 125	C 147 or C 148	3
Washington	Hurunui-Bluff	--	--	K 88	
Wallaby	Foxton	--	--	--	
Waverley	Otago	11	--	F 38	2
Weka	Otago	26	--	--	1, 3
Werner	Otago	3	--	M 3	

Schnapper; the photograph showing this name is believed to be spurious.

Lady Mordaunt; the reminiscence of Thomas Galloway, who erected this locomotive, relates that he christened the locomotive during a stop at Burke's Brewery on its trial run. Although it was known throughout its service by this name, no evidence has been found that the name was carried.

These names have also been noticed, but evidence is not available to verify them, or to assign them to locomotives: *Cat, Carrickfergus, Makarewa* and *Oreti* (said for the Oreti Railway locomotives numbers 2 and 3), *Sanspareil, Taringatura* (reported as the fourth engine at Winton), *Tuapeka numbers 1 and 2* (Fairlies for the Lawrence branch railway) and *Penguin* (said for the Fairlie E 22 at Wanganui).

124 - Locomotive Names

ABOVE: "Two new engines of improved tank and pattern... have been put together in the newly built shed on the reserve facing the Dunedin station... Messrs. Burton Brothers took a photograph of one of them yesterday, the *Rob Roy*, and with its fresh coat of green paint and name in gold letters with its gleaming 'Nº 10', it presents a very handsome appearance..." So said the *Otago Witness* on 11 July 1874. (Burton Brothers, G. W. Emerson Collection)

BELOW: The Otago style of painting varied. *Weka*, Otago Nº 27, shows subtle differences in lining-out when compared with *Rob Roy*. (Alexander Turnbull Library Collection)

Locomotive Names - 125

ABOVE: Kaipara section D 16, later D 51 and then D 240, is recorded as being christened *Schnapper.* This name, almost certainly, has been interpolated into the illustration. (A. P. Godber Collection, Alexander Turnbull Library)

BELOW: *Passchendaele,* the 1914-1918 War Memorial locomotive, was prepared at Hillside Workshops for display at the Dunedin and South Seas Exhibition held from November 1925 to April 1926. Two alterations from new are visible; electric lighting is fitted and the air compressor has been moved from its original location alongside the smokebox. A^B 608, Hillside, November 1925.
(D. J. Sherriff, E. J. McClare Collection)

CHAPTER EIGHT

THE MAKERS OF NZR LOCOMOTIVES

This chapter serves two purposes. Firstly, it summarises the contribution of the many locomotive builders to the NZR fleet. Secondly, it provides a ready means of cross-reference between the separate schemes of numbers which were issued at various times.

The column headed "1874 Series" is the Public Works Department's numbering of Otago and Canterbury Railways, together with the placement of the South Island Isolated Sections locomotives. All of these were renumbered into the PWD "South Island" List commencing in 1877, which carried over as the early portion of the "1890 List", except for the few Isolated engines. The locomotives of the PWD "North Island" List and the South Island Isolated Section engines were renumbered by the Railways Department's "1882 System" and later into the "1890 List". The latter had currency until the end of steam in 1971.

Where there is a sequence of numbers these have not been quoted individually. For example, Avonside 1202-4 belonged to three locomotives, respectively numbers 12, 13 and 14 in the North Island series, L 52, L 53 and L 54 in the 1882 system, and L 265, L 266 and L 267 in the 1890 list.

The Avonside Engine Co. Ltd. issued two numbers to every Fairlie double locomotive: e.g. Avonside 1060/1 is one locomotive.

Some locomotives were renumbered during the currency of a number series: e.g.. Avonside 1093 in the South Island list was at first numbered F 39 and later F 19, Avonside 1222 in the 1882 list was R 3 at Wellington and on transfer to Auckland was renumbered R 53.

The abbreviations used in this table are:

ADR	Auckland and Drury Railway		Ak.	Auckland section
BHIR	Bluff Harbour and Invercargill Railway		Gy.	Greymouth Section
CR	Canterbury Railways		Nn.	Nelson Section
DPCR	Dunedin and Port Chalmers Railway		Np.	Napier Section
NZMR	New Zealand Midland Railway		Pn.	Picton Section
Oreti	Oreti Railway		Wg.	Wanganui Section
Otago	Otago Railways		Wn.	Wellington Section
RAFR	Rakaia and Ashburton Forks Railway		Wpt.	Westport Section
WMR	Wellington and Manawatu Railway			

THE AMERICAN LOCOMOTIVE COMPANY

Brooks Works, Dunkirk, N.Y. USA.			Richmond Works, Richmond, Va. USA.		
Maker's Number	Type	1890 List	Maker's Number	Type	1890 List
Brooks 3925	4-6-0	U^B 17	Richmond 3275	4-6-0	U^B 371

AVONSIDE ENGINE COMPANY LIMITED

Bristol, England.   (Late Slaughter Gruning & Company)

Maker's Number	Type	Canterbury Railways Broad-Gauge	Maker's Number	Type	Canterbury Railways Broad-Gauge
699	2-4-0T	3	855	0-4-2T	7
740	0-4-2WT	5	964	0-4-2T	8
741	0-4-2WT	6	1021	0-4-2T	10
742	2-4-0T	4			

ABOVE: A quarter of all New Zealand Railways steam locomotives were manufactured in the Scottish city of Glasgow, in the workshops of the North British Locomotive Company or its constituents, one of which was Dubs and Company. Dubs' portrait of F 226. (E. J. McClare Collection)

BELOW: Another constituent was Neilson and Company. The Neilson class H locomotives were unique in New Zealand, being fitted with outside Joy valve gear. For comparison with the Avonside class H refer to illustrations of H 200 on page 51 and H 201 on page 121. Neilson's portrait of H 6, later H 204. (E. J. McClare Collection)

AVONSIDE ENGINE COMPANY LIMITED (continued)						
Maker's Number	Type	1874 Series	South Island	North Island	1882 System	1890 List
1022/3	0-4-4-0T	--	--	1 later 10	Ak. B 51	B 238
1038	2-6-0	CR 15-20	J 81	--	--	J 81
1039	2-6-0	CR 15-20	J 83	--	--	J 83
1040	2-6-0	CR 15-20	J 82	--	--	J 82
1041	2-6-0	CR 15-20	J 85	--	--	J 85
1042	2-6-0	CR 15-20	J 84	--	--	J 84
1043	2-6-0	CR 15-20	J 86	--	--	J 86
1044/5	0-4-4-0T	Otago 18	B 21/B 27	--	Wg. B 27	B 165
1060/1	0-4-4-0T	Otago 23	E 23	--	Wg. E 26	E 177
1062/3	0-4-4-0T	Otago 25	E 25	--	Wg. E 25	E 176
1064/5	0-4-4-0T	Otago 24	E 24	--	Wg. E 27	E 178
1066/7	0-4-4-0T	--	--	30	Wg. E 23	E 174
1068/9	0-4-4-0T	--	--	24	Wg. E 22	E 173
1070/1	0-4-4-0T	--	--	17 later 23	Wg. E 21	E 172
1072	0-4-2T	--	--	37	Wn. H 3	H 201
1073	0-4-2T	--	--	38	Wn. H 4	H 202
1074	0-4-2T	--	--	36	Wn. H 2	H 200
1075	0-4-2T	--	--	35	Wn. H 1	H 199
1084	0-6-0ST	--	--	27	Wg. F 23	F 181
1085	0-6-0ST	Otago 31	F 80	--	--	F 80
1086	0-6-0ST	--	--	18 or 19	Np. F 41	F 224
1087	0-6-0ST	--	--	--	Ak. F 68	F 160
1088	0-6-0ST	CR	F 75	--	--	F 75
1089	0-6-0ST	--	--	18 or 19	Np. F 42	F 225
1090	0-6-0ST	Otago 29	F 40	--	--	F 40
1091	0-6-0ST	Otago 30 or 32	F 44	--	--	F 44
1092	0-6-0ST	--	--	--	Ak. F 67	F 159
1093	0-6-0ST	Otago 30 or 32	F 39/F 19	--	--	F 19
1094	0-6-0ST	Otago	F 10	--	--	F 10
1095	0-6-0ST	Otago	F 1	--	--	F 1
1131	0-6-0ST	CR	F 77	--	--	F 77
1132	0-6-0ST	CR	F 76	--	--	F 76
1133	0-6-0ST	Otago	F 8	--	--	F 8
1134	0-6-0ST	Otago	F 7	--	--	F 7
1135	0-6-0ST	--	--	29	Wg. F 25	F 183
1136	0-6-0ST	--	--	28	Wg. F 24	F 182
1137	0-6-0ST	Otago	F 9	--	--	F 9
1138	0-6-0ST	CR	F 78	--	--	F 78
1139	0-6-0ST	CR	F 79	--	--	F 79
1140	0-6-0ST	Otago	F 41	--	--	F 41
1141	0-6-0ST	Otago	F 2	--	--	F 2
1142	0-6-0ST	Otago	F 42	--	Gy. F 2	F 151
1143	0-6-0ST	Otago	F 43	--	--	F 43
1144	0-6-0ST	Otago	F 45	--	--	F 45
1199	2-4-0T	--	L 91	--	--	L 91
1200-1	2-4-0T	--	--	39-40	Wn. L 1-2	L 205-6
1202-4	2-4-0T	--	--	12-14	Ak. L 52-54	L 265-7
1205-6	2-4-0T	--	--	41-42	Wn. L 3-4	L 207-8
1207	2-4-0T	--	--	30	Wg. L 21	L 219
1208	2-4-0T	--	--	11	Ak. L 51	L 264
1217-18	0-6-4T	--	R 28-9	--	--	R 28-9
1219-20	0-6-4T	--	--	--	Ak. R 51-2	R 271-2
1221	0-6-4T	--	--	--	Wn. R 1	R 209

AVONSIDE ENGINE COMPANY LIMITED (continued)

Maker's Number	Type	1874 Series	South Island	North Island	1882 System	1890 List
1222	0-6-4T	--	--	--	Wn. R 3/Ak. R 53	R 273
1223	0-6-4T	--	R 30	--	Wn. R 3	R 211
1224	0-6-4T	--	--	--	Wg. R 21	R 187
1225	0-6-4T	--	R 31	--	Gy. R 1	R 153
1226	0-6-4T	--	--	--	Wn. R 2	R 210
1227-28	0-6-4T	--	--	--	Wg. R 22-3	R 188-9
1229	0-6-4T	--	R 32	--	--	R 32
1230-31	0-6-4T	--	--	--	Wg. R 24-5	R 190-1
1232	0-6-4T	--	R 33	--	--	R 33
1233	0-6-4T	--	R 22	--	--	R 22
1234	0-6-4T	--	R 112	--	--	R 112
1279-80	0-6-4T	--	--	--	Wn. S 1-2	S 212-3
1281-82	0-6-4T	--	--	--	Wn. S 6-7	S 217-8
1283	0-6-4T	--	--	--	Wn. S 4	S 215
1284	0-6-4T	--	--	--	Wn. S 3	S 214
1285	0-6-4T	--	--	--	Wn. S 5	S 216

Avonside 1022/3, 1044/5 and 1060-71. It was the custom of the company to allocate two maker's numbers to each double-boiler locomotive.
Avonside 1038-43 were Canterbury Railways 15-20, the order is not certain.
Avonside 1088, 1131/2/8/9 were Canterbury Railways 24-28, order not certain.
Avonside 1091/3 were Otago Railways 30 and 32, may be transposed.
Avonside 1094/5, 1133/4/7 and 1140-4 were delivered to Otago Railways. There is some doubt as to how many received an Otago Railways number.

THE BALDWIN LOCOMOTIVE WORKS

Philadelphia and Eddystone, Pennsylvania, USA.

Maker's Number	Type	WMR Number	1890 List	Maker's Number	Type	WMR Number	1890 List
4660-1	2-8-0	--	T 101-2	15055	2-8-0	16	O^C 458
4664-7	2-8-0	--	T 103-6	16042-51	4-6-0	--	U^B 278-287
7565	2-8-0	--	O 54	16166-67	2-6-2T	--	W^B 297-298
7566	2-8-0	--	O 98	16168-69	2-6-2T	--	W^B 295-296
7567	2-8-0	--	O 69	16170	2-6-2T	--	W^B 294
7568	2-8-0	--	O 100	16171-72	2-6-2T	--	W^B 291-292
7569	2-8-0	--	O 99	16173	2-6-2T	--	W^B 290
7571	2-6-2	--	N 30	16174	2-6-2T	--	W^B 293
7572	2-8-0	--	O 31	16175-7	2-6-2T	--	W^B 299-301
7573	2-6-2	--	N 37	18543-54	2-6-4T	--	W^D 316-327
7574	2-6-2	--	N 42	18574-83	4-6-0	--	U^B 328-337
7575	2-6-2	--	N 34	19202-7	4-6-2	--	Q 338-343
7576	2-6-2	--	N 27	19248-54	4-6-2	--	Q 344-350
7579	2-6-2	--	N 36	19259-64	2-6-4T	--	W^D 355-360
9018	2-8-0	11	O^B 455	19270-73	2-6-2	--	N 351-354
9021	2-8-0	12	O^B 456	19796	2-8-2	17	B^C 463
12104	2-6-2	9	N 453	19797	2-6-2	5	N^C 461
12106	2-6-2	10	N 454	23594	2-6-2	18	N^C 462
13908	2-8-0	13	O^A 457	23596	2-8-4T	3	W^J 466
13913	2-6-2	14	N^A 459	24086-87	4-6-0	19-20	U^D 464-465
15054	2-6-2	15	N^A 460	41826-35	4-6-2	--	A^A 648-657

BEYER PEACOCK and COMPANY Ltd
Manchester, England.

Maker's Number	Type	1890 List
6484-6	4-6-2+2-6-4	G 98-100

BLACK HAWTHORN and COMPANY
Gateshead-on-Tyne, England

Maker's Number	Type	1874 Series	South Island	1890 List
277	0-6-0ST	Otago 12	F 34	F 231
278	4-4-0ST	CR 1-4 (Order not known)	G 55	G 55
279	4-4-0ST		G 58	G 58
281	4-4-0ST		G 57	G 57
282	4-4-0ST		G 56	G 56

CLAYTON WAGONS LIMITED
Abbey Works, Lincoln, England.

Maker's Number	Type	1890 List
AW 637	0-4-0T	D 1

ALEXANDER CHAPLIN and COMPANY
Cranstonhill Engine Works, Glasgow, Scotland.

Maker's Number	Type	1874 Series
1455	0-4-0VBT	Otago 21

JAMES DAVIDSON and COMPANY
Otago Foundry, Dunedin, New Zealand.

Maker's Number	Type	1874 Series	South Island
1	0-6-0ST	Otago 26	P 54
3	0-6-0ST	Otago 27	P 59

This company erected three six-coupled saddle-tank locomotives from parts supplied by the Hunslet Engine Company of Leeds. The second machine put together, *Jerusalem*, was delivered to the Kaitangata Railway and Coal Co., and subsequently sold for the Greymouth harbour works construction in 1885, where it was named *Cobden*. The maker's numbers are allocated in delivery date order.

ABOVE: The Avonside Engine Company, late Slaughter Gruning and Company, as written on the maker's plate, was the most innovative of the British locomotive manufacturers. Its Design Engineer, Mr. H. W. Widmark, drew out the largest medium-gauge locomotives of the time in the NZR class J, and created the only successful Fell-type mountain railway locomotive, New Zealand Railways class H. Avonside company portrait of J 84. (E. J. McClare Collection)

BELOW: The Otago Provincial Council imported four locomotives from the Hunslet Engine Company. The first, Otago Railways Nº 1, later M 90, was photographed in works grey livery before dispatch from England. (W. W. Stewart Collection)

DUBS and COMPANY						
Glasgow (Queen's Park) Locomotive Works, Glasgow, Scotland Incorporated into the North British Locomotive Co. Ltd. in 1903						
Maker's Number	Type	1874 Series	South Island	North Island	1882 System	1890 List
645	0-4-0T		--	44	Wg. A 22	A 215
646	0-4-0T	CR	--	43	Wg. A 21	A 192
647	0-4-0T	numbers	A 67	--	--	A 67/A 5
648	0-4-0T	5-14	A 66	--	--	A 66
649	0-4-0T		A 70	--	Np. A 41	--
650	0-4-0T	Order	A 61	--	Wg. A 23/Ak. A51	A 161
651	0-4-0T	not	A 64	--	--	A 64
652	0-4-0T	known	A 68	--	--	A 68
653	0-4-0T		A 65	--	--	A 65
654	0-4-0T		A 69	--	Wn. A 1	A 220
655	0-4-0T	--	A 60	--	Wn. A 2	A 193
656	0-4-0T	--	A 62	--	--	A 62/A 196
800	0-4-0ST	--	--	15	Ak. C 51	C 239
801	0-4-0ST	Wpt.	--	46	Wg. C 22	C 167
802	0-4-0ST	--	--	4(23)	Wpt. C 3	--
803	0-4-0ST	Wpt.	C 126	--	Wpt. C 2	--
804	0-4-0ST	Wpt.	C 127	--	Wpt. C 1	C 158
885	0-4-0ST	Gy.	C 132	--	Gy. C 2	--
1164	2-4-0T	--	D 50	--	--	D 50
1165	2-4-0T	--	D 49	--	--	D 49
1166-7	2-4-0T	--	D 47-8	--	--	D 47-8
1168	2-4-0T	--	D 46	--	--	D 46
1169-70	0-6-0ST	--	--	46-47	Np. F 43-4	F 226-7
1171	0-6-0ST	--	F 100	--	Wg. F 27	F 185
1172	0-6-0ST	--	F 99	--	Nn. F 1	F 146
1173	0-6-0ST	--	F 98	--	Gy. F 3	F 152
1212-4	2-6-0	--	J 107-9	--	Np. J 41-3	J 234-6
1215	2-6-0	--	J 110	--	--	J 110
1233	0-6-0ST	--	F 111	--	--	F 111
1362	0-6-0ST	--	--	--	Ak. F 60	F 249
1363	0-6-0ST	--	--	--	Ak. F 61	F 162
1364	0-6-0ST	--	--	--	Ak. F 65/Np. F 47	F 230
1365	0-6-0ST	--	--	--	Np. F 45	F 228
1366	0-6-0ST	--	--	--	Ak. F 64	F 251
1367	0-6-0ST	--	--	--	Ak. F 63	F 163
1368	0-6-0ST	--	--	--	Ak. F 62	F 250
1369	0-6-0ST	--	--	--	Ak. F 66/ Np. F 46	F 229
1370	0-6-0ST	--	--	--	Wpt. F 4	F154
1371	0-6-0ST	--	--	--	Gy. F 1	F 150
1372	0-6-0ST	--	--	--	Wg. F 26	F 184
1884-5	0-6-0ST	--	--	--	Ak. F65-6	F 252-3
1886-7	0-6-0ST	--	--	--	Ak. F 69-70	F 254-5

Dubs 801-804: three of these locomotives were delivered to Westport and the fourth to Napier. Records compiled many years ago show 802 as the Napier locomotive. It is not certain which of 803 or 804 carried the numbers C 126 and C 127 after 1877. The numbers of the Greymouth and Westport locomotives prior to this date have still to be established.

Dubs 1884-1887 were built for the Thames Valley and Rotorua Railway Company. TVRR Numbers F 1-F 4.

HUDSWELL and CLARKE
Railway Foundry, Leeds, England.

Two 0-4-0ST locomotives, maker's numbers 23 and 24, BHIR and Otago 2 and 3. It has not been ascertained which road number applied to either locomotive.

HENRY HUGHES and COMPANY
Falcon Works, Loughborough, England.

One 0-4-0ST locomotive, maker's number unknown, Otago 28, South Island S 52.

HUNSLET ENGINE COMPANY LIMITED
Leeds, England

Maker's Number	Type	1874 Series	South Island	1890 List
141	0-6-0T	Otago 1	M 1/M 90	M 90
142	0-6-0T	Otago 2	M 2/M 89	M 89
143	0-6-0T	Otago 3	M 3	M 3
144	0-6-0T	Otago 22	M 4	M 4
1443	0-6-0T	--	--	Y 543
1444	0-6-0T	--	--	Y 542
1445	0-6-0T	--	--	Y 544

HUNT and OPIE
Victoria Ironworks, Ballarat, Victoria, Australia.

One locomotive, known as *Lady Barkly,* for the Oreti Railway

MANNING WARDLE and COMPANY
Boyne Engine Works, Leeds, England.

Maker's Number	Type	Gauge	Company Number	1890 List
162	0-6-0ST	4' 8½"	ADR	--
201	0-6-0ST	4' 8½"	ADR	--
920-1	2-6-2T	3' 6"	WMR 1-2	W^H 447-8
922	2-6-2T	3' 6"	WMR 3	--
923	2-6-2T	3' 6"	WMR 4	W^H 449
924	2-6-2T	3' 6"	WMR 5	--

E. W. MILLS
Lion Foundry, Wellington, New Zealand.

E. W. Mills built three tiny locomotives in 1875 for the wooden-railed Foxton Tramway. *Opossum* was transferred from Foxton to Greymouth in April 1877 for harbour works construction purposes. The other two, *Skunk* and *Wallaby*, remained on the Foxton-Wanganui section where in 1881 they were listed as "two small locomotives built in Wellington - not numbered"

NEILSON and COMPANY

Hyde Park Locomotive Works, Glasgow, Scotland.
Incorporated into the North British Locomotive Co. Ltd. in 1903.

Maker's Number	Type	1874 Series	South Island	North Island	1882 System	1890 List
1691	0-6-0ST	Otago 4	F 11	--	--	F 11
1692	0-6-0ST	Otago 8	F 36/F13	--	--	F 13
1706	0-6-0ST	--	--	2	Ak. F 51	F 241
1764	0-4-0ST	--	--	32	Wn. C 1	--
1765	0-4-0ST	--	--	31/45	Wg. C 21	C 166
1766	0-4-0ST	Pn.	--	--	Pn. C 2	C 148/577
1767	0-4-0ST	Pn.	--	--	Pn. C 1	C 147
1768	0-4-0ST	Otago 5	C 5	--	--	C 5
1769	0-4-0ST	Otago 9	C 22	--	Wg. C 23	C 168
1770	0-4-0ST	--	C 6	1(20)	--	--
1771	0-4-0ST	--	C 31	2(21)	Wn. C 1	C 194
1772	0-4-0ST	Gy.	C 131	--	Gy. C 1	--
1773	0-4-0ST	CR 21	C 53	--	--	C 53
1798	0-4-0T	CR (brd-gauge) 9	--	--	--	--
1841	0-6-0ST	Otago 11	F 38	--	--	F 38
1842	0-6-0ST	Otago 10	F 37	--	--	--
1843	2-4-0T	--	--	16	Ak. D 51	D 240
1844	2-4-0T	--	--	3(22)	Wn. D 3	D 197
1845	2-4-0T	--	--	34	Wn. D 2	D 196
1846	2-4-0T	--	--	33	Wn. D 1	D 195
1847	2-4-0T	Nn. 12	D 128	--	Nn. D 1	D 143
1848	2-4-0T	Otago 13	D 51	--	Wg. D 21	D 169
1849	2-4-0T	Nn. 13	D 129	--	Nn. D 2	D 144
2306	2-4-0T	--	D 16	--	--	D 16
2307	2-4-0T	--	D 17	--	Pn. D 1	D 149
2308	2-4-0T	--	D 18	--	--	D 18
2309	2-4-0T	--	D 15	--	Nn. D 3	D 145
2409	0-6-0ST	-	F 39	--	--	F 39
2410	0-6-0ST	--	F 21	--	--	F 21
2411	0-6-0ST	--	F 114/F 24	--	--	F 24
2412	0-6-0ST	--	F 20	--	--	F 20
2413	0-6-0ST	--	F 113	--	--	F 113
2414	0-6-0ST	--	F 112/F 23	--	--	F 23
2460-64	2-6-0	--	J 115-119	--	--	J 115-119
2561	2-4-0T	--	--	--	Wn. D 4	D 198
2562	2-4-0T	--	--	--	Wg. D 23	D 171
2563	2-4-0T	--	--	--	Wg. D 22	D 170/576
2564	2-4-0T	--	D 6	--	Wg. 24	D 6
2565-6	2-4-0T	--	--	--	Np. D 41-42	D 221-222
3468	0-4-2T	--	--	--	Wn. H 6	H 204
3469	0-4-2T	--	--	--	Wn. H 5	H 203
3751	0-6-0ST	--	--	--	--	F 216

Neilson 1766 and 1767 were delivered to Picton late in 1873. In 1882 they were listed as 11 (1877 Series) and 125 (South Island List). It is not known which of these two numbers was relevant to the two locomotives.
Neilson 1770 and 1771 were the first two locomotives delivered to Napier and are certainly the numbers 1 and 2 recorded in the 1881 lists. It is deduced that they were allocated numbers 20 and 21 in the 1878 North Island List. These numbers may be transposed.
Neilson 1847 and 1849. The numbers D 128 and D 129 in the South Island List may be transposed.

ABOVE: U^B 329, one of the ten piston-valve machines of 1901, soon after arrival. The road number painted on the sand dome was a typical American feature of the era which soon disappeared. (S. A. Rockcliff Collection)

BELOW: The final development of the Addington 4-6-0 locomotives were the Scottish-built class U^C. Sharp Stewart's portrait of U^C 369. (S. A. Rockliff Collection)

NASMYTH WILSON and COMPANY LIMITED

Patricroft Ironworks, Manchester, England.

Maker's Number	Type	Company Number	South Island	1882 System	1890 List
252	2-6-2	--	V 136	--	V 136
253	2-6-2	--	V 132	--	V 132
254	2-6-2	--	V 128	--	V 128
255	2-6-2	--	V 127	--	V 127
256	2-6-2	--	V 114	--	V 114
257	2-6-2	--	V 125	--	V 125
258	2-6-2	--	V 129	--	V 129
259	2-6-2	--	V 35	--	V 35
260	2-6-2	--	V 63	--	V 63
261	2-6-2	--	V 126	--	V 126
272	2-8-0	--	--	Ak. P 51	P 268
273	2-8-0	--	--	Ak. P 52	P 269
274	2-8-0	--	P 134	--	P 134
275	2-8-0	--	P 135	--	P 135
276	2-8-0	--	--	Ak. P 53	P 270
277	2-8-0	--	P 52	--	P 52
278	2-8-0	--	P 107	--	P 107
279	2-8-0	--	P 60	--	P 60
280	2-8-0	--	P 133	--	P 133
281	2-8-0	--	P 25	--	P 25
282-4	2-6-2	WMR 6-8	--	--	V 450-2
311	4-4-0T	NZMR 1	--	--	L^A 310
312	4-4-0T	NZMR 5	--	--	L^A 314
315	4-4-0T	NZMR 2	--	--	L^A 311
322-3	4-4-0T	NZMR 3-4	--	--	L^A 312-3

NEW ZEALAND RAILWAYS

Locomotives were built at NZR workshops at Petone and Hutt (Wellington), Newmarket (Auckland), Addington (Christchurch), and Hillside (Dunedin). Major modifications were made at East Town (Wanganui), Otahuhu (Auckland) and Westport. The originating workshop is detailed in the 1890 List.

Maker's Number	Type	1890 List	Maker's Number	Type	1890 List
1	2-6-2T	W 192	18	0-6-2T	F^A 9
2	2-6-2T	W 238	19	2-6-2T	W^A 165
3	2-6-2T	W^A 64	20	4-6-0	U 51
4	2-6-2T	W^A 67	21	4-6-0	U 65
5	0-6-2T	F^A 250	22	4-6-0	U 194
6	0-6-2T	F^A 251	23	4-6-0	U 215
7	0-6-2T	F^A 10	24	4-8-0	B 302
8	0-6-2T	F^A 41	25	2-6-2T	W^A 289
9	2-6-2T	W^A 217	26	4-8-0	B 303
10	4-6-0	U 237	27	2-6-2T	W^A 288
11	4-6-0	U 239	28	0-6-2T	F^A 242
12	0-6-2T	F^A 157	29	0-6-2T	F^A 247
13	2-6-2	N 27	30	0-6-2T	F^A 226
14	2-6-2T	W^A 220	31	4-4-2T	L^A 267
15	2-6-2T	W^A 275	32	0-6-2T	F^A 182
16	4-6-0	U 193	33	0-6-2T	F^A 179
17	4-6-0	U 274	34	4-4-2T	L^A 265

The Makers of NZR Locomotives - 137

\multicolumn{6}{c}{**NEW ZEALAND RAILWAYS (continued)**}						
Maker's Number	Type	1890 List	Maker's Number	Type	1890 List
35	0-6-2T	F^A 244	112	4-6-4T	W^G 170
36	0-6-2T	F^A 186	113-121	4-6-4T	W^G 488-496
37	0-6-2T	F^A 276	122	4-8-0	B^A 148
38	4-4-2T	L 205	123-126	4-8-0	B^A 497-500
39	4-4-2T	L 266	127-131	4-8-0	B^A 551-555
40	4-4-2T	L 264	132-151	4-6-4T	W^W 556-575
41	4-4-2T	L 206	152-161	4-8-2	X 588-597
42	4-4-2T	L 91	162	4-4-2T	L 219
43	4-8-0	B 304	163-168	4-6-2	A^B 608-613
44	0-6-2T	F^A 315	169	4-6-2	A^B 658
45	0-6-2T	F^A 372	170-172	4-6-2	A^B 615-617
46	0-6-2T	F^A 373	173-182	4-6-4T	W^W 638-647
47	2-6-2T	W^A 50	183	4-6-2	A^B 614
48	2-6-2T	W^A 68	184-190	4-6-2	A^B 659-665
49	2-6-2T	W^A 137	191-192	4-6-2	A^B 688-689
50	4-4-2T	L 207	193-202	4-6-4T	W^W 668-677
51	4-4-2T	L 208	203-204	4-6-4T	W^W 682-683
52	4-4-2T	L 219	205	4-6-4T	W^W 131
52	0-6-2T	F^A 374	206	4-6-4T	W^W 449
53-55	4-8-0	B 305-307	207-208	4-6-4T	W^W 684-685
56-57	0-6-2T	F^A 375-376	209-212	4-6-4T	W^W 678-681
58	4-6-0	U 378	213-214	4-6-4T	W^{AB} 686-687
59-68	2-6-4T	W^F 379-388	215-222	4-6-2	A^B 690-697
69	2-6-6-0T	E 66	223-232	4-6-4T	W^{AB} 763-772
70	4-6-2	A 71	233-242	4-6-2	A^B 776-785
71	4-6-2	A 161	243-252	4-6-4T	W^{AB} 786-795
72	4-6-2	A 178	253-276	2-6-2	C 845-868
73	4-6-2	A 399	277-306	4-8-4	K 900-929
74-79	2-6-4T	W^F 400-405	307-312	4-6-2	G 95-100
80-83	4-6-2	A 406-409	313-347	4-8-4	K^A 930-964
84	2-6-4T	W^F 62	348-353	4-8-4	K^B 965-970
85-93	2-6-4T	W^F 430-438	354-362		See note
94-101	4-8-2	X 439-446	363-397	4-8-2	J^A 1240-1274
102	4-6-4T	W^G 166	398-449		See note
103-111	4-6-4T	W^G 479-487	450-458		See note

NZR 13 was issued to N 27 when it was rebuilt as a Vauclain compound. Some authorities state that the number was deleted from the records. It was so identified until 1925.

NZR 43 is the correct maker's number for B 304. However, the worksplate on the tender of this engine carried the number 27, by which number the locomotive was recorded in the Boiler Register. To further complicate the issue this tender was coupled to B 308 in later years.

NZR 52 was issued to both L 219 and F^A 374. The duplication was rectified in 1913 by the issue of number 162 to L 219.

NZR 354-362 were class E^D electric locomotives, road numbers E^D 102-110. Seven were built at Hutt workshops and the final two at Addington.

NZR 388-391 were allocated to J^A 1265-8. These locomotives, constructed out of order, carried maker's plates numbered 379-382, which properly belonged to J^A 1256-9. The latter engines had no maker's plates affixed.

NZR 398-449 were class D^{SC} diesel-electric shunting locomotives, road numbers 418-469. Note that the road number sequence is greater by 20 than the maker's sequence. NZR 398-407, 418-423 and 430-439 were built at Addington Workshops, while NZR 408-417, 424-429 and 440-449 were built at Hillside Workshops.

NZR 450-458 were class T^R diesel-mechanical shunting tractors, road numbers 183-191, built at Hillside Workshops between 1973 and 1977.

138 - The Makers of NZR Locomotives

NORTH BRITISH LOCOMOTIVE COMPANY LIMITED					
Glasgow, Scotland.					
Formed in 1903 by the amalgamation of Dubs & Co. Queen's Park works, Neilson Reid & Co. (formerly Neilson & Co.) Hyde Park Works, and Sharp Stewart & Co. Atlas Works.					
Maker's Number	Type	1890 List	Maker's Number	Type	1890 List
22836-37	4-6-2	A^B 747-748	22874	4-6-2	A^B 744
22838	4-6-2	A^B 733	22875-77	4-6-2	A^B 726-728
22839-40	4-6-2	A^B 749-750	22878-79	4-6-2	Lost at sea
22841	4-6-2	A^B 736	22880	4-6-2	A^B 745
22842-43	4-6-2	A^B 751-752	22881	4-6-2	A^B 729
22844	4-6-2	A^B 735	22882	4-6-2	A^B 761
22845	4-6-2	A^B 734	22883-84	4-6-2	A^B 730-731
22846	4-6-2	A^B 753	22885	4-6-2	A^B 746
22847	4-6-2	A^B 737	23039	4-6-2	A^B 762
22848-49	4-6-2	A^B 718-719	23040-42	4-6-2	A^B 773-775
22850-51	4-6-2	A^B 754-755	23043	4-6-2	A^B 732
22852	4-6-2	A^B 738	23173-76	4-6-2	A^B 804-807
22853	4-6-2	A^B 720	23177-80	4-6-2	A^B 814-817
22854	4-6-2	A^B 756	23181	4-6-2	A^B 829
22855	4-6-2	A^B 739	23182	4-6-2	A^B 812
22856-57	4-6-2	A^B 721-722	23183-86	4-6-2	A^B 808-811
22858	4-6-2	A^B 757	23187	4-6-2	A^B 813
22859	4-6-2	A^B 740	23188-90	4-6-2	A^B 830-832
22860	4-6-2	A^B 723	23191-98	4-6-2	A^B 818-825
22866-67	4-6-2	A^B 758-759	23199-202	4-6-2	A^B 833-836
22868	4-6-2	A^B 741	23203-04	4-6-2	A^B 826-827
22869	4-6-2	A^B 724	23205-06	4-6-2	A^B 837-838
22870	4-6-2	A^B 760	23207	4-6-2	A^B 828
22871	4-6-2	A^B 743	24523-62	4-8-2	J 1200-1239
22872	4-6-2	A^B 742	27104-19	4-8-2	J^A 1275-1290
22873	4-6-2	A^B 725			

North British 22878-9, Class A^B locomotives were lost in the wreck of *TSS Wiltshire* at Great Barrier Island on 31 May 1922.

A. & G. PRICE LIMITED					
Thames, New Zealand.					
Maker's Number	Type	1890 List	Maker's Number	Type	1890 List
1-10	2-6-4T	W^F 389-398	86	4-8-0	B^B 144
11-12	2-6-4T	W^F 467-468	87	4-8-0	B^B 147
13-32	4-6-2	A 410-429	88	4-8-0	B^B 167
33-42	4-6-2	A 469-478	89	4-8-0	B^B 169
43-52	4-6-2	A 578-587	90	4-8-0	B^B 171
53-62	4-6-2	A-598-607	91	4-8-0	B^B 197
63-82	4-8-0	B^B 618-637	92	4-8-0	B^B 222
83	4-8-0	B^B 55	93-112	4-6-2	A^B 698-717
84	4-8-0	B^B 109	113-120	4-6-4T	W^{AB} 796-803
85	4-8-0	B^B 143	121-123	2-6-4T	W^F 842-844

The Makers of NZR Locomotives - 139

ABOVE: A & G Price of Thames built 123 steam locomotives for the New Zealand Railways. The first, W^F 389, was photographed on completion in September 1904.   (E. J. McClare Collection)

BELOW: The North British Locomotive Company supplied the New Zealand Railways with an official photograph for the 1925 order of class A^B engines. The diamond shaped works' plate on the smokebox indicates that the locomotive was constructed at the former Dubs factory, the Queen's Park Works. (E. J. McClare Collection)

ROBINSON, THOMAS and COMPANY

Soho Foundry, Ballarat, Victoria, Australia.

Two locomotives, maker's numbers unknown.
Oreti Railway numbers 2 and 3

ROGERS LOCOMOTIVE and MACHINE WORKS

Paterson, New Jersey, USA.

Maker's Number	Type	Company Number	South Island and 1890 List
2510	2-4-4T	RAFR 1	Q 51
2512	2-4-4T	RAFR 2	Q 17
2454	2-4-2	--	K 88
2455	2-4-2	--	K 87
2468-71	2-4-2	--	K 92-95
2473-74	2-4-2	--	K 96-97

The maker's record allocates 2471 to a 2-6-0 locomotive for the Leopoldina Railway, Brazil, and 2472 to NZR K 95. Photographic evidence shows that K 95 carried a maker's plate with the number 2471.

SCOTT BROTHERS LIMITED

Christchurch, New Zealand.

Maker's Number	Type	Company Number	South Island and 1890 List
30	2-4-0T	--	D 108
31-33	2-4-0T	--	D 137-139
34	2-4-0T	--	D 109
35	2-4-0T	--	D 130
36-37	2-4-0T	--	D 140-141
38	2-4-0T	--	D 131
39	2-4-0T	--	D 142
40	2-4-0T	NZMR 6	D 315

ALEXANDER SHANKS and SONS LIMITED

Dens Iron Works, Arbroath, Scotland.

Maker's Number	Type	South Island	Name
Not Known	0-4-0ST	A 6	*Mouse*
Not Known	0-4-0ST	--	*Kangaroo*

SHARP STEWART and COMPANY LIMITED

Atlas Works, Springburn, Glasgow, Scotland.

Incorporated into the North British Locomotive Company Limited in 1903

Maker's Number	Type	1890 List	Maker's Number	Type	1890 List
4502-04	4-6-0	U^A 172-174	4509	4-8-0	B 198
4505	4-6-0	U^A 177	4510	4-8-0	B 309
4506-07	4-6-0	U^A 175-176	4511	4-8-0	B 308
4508	4-8-0	B 178	4745-54	4-6-0	U^C 361-370

SLAUGHTER GRUNING and COMPANY

Avonside Ironworks, Bristol, England.

Incorporated as the Avonside Engine Company Limited in 1864

Maker's Number	Type	Road Number
488	2-4-0T	CR (broad-gauge) N° 1
531	2-4-0T	BHIR & Otago (standard-gauge) N° 1
532	2-4-0T	CR (broad-gauge) N° 2

The maker's number of Bluff Harbour and Invercargill Railway N° 1 is not known. Circumstantial evidence indicates that it is one of the batch 525-531, six numbers of which belong to locomotives built for the Santiago and Valparaiso Railway in Chile. The considered opinion is that it is 531, and unless the maker's plate can be recovered from the sea-bed at Big Bay, Westland, this is the best option.

ROBERT STEPHENSON and COMPANY

Forth Street Works, Newcastle-upon-Tyne, England.

Maker's Number	Type	South Island	North Island	1882 System	1890 List
2085	0-6-0ST	--	5	Ak. F 53	F 243
2086	0-6-0ST	--	1	Ak. F 52	F 242
2087	0-6-0ST	--	6	Ak. F 54	F 244
2367-71	2-6-0	J 120-124	--	--	J 120-124
2593	0-6-0ST	--	--	Np. F 50	F 233
2594	0-6-0ST	--	--	--	F 166/839
2595	0-6-0ST	--	--	Np. F40	F 223
2596	0-6-0ST	--	--	--	F 841
2597	0-6-0ST	--	--	--	F 277
2598	0-6-0ST	--	--	Wpt. F 5	F 155
2599	0-6-0ST	--	--	Ak. F 71	F 256
2600	0-6-0ST	--	--	Ak. F 72	F 257
2611	0-6-0ST	--	--	--	F 5

SOUTHLAND PROVINCIAL COUNCIL

Invercargill, New Zealand.

One locomotive, converted from a portable engine, for the Oreti Railway

VULCAN FOUNDRY LIMITED

Newton-le-Willows, Lancashire, England

Maker's Number	Type	1874 Series	South Island	North Island	1882 System	1890 List
636	0-4-4-0T	DPCR 1/Otago 6	E 27	--	--	--
637	0-4-4-0T	DPCR 2/Otago 7	E 26	--	Wg. E 24	E 175
735	0-6-0ST	--	--	7	Ak. F 57	F 246
736	0-6-0ST	--	--	9	Ak. F 59	F 248
737	0-6-0ST	--	--	8	Ak. F 58	F 247
998	2-6-0	--	--	--	Ak. J 52	J 259
999	2-6-0	--	J 26	--	--	J 26
1000	2-6-0	--	J 15	--	--	J 15
1001	2-6-0	--	--	--	Ak. J 51	J 258
1002	2-6-0	--	J 59	--	--	J 59
1003	2-6-0	--	--	--	Ak. J 53	J 260
1004	2-6-0	--	J 61	--	--	J 61
1005	2-6-0	--	--	--	Ak. J 54	J 261
1006	2-6-0	--	--	--	Ak. J 55	J 262
1007	2-6-0	--	J 70	--	--	J 70
1008	2-6-0	--	Class J lost at sea	--	--	--
1009	2-6-0	--	--	--	Ak. J 56	J 263
1076	2-6-0	--	J 14	--	--	J 14
1180	0-6-0ST	--	--	--	--	F 840
1181	0-6-0ST	--	--	--	Wpt. F 6	F 156

The Vulcan Foundry also manufactured a substantial quantity of parts for fifteen K[A] class locomotives. See note 44, page 117.

YORKSHIRE ENGINE COMPANY LIMITED

Meadowhall Works, Sheffield, England

Maker's Number	Type	1874 Series	South Island	North Island	1882 System	1890 List
239	0-6-0ST	--	--	3	Ak. F 55	F 164
240	0-6-0ST	--	--	4	Ak. F 56	F 245
241	0-6-0ST	Otago 14	F 12	--	--	F 12
242	0-6-0ST	Otago 15	F 13	--	Wg. F 28	F 186
243	0-6-0ST	Otago 16	F 14	--	Wpt. F 14	F 157
244	0-6-0ST	--	--	26	Wg. F 22	F 180
245	0-6-0ST	--	--	25	Wg. F 21	F 179
246	0-6-0ST	Otago xx or 19	F 72	--	--	F 72
247	0-6-0ST	Otago 20	F 73	--	--	F 73
248	0-6-0ST	Otago 17	F 35	--	Np. F 49	F 232
249	0-6-0ST	Otago xx or 19	F 74	--	--	F 74
255	0-4-0T	CR 22	A 71	--	--	A 71
256	0-4-0T	CR 23	A 63	--	Np. A 41	A 237

Yorkshire 241-3 were Otago 14-16, the order is uncertain.
Yorkshire 246 and 249 were Otago 19, *Talisman*, and the probably unnumbered *Roswal*, and may be transposed.
Yorkshire 255-6 were Canterbury 22-23 and may be transposed.

ABOVE: J^A 1243, the second of the class to be completed, was temporarily painted in a photographic grey finish for a formal portrait. Hillside Workshops, 22 February 1947. (NZR Publicity)

BELOW: K^A 955, the first of the class built without streamlining, was released into service fitted with a streamline-type funnel and ran in this configuration for about a year until fitted with a standard K^A funnel. Both K^As 955 and 956 were briefly painted in a grey livery before entering service. Hutt Workshops, December 1944. (NZR Publicity)

CHAPTER NINE

DISPOSAL OF LOCOMOTIVES FOR INDUSTRIAL AND OTHER RAILWAY USE

From the very earliest times contractors required locomotives for construction work. Canterbury Railways Nº 1, known as *Pilgrim,* and the Oreti Railway's *Lady Barkly* were both imported by the contractors undertaking the construction of those lines. So it was with the narrow-gauge; Walkem and Peyman, the builders of the Oamaru breakwater, took delivery of another within a month of the arrival of the Government's first narrow-gauge locomotive. Even before the broad-gauge machines were landed; horse, rope and gravity lines were at work at the Lewis coalmine near Kaitangata and on the Dun Mountain in Nelson.

As industrial development expanded, more substantial motive power was required for harbour works, both cargo operations and breakwater construction, for mines and bush railways, and for manufacturing, particularly the meat freezing industry. Locomotives were bought new from both overseas and local manufacturers, whilst many were acquired second-hand from the Railways Department. This chapter is concerned solely with those in the latter category.

The details of the former broad-gauge locomotives have already been set out in chapter two and are therefore not repeated here.

The record of industrial users has been compiled mainly from boiler records of the Public Works and later the Marine Departments. These bodies were charged with the registration and inspection of boilers following explosions causing fatal accidents in the 1870s. The dates show the period for which a boiler certificate was issued to a locomotive. In many cases the machines were in existence, but not working, long after the latest certificates had expired.

LOCOMOTIVE SALES PRIOR TO 1890	In Private Service
Chaplin 1455. Otago Nº 21 (0-4-0VBT).	
Imported by Walkem and Peyman, Contractors, Oamaru.	Jan 1873
Purchased by Otago Provincial Council, number Otago 21.	Jan 1876
Miller and Smillie.	1879-1881
Believed taken over by the Oamaru Harbour Board.	1881
Davidson 1. Hurunui-Bluff *Weka* (0-6-0ST).	
J. Saunders, Wellington.	1885-1887
Wellington &Manawatu Railway Co.	1887-1898
Manawatu County Council. Sanson Tramway.	1898-1922
Mangawhero Timber Co., Karioi.	1922-1929
Davidson 3. Hurunui-Bluff *Kiwi* (0-6-0ST).	
J. Saunders, Wellington.	1883-1885
Whereabouts unknown.	1885-1907
Bartholomew Land and Timber Co., Ngatira.	1907-1909
Morningside Quarries Ltd., Morningside.	1914-1915
Woolsey Allen Jnr, Taita.	1916-1918
T. Hawkins, Taita.	1918-1920
Northern Timber Co., Wairoa.	1921-1922
Matiere Sawmilling Co. } John Endean, Maharahau.	} 1923-1928
Derelict near Raurimu, 1956.	

LOCOMOTIVE SALES PRIOR TO 1890 (continued)	In Private Service

Dubs 645. Wanganui A 22 *Ferret* (0-4-0T).
    Kaihu Valley Railway, Dargaville.
    Returned to NZR in 1893 as A 215.
	1888-1893

Dubs 646. Wanganui A 21 *Fox* allocated A 192 in the 1890 list (0-4-0T). Manawatu County Council, Sanson Tramway.	1889-1910
Dubs 649. Napier A 41, formerly Hurunui-Bluff A 70 (0-4-0T). Napier Harbour Board, Napier.	1886-1925

Dubs 802, Westport C 3, formerly Napier 4/22, class C (0-4-2ST).
    Westport Harbour Board, Westport.
    Bowater and Bryan, Fairdown, Westport.
    Bruce Bay Timber Co., Bruce Bay.
    New Forest Sawmilling Co., Ngahere.
	1887-1921
	1921-1925
	1939-1945
	1950-1961

Dubs 803. Westport C 2 (0-4-2ST).
    Westport Harbour Board. Westport C 236.
    Marine Department, Westport.
    NZR Maintenance Branch.
    Public Works Department.
    Dumped at Te Kaha, Buller, 1929. Recovered 1995.
    Preserved.
	1887-1920
	1921
	1921-1925
	1925

Dubs 885. Greymouth C 132/C 1. *Pounamu* (0-4-2ST).
    Public Works Department (PWD 512).
    J. F. Mackley.
    Renown Colliery, Rotowaro.
    State Mines Department, Rotowaro.
    Preserved.
	1885-1927
	1927
	1928-1951
	1951-1971

Hughes (maker's number not known), Hurunui-Bluff S 52 (0-4-0ST).
    Gisborne Harbour Board.
    Langland and Co., Gisborne.
    Langland and Co., Tirohanga.
    Waitomo Sawmilling Co., Otorohanga.
    Waitomo Sawmilling Co., Waitomo Valley.
	1886-1913
	1914-1915
	1916-1918
	1919-1921
	1921-1925

Mills. Foxton. *Skunk* (0-4-0T).
    Wilkie Brothers and Wilson, Westport.
    Tim Corby. Mokihinui.
    Mokihinui Sawmilling Co., Mokihinui.
    W. J. Marris. Mokihinui.
    A. Griffiths. Birchfield.
    Ngahere Sawmilling Co., Ngahere.
    Wanganui Harbour Board, Wanganui.
	circa 1882
	Dates not
	certain
	1898-1899
	1904-1905
	1906-1907
	1910-1918

Mills. Foxton. *Wallaby* (0-4-0T). Manawatu County Council, Sanson Tramway.	1885-1889

Mills. Greymouth number not known, formerly at Foxton. *Opossum* (0-4-0T).
    Public Works Department. Greymouth Harbour Works.
    Greymouth Harbour Board. Greymouth.
    Ogilvie and Co., Gladstone.
    Preserved.
	1878-1884
	1885-1910
	1911-1952

146 - Disposal of Locomotives

ABOVE: From the north end of Belfast yard C 5 worked for the Canterbury Frozen Meat Company for fifty-eight years. As with many industrial locomotives its appearance altered significantly over the years. Belfast, 1950. (G. W. Emerson)

BELOW: The South Otago Freezing Company acquired C 53 from NZR in 1920. Fitted with a replacement sheet metal cab, it had also made its last run. Finegand, 1942. (S. A. Rockliff)

Disposal of Locomotives - 147

LOCOMOTIVE SALES PRIOR TO 1890 (continued)	In Private Service

Neilson 1692. Hurunui-Bluff F 36. *Edie Ochiltree* **(0-6-0ST).**
    Public Works Department.
    Returned to NZR in 1886 as F 13.
    Preserved.
	1879-1886

Neilson 1764. Wellington 32. *Belmont* **(0-4-0ST).**
    J. Saunders.
    Wilkie and Wilson, Helensville.
    Wilkie Brothers and Wilson, Westport.
    Castlecliff Railway Co., Wanganui.
    Tauranga Rimu Timber Co., Tauriko.
	1882-1888
	1888-1889
	1889-1890
	1891-1918
	1918-1926

Neilson 1770. Hurunui-Bluff C 6 (0-4-2ST).
    Palliser and Jones. Timaru.
    Allendale Coal Co., Bushey.
    Taupiri Coal Co., Huntly.
	1888-1890
	1893-1909
	1909-1960

Neilson 1772. Greymouth C 131/C 2. *Ahaura* **(0-4-2ST)** Greymouth Harbour Board. Greymouth.	1885-1940
Neilson 1842. Hurunui-Bluff F 37. *Rob Roy* **(0-6-0ST).** Public Works Department PWD 503.	1879-1940

Shanks. Greymouth number not known. *Kangaroo* **(0-4-0ST).**
    Public Works Department. Greymouth Harbour Works
    Greymouth Harbour Board.
    Ogilvie and Co., Gladstone.
    Butler Brothers, Rautapu.
    Waitaha Timber Co., Waitaha.
    Lake Brunner Sawmilling Co., Ruru.
	1878-1910
	1885-1916
	1916-1918
	1919-1929
	1929
	1936-1941

Shanks. Hurunui-Bluff A 6. *Mouse* **(0-4-0ST).**
    A. Tapper, Longbush.
    New Zealand Pine Co., Colac Bay.
    H. A. Massey, Colac Bay.
    Otago Harbour Board, Aramoana.
	1883-1889
	1889-1899
	1899-1923
	1923-1930

\multicolumn{5}{c}{LOCOMOTIVE SALES AFTER 1890}

Number	Maker's Number	Type	PRIVATE OWNER	In Private Service
F 2	Avonside 1141	0-6-0ST	Charming Creek Coal Co., Ngakawau.	1954-1959
A 5	Dubs 647	0-4-0T	Lovell's Flat Coal Co., Lovell's Flat. Real Mackay Coal Co., Milton. Bruce Railway and Coal Co., Milton. Milburn Lime and Cement Co. Ltd., Milburn. Preserved (as A 67).	1896-1906 1906-1907 1908-1921 1921-1968
C 5	Neilson 1768	0-4-2ST	Hokonui Railway and Coal Co. Winton. Canterbury Frozen Meat Co, Ltd., Belfast.	1893-1897 1899-1957
D 6	Neilson 2564	2-4-0T	Taratu Coal Co, Lovell's Flat. McDonald's Oamaru Lime Co. Whitecraig. Preserved.	1917-1940 1940-1964

148 - Disposal of Locomotives

ABOVE: D 6 served the Taratu Coal Company for twenty-four years and from 1940 for a similar period at McDonald's Lime Company near Kakanui. One of its last steamings took place on 3 July 1965 just prior to delivery to the Ocean Beach Railway for preservation. (G. W. Emerson)

All thirty three class D locomotives, having ample power and a short-coupled wheelbase, were popular with industry. Some had multiple owners.

BELOW: In 1973 D 16, after working for fifty-five years at the Pukeuri Freezing Works for two owners, went on static display there. D 16 is now in active preservation at the Pleasant Point Railway. (G. W. Emerson)

Disposal of Locomotives - 149

ABOVE: Thomas Borthwick and Company operated D 138 at its Belfast Freezing Works for forty years. When photographed in 1950 it still had five years of active life left. (G. W. Emerson)

BELOW: For a similar period D 140 was visible to passengers on the South Express from Christchurch passing the Kempthorne Prosser fertiliser works at Hornby. It went to static display in Christchurch and is now being restored to operating condition at the Ferrymead Railway. D 140, Hornby 1950. (G. W. Emerson)

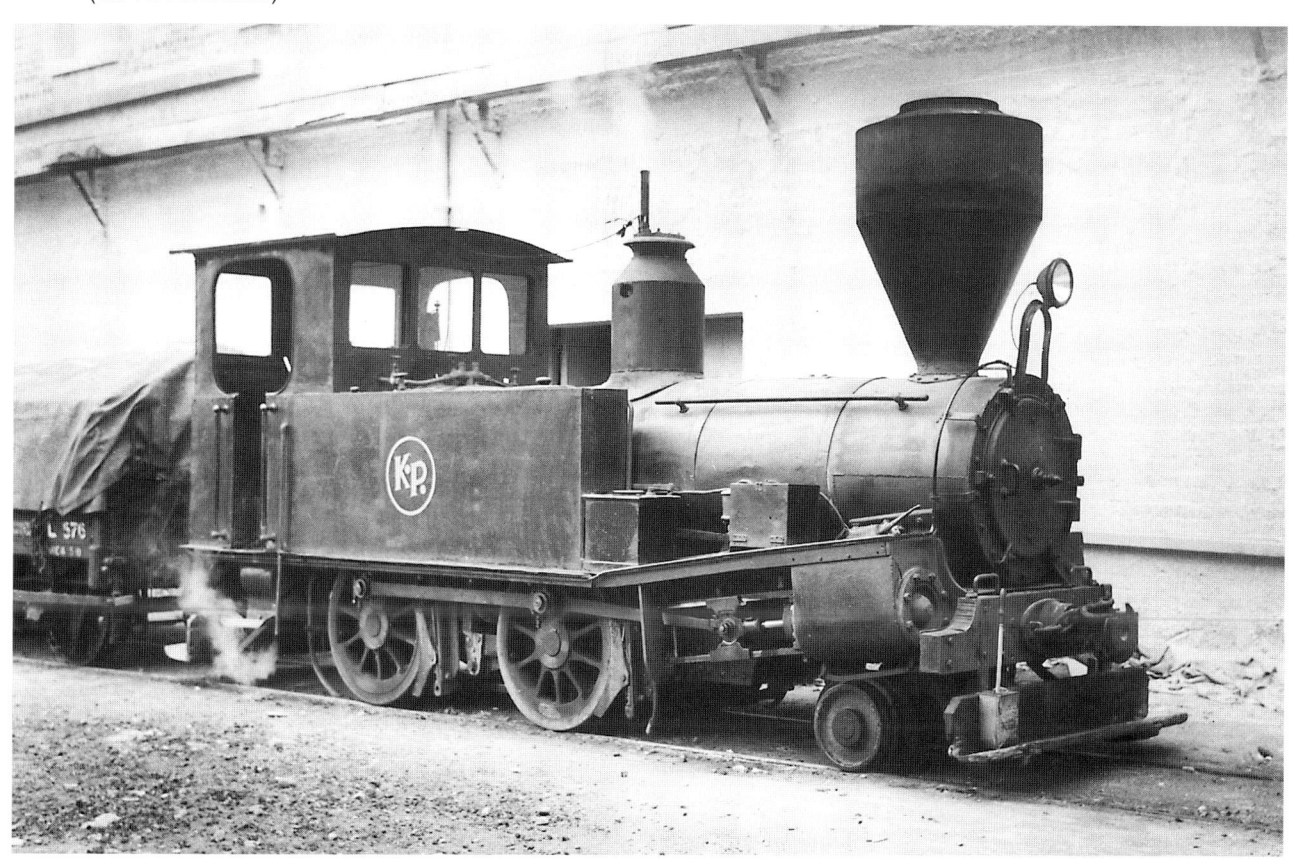

150 - Disposal of Locomotives

LOCOMOTIVE SALES AFTER 1890 (continued)

Number	Maker's Number	Type	Private Owner	In Private Service
FA 9	NZR 18	0-6-2T	Auckland Farmers' Freezing Co. Ltd., Horotiu.	1944-1952
FA 10	NZR 7	0-6-2T	Ohai Railway Board, Wairio. Blackburn Coal Co., Mount Somers.	1919-1927 1930-1940
F 12	Yorkshire 241	0-6-0ST	Waitaki Farmers' Freezing Co. Ltd., Pukeuri. Preserved.	1957-1967
D 16	Neilson 2306	2-4-0T	N. Z. Refrigerating Co. Ltd., Pukeuri. Waitaki Farmers' Freezing Co. Ltd., Pukeuri Preserved.	1918-1922 1922-1973
D 18	Neilson 2308	2-4-0T	Bruce Railway and Coal Co., Milton. Kaitangata Coal and Railway Co., Kaitangata.	1920-1930 1932-1941
R 28	Avonside 1217	0-6-4T	Timaru Harbour Board, Timaru. Burkes Creek Colliery, Reefton. State Mines Department, Reefton. Preserved.	1934-1940 1944-1947 1947-1948
R 29	Avonside 1218	0-6-4T	Manawatu County Council, Sanson Tramway.	1944-1946
R 33	Avonside 1232	0-6-4T	Public Works Department (PWD 516).	1917-1932
F 40	Avonside 1090	0-6-0ST	Stuart and Chapman Ltd., Ross.	1934-1948
FA 41	NZR 8	0-6-2T	Whakatane Board Mills, Whakatane.	1937-1960
F 43	Avonside 1143	0-6-0ST	McDonald's Oamaru Lime Ltd, Whitecraig, Bought for spare parts in 1953, scrapped about 1968.	
D 46	Dubs 1168	2-4-0T	N. Z. Refrigerating Co. Ltd., Burnside. Broken up about 1953.	1920-1939
D 47	Dubs 1166	2-4-0T	Lauriston Timber Co., Tahakopa. Lake Brunner Sawmilling Co., Ruru. Derelict 1972.	1917-1928 1928-1952
D 48	Dubs 1167	2-4-0T	Kempthorne Prosser and Co. Ltd., Aramoho.	1925-1950
D 49	Dubs 1165	2-4-0T	Waitahu Coal Co., Reefton. Reefton Coal Co., Reefton. Burke's Creek Colliery, Reefton.	1919-1922 1923-1930 1930-1935
D 50	Dubs 1164	2-4-0T	Fortification Coal Co., Milton. Bruce Railway and Coal Co., Milton Waronui Coal Co., Milton. Kauri Timber Co. Ltd., Puketi Bush. Kauri Timber Co. Ltd., Kairanga. Challenge Phosphate Co. Ltd., Otahuhu.	1902-1905 1905-1907 1907-1908 1909-1919 1922-1928 1928-1950
C 53	Neilson 1773	0-4-2ST	South Otago Freezing Co. Ltd, Finegand. Broken up about 1955.	1920-1941

LOCOMOTIVE SALES AFTER 1890 (continued)

Number	Maker's Number	Type	Private Owner	In Private Service
G 55	Black Hawthorn 278	4-4-0ST	N. Z. Coal and Oil Co. Ltd, Kaitangata. Shag Point Coal Co., Shag Point.	1915-1927 1927-1936
G 56	Black Hawthorn 282	4-4-0ST	Manawatu County Council, Sanson Tramway.	1918-1944
G 57	Black Hawthorn 281	4-4-0ST	Castlecliff Railway Co., Castlecliff.	1917-1956
G 58	Black Hawthorn 279	4-4-0ST	Gamman and Co., Ohakune. Gamman and Co., Mamaku.	1919-1924 1925-1938
A 64	Dubs 651	0-4-0T	Canterbury Frozen Meat Co. Ltd., Fairfield. Preserved.	1890-1960
A 65	Dubs 653	0-4-0T	John Harrison, Aratapu. White Pine Sawmilling Co., Naumai. Stuart and Chapman Ltd., Ross	1897-1901 1902-1917 1918-1936
A 66	Dubs 648	0-4-0T	N. Z. Pine Co., Colac Bay. Dunedin City Corporation Gas Works, Dunedin. On loan to Otago Harbour Board, Dunedin. Preserved.	1904 1904-1949 1913-1920
A 67	Dubs 647	0-4-0T	Hokonui Coal Co., Winton. Returned to NZR as A 5.	1891-1892
W^A 67	NZR 4	2-6-2T	Castlecliff Railway Co., Castlecliff.	1941-1956
A 68	Dubs 652	0-4-0T	Black and Stumbles, Timaru. Timaru Harbour Board, Timaru. Ellis and Burnand Ltd, Manunui.	1900-1901 1901-1907 1908-1929
A 71	Yorkshire 255	0-4-0T	Taupo Totara Timber Co., Putaruru. NZ Farmers' Fertiliser Co. Ltd., Te Papapa.	1905-1921 1922-1930
F 72	Yorkshire 246	0-6-0ST	Canterbury Frozen Meat Co. Ltd., Pareora.	1954-1959
F 75	Avonside 1088	0-6-0ST	Stuart and Chapman Ltd, Ross. Butler Brothers, Ruatapu.	1925-1955 1956
F 80	Avonside 1085	0-6-0ST	Otago Harbour Board, Aramoana.	1933-1946
D 108	Scott 30	2-4-0T	Public Works Department (PWD 519).	1920-1930
D 109	Scott 34	2-4-0T	Auckland Farmers' Freezing Co. Ltd, Southdown.	1916-1956
F 111	Dubs 1233	0-6-0ST	Oamaru Harbour Board, Oamaru. Preserved.	1934-1966
F 113	Neilson 2413	0-6-0ST	Butler Brothers, Ruatapu.	1941-1956
D 130	Scott 35	2-4-0T	McDonald's Oamaru Lime Ltd, Whitecraig. Broken up 1964.	1927-1940
D 131	Scott 38	2-4-0T	Christchurch Meat Co. Ltd., Smithfield.	1916-1930

152 - Disposal of Locomotives

ABOVE Clean, lined and proudly displaying its ownership, F^A 41 worked in this guise between 1937 and 1963. Awakeri Junction, June 1951. (J. A. T. Terry)

BELOW: W^A 67 was the largest and last of four locomotives purchased from NZR by the Castlecliff Railway Company at Wanganui. Only the lack of a number plate betrays that it is not an NZR locomotive. Castlecliff, November 1951. (W. W. Stewart)

Disposal of Locomotives - 153

ABOVE: NZR sold eight class W^F locomotives to the Tasmanian Government Railways, four each in 1939 and 1944. These were used on suburban trains around Hobart. Tasmanian DS2, formerly NZR W^F 385, was one of the early sales. A number of alterations were made before the locomotives entered service in Tasmania. Screw couplings and side buffers, vacuum braking and electric classification lights were fitted. The NZR cowcatchers were removed prior to shipping. Launceston, Tasmania about 1950. (Australian Railway Historical Society, Tasmanian Division Archives)

BELOW: The Ohai Railway Board operated big power to move coal over its steeply graded line from Ohai to Wairio in Southland. With the Board for nearly a quarter century from 1944, X 442 saw little use after 1955 except on excursion trains. In January 1960 it worked the Otago and Southland Railtour over the Board's line. (G. W. Emerson)

LOCOMOTIVE SALES AFTER 1890 (continued)

Number	Maker's Number	Type	Private Owner	In Private Service
D 137	Scott 31	2-4-0T	Gear Meat Co. Ltd., Petone. Preserved.	1901-1963
D 138	Scott 32	2-4-0T	Thomas Borthwick and Co. Ltd., Belfast.	1916-1955
D 139	Scott 33	2-4-0T	New Plymouth Harbour Board, New Plymouth. N. Z. Farmers' Fertiliser Co. Ltd., Smart Road, New Plymouth.	1919-1930 1930-1953
D 140	Scott 36	2-4-0T	Kempthorne Prosser and Co. Ltd, Hornby, Christchurch. Preserved.	1920-1960
D 141	Scott 37	2-4-0T	Shag Point Coal Co., Shag Point.	1920-1927
D 142	Scott 39	2-4-0T	Public Works Department (PWD 520).	1920
D 143	Neilson 1847	2-4-0T	Dominion Portland Cement Co. Ltd., Portland. Wilson's NZ Portland Cement Co. Ltd., Portland. Preserved.	1916-1927 1928-1968
D 144	Neilson 1849	2-4-0T	Mount Burnett Coal Co. Ltd., Pakawau. Kanieri-Hokitika Sawmilling Co., Hokitika.	1915-1923 1928-1951
D145	Neilson 2309	2-4-0T	Public Works Department (PWD 517).	1919-1955
C 147	Neilson 1767	0-4-2ST	Auckland Farmers' Freezing Co. Ltd., Auckland. Auckland Farmers' Freezing Co. Ltd., Horotiu.	1915-1919 1920-1921 1919-1920 1921-1930
D 149	Neilson 2307	2-4-0T	Gamman and Co., Ohakune. Gamman and Co., Mamaku.	1920-1924 1924-1931
F 152	Dubs 1173	0-6-0ST	Stuart and Chapman Ltd, Ross. Butler Brothers, Ruatapu.	1954-1957 1957-1958
F 154	Dubs 1370	0-6-0ST	Marine Department, Westport. Westport Harbour Board, Westport. Charming Creek Coal Co., Ngakawau (on loan).	1929-1936 1936-1946 1946-1955
F 155	Stephenson 2598	0-6-0ST	Charming Creek Coal Co., Ngakawau.	1934-1946
FA 157	NZR 12	0-6-2T	Ohai Railway Board, Wairio.	1923-1927
C 158	Dubs 804	0-4-2ST	N. Z. Pine Co., Colac Bay. Otago Harbour Board, Aramoana.	1920-1927 1927-1933
A 161	Dubs 650	0-4-0T	Canterbury Frozen Meat Co. Ltd., Pareora. Canterbury Frozen Meat Co. Ltd., Belfast.	1904-1954 1954-1955
C 166	Neilson 1765	0-4-2ST	John McLean and Sons, Helensville. Castlecliff Railway Co., Castlecliff.	1896-1897 1899-1956
F 166	Stephenson 2594	0-6-0ST	Westport Harbour Board, Westport. Returned to NZR as F 839.	1909-1923
Number	Maker's Number	Type	Private Owner	In Private Service

\multicolumn{5}{c}{**LOCOMOTIVE SALES AFTER 1890 (continued)**}
Number	Maker's Number	Type	Private Owner	In Private Service
C 167	Dubs 801	0-4-2ST	Wairio Railway and Coal Co., Wairio. Ohai Railway Board, Wairio. New Brighton Coal Co., Nightcaps. Black Diamond Coal Co., Nightcaps. State Mines Department, Black Diamond Mine. Downer and Co. Ltd., Nightcaps.	1915-1917 1917-1925 1925-1926 1930-1947 1947-1949 1949-1950
C 168	Neilson 1769	0-4-2ST	Taranaki Farmers' Meat Co. Ltd, Smart Road, New Plymouth. N. Z. Farmers' Fertiliser Co. Ltd, Smart Road, New Plymouth.	1919-1924 1924-1930
D 169	Neilson 1848	2-4-0T	Kauri Timber Co. Ltd., Thames and Parawai.	1914-1928
D 171	Neilson 2562	2-4-0T	Wellington Farmers' Meat Co. Ltd.. Waingawa. Wilsons Portland Cement Co. Ltd., Portland.	1915-1922 1922-1957
E 175	Vulcan 637	0-4-4-0T	Public Works Department (PWD 504). Otago Iron Rolling Mills, Green Island. Preserved.	1900-1917 1917-1925
F 184	Dubs 1372	0-6-0ST	Burke's Creek Colliery, Reefton. State Mines Department. Reefton. Butler Brothers, Ruatapu.	1934-1945 1947 1948-1955
F 185	Dubs 1171	0-6-0ST	Taupiri Coal Co., Rotowaro. State Mines Department, Rotowaro. Preserved.	1936-1951 1951-1972
A 192	Dubs 646	0-4-0T	1890 number allocated, sold 8-1889. See page 145.	
A 193	Dubs 655	0-4-0T	Gear Meat Co. Ltd., Petone. Thomas Borthwick and Sons Ltd., Pakipaki, Hawke's Bay. Thomas Borthwick and Sons Ltd., Aorangi, Feilding.	1894-1915 1915-1931 1931-1934
C 194	Neilson 1771	0-4-2ST	Public Works Department (PWD 505). Nelson Brothers Ltd., Tomoana.	1893-1945 1946
D 195	Neilson 1846	2-4-0T	Napier Harbour Board, Napier.	1919-1931
D 196	Neilson 1845	2-4-0T	Public Works Department (PWD 513).	1914-1955
D 197	Neilson 1844	2-4-0T	N. Z. Powell Wood Processing Co. Ltd., Rangataua. Gisborne Harbour Board, Gisborne. Waitaha Timber Co., Waitaha. Lake Brunner Sawmilling Co., Ruru.	1917-1925 1925-1930 1930-1947 1947-1951
D 198	Neilson 2561	2-4-0T	Public Works Department (PWD 506).	1899-1930
L 207	Avonside 1205	2-4-0T	Public Works Department (PWD 507). New Plymouth Harbour Board, New Plymouth. Wilson's Portland Cement Co. Ltd., Portland. Preserved.	1901-1931 1931-1954 1954-1972
L 208	Avonside 1206	2-4-0T	Public Works Department (PWD 508). Wilson's Portland Cement Co. Ltd, Portland. Preserved.	1901-1931 1945-1974

156 - Disposal of Locomotives

ABOVE: When scrap iron had little value locomotives were dumped. R 271, with at least a dozen others, were placed on the Oamaru foreshore in 1936 to control erosion. (S. A. Rockliff)

BELOW: Just dumped. An L, N 354 and N 353 amongst others at Westfield in the mid-1930s, were all later exhumed and sold for scrap. (W. W. Stewart)

Disposal of Locomotives - 157

ABOVE: Others were used for riverbank protection. In 1941 V 63, K 88 and the separated boiler and chassis of P 60 were visible, a few of many dumped at Branxholme in 1927. (A. R. Schmidt)

BELOW: R 28, derelict in the bush at Burkes Creek, Reefton in August 1955. Now on covered display it has honoured retirement as the sole remaining original single Fairlie locomotive in the world. (W. W. Stewart)

158 - Disposal of Locomotives

LOCOMOTIVE SALES AFTER 1890 (continued)

Number	Maker's Number	Type	Private Owner	In Private Service
R 211	Avonside 1223	0-6-4T	Manawatu County Council, Sanson Tramway.	1926-1933
S 215	Avonside 1283	0-6-4T	Western Australian Government Railways (I 25).	1891-1900
A 215	Dubs 645	0-4-0T	Taupiri Coal Co. Ltd., Kimihia. Taupiri Coal Co. Ltd., Rotowaro.	1896-1919 1919-1937
S 216	Avonside 1285	0-6-4T	Western Australian Government Railways (I 26).	1891-1900
S 217	Avonside 1281	0-6-4T	Western Australian Government Railways (I 27).	1891-1900
L 219	Avonside 1207	2-4-0T	Public Works Department (PWD 509). Wilson's Portland Cement Co. Ltd., Portland. Preserved.	1903-1948 1948-1973
A 220	Dubs 654	0-4-0T	Nelson Brothers Ltd., Tomoana. Nelson Harbour Board, Nelson. Taupo Totara Timber Co. Ltd., Putaruru. Gamman and Co., Ohakune. Wellington Farmers' Meat Co. Ltd., Waingawa. Ellis and Burnand Ltd., Ongarue.	1891-1901 1901-1907 1907-1914 1915-1919 circa 1920 1923-1925
W^A 220	NZR 14	2-6-2T	Napier Harbour Board, Napier.	1946-1956
D 221	Neilson 2565	2-4-0T	Leyland O'Brien Timber Co., Kaingaroa. Preserved.	1918-1928
D 222	Neilson 2566	2-4-0T	Nelson Brothers Ltd, Tomoana.	1915-1932
F 225	Avonside 1089	0-6-0ST	Butler Brothers, Ruatapu.	1935-1955
F 228	Dubs 1365	0-6-0ST	Auckland Farmers' Freezing Co. Ltd.	1936
F 230	Dubs 1364	0-6-0ST	Napier Harbour Board, Napier. Ellis and Burnand Ltd., Mangapehi. Preserved.	1933-1946 1946-1956
F 233	Stephenson 2593	0-6-0ST	Auckland Farmers' Freezing Co. Ltd., Southdown. Preserved.	1936-1964
A 237	Yorkshire 256	0-4-0T	New Plymouth Sash and Door Co., Ngaire. Lyttelton Harbour Board, Lyttelton. Dominion Cement Co. Ltd., Whangarei. Westland Sawmilling Co., Marsden. Malfroy and Co. Hokitika Ltd., Houhou. T. Wall and Co., Houhou. Westland Boxes Ltd., Houhou.	1891-1909 1909-1915 1915-1916 1916-1920 1920-1950
C 239	Dubs 800	0-4-2ST	D. Fallon, Freemans Bay. Butler Brothers, Ruatapu.	1890-1901 1915-1936
D 240	Neilson 1843	2-4-0T	Union Box and Packing Co., Rawene. McDonald's Oamaru Lime Ltd., Totara.	1919-1925 1925-1939

LOCOMOTIVE SALES AFTER 1890 (continued)

Number	Maker's Number	Type	Private Owner	In Private Service
F 243	Stephenson 2085	0-6-0ST	Matahina Tramway, Edgecumbe. Bought for Spare Parts 1934.	
F 248	Vulcan 736	0-6-0ST	Matahina Tramway, Edgecumbe.	1930
F^A 250	NZR 5	0-6--2T	Whakatane Board Mills, Whakatane. Preserved.	1943-1966
F^A 251	NZR 6	0-6--2T	Stuart and Chapman Ltd., Ross.	1939-1954
L^A 311	Nasmyth Wilson 315	4-4-0T	Auckland Farmers' Freezing Co. Ltd., Moerewa.	1920-1934
L^A 314	Nasmyth Wilson 312	4-4-0T	New Forest Sawmilling Co., Ngahere.	1926-1950
D 315	Scott 40	2-4-0T	Public Works Department (PWD 510).	1901-1930
W^D 316	Baldwin 18543	2-6-4T	Wilton Collieries Ltd., Ngaruawahia.	1934
W^D 317	Baldwin 18544	2-6-4T	Ohai Railway Board, Wairio.	1934-1944
W^D 356	Baldwin 19260	2-6-4T	Wilton Collieries Ltd., Ngaruawahia.	1933
W^D 357	Baldwin 19261	2-6-4T	Timaru Harbour Board, Timaru. Preserved.	1938-1964
W^F 381	NZR 61	2-6-4T	Tasmanian Government Railways (DS 2).	1939-1951
W^F 385	NZR 65	2-6-4T	Tasmanian Government Railways (DS 1). Mount Lyell Railway Co. Ltd.	1939-1952 1952-1953
W^F 392	Price 4	2-6-4T	Tasmanian Government Railways (DS 8).	1944-1953
W^F 405	NZR 79	2-6-4T	Tasmanian Government Railways (DS 5). Emu Bay Railway Co (hired).	1944-1956 1953
W^F 431	NZR 86	2-6-4T	Tasmanian Government Railways (DS 6).	1944-1953
W^F 434	NZR 89	2-6-4T	Tasmanian Government Railways (DS 7).	1944-1958
W^F 436	NZR 91	2-6-4T	Tasmanian Government Railways (DS 4). Mount Lyell Railway Co. Ltd.	1939-1951 1952-1953
W^F 437	NZR 92	2-6-4T	Tasmanian Government Railways (DS 3).	1939-1953
X 442	NZR 97	4-8-2	Ohai Railway Board, Wairio. Preserved.	1944-1968
X 446	NZR 101	4-8-2	Ohai Railway Board, Wairio.	1946-1959
W^H 447	Manning Wardle 920	2-6-2T	Collett and Co., Dannevirke. Purchased 1929. Never used, derelict 1945.	
W^H 448	Manning Wardle 921	2-6-2T	Mangawhero Timber Co., Raetihi. Challenge Phosphate Co. Ltd., Otahuhu.	1926-1927 -1943

ABOVE: Parts of a few found new uses. Steam crane Nº 103, constructed at Petone about 1900 was carried on bogies of class B and E Fairlies. (A. P. Godber, Alexander Turnbull Library)

BELOW: Although its boiler certificate had expired in 1936, A 65 continued to serve its owners for many years after conversion to diesel power. Stuart and Chapman's Mill, Ross, January 1958. (J. A. Herbert)

Disposal of Locomotives - 161

ABOVE: A few were used as childrens' playthings. W^A 68 was placed on the Napier foreshore in August 1960. After a decade of exposure to the salt air, the rusty and hazardous hulk was broken up for scrap. Napier, February 1962. (J.A.T. Terry)

BELOW: For most of the NZR's fleet of steam locomotives the end was ignominious. W^B 298 being cut up for scrap at Dunedin, 1958. (G. W. Emerson)

162 - Disposal of Locomotives

Number	Maker's Number	Type	Private Owner	In Private Service
W^H 449	Manning Wardle 923	2-6-2T	Waipa Railway and Colliery Co., Ngaruawahia.	1914-1933
Y 542	Hunslet 1444	0-6-0T	Wilson's Portland Cement Co. Ltd., Portland. Preserved.	1957-1985
D 576 (D 170)	Neilson 2563	2-4-0T	Hawke's Bay Farmers' Meat Co. Ltd, Whakatu. Preserved.	1923-1960
C 577 (C 148)	Neilson 1766	0-4-2ST	Butler Brothers, Ruatapu.	1922-1953
W^AB 794	NZR 251	4-6-4T	Ohai Railway Board, Wairio. Preserved.	1955-1968
F 839	Stephenson 2594	0-6-0ST	Charming Creek Coal Co., Ngakawau.	1930-1947
F 840	Vulcan 1180	0-6-0ST	Butler Brothers, Ruatapu.	1928-1955
F 841	Stephenson 2596	0-6-0ST	Marine Department, Westport. Burkes Creek Colliery, Reefton.	1930-1947

LOCOMOTIVE SALES AFTER 1890 (continued)

BELOW: Unlike some class mates sold into industrial service and extensively modified by their new owners, Neilson 1770, other than being fitted with an extended cab and bogie, retained some semblance of its original appearance. The former Hurunui-Bluff C 6 worked for its third owner, the Taupiri Coal Company, for over fifty years. Rotowaro, 22 December 1949. (J. A. T. Terry)

CHAPTER TEN

NOSTALGIA

There is a sentimental attachment to antique machinery, none more so than to the steam locomotive. *Josephine*, the first 3 foot 6 inch (1067mm) gauge main line steam locomotive to turn a wheel in this country was given a cosmetic restoration for display at the New Zealand and South Seas Exhibition held in Dunedin in 1925-26. For half a century after this display E 175 sat rusting outside the Otago Early Settlers' Museum. Public affection for *Josephine* eventually provided the finance for a second restoration and the provision of a weatherproof showcase in 1968.

About 1960, as the steam era was drawing to a close, it was realised that the steam locomotive needed a better memorial than as a mouldering relic. Thus was born the Ocean Beach Railway at St. Kilda, set up with the intention of preserving and operating a small industrial locomotive. This modest beginning provided the impetus for several working railway museums and steam locomotive restoration depots throughout the country. Some were laid anew or relaid on long abandoned railway formations, others inherited formations, track and buildings of recently closed lines.

The New Zealand Railways Department realised the heritage value of its steam locomotives and vintage rolling stock. In 1971 it commenced the operation of the *Kingston Flyer* between Lumsden and Kingston, alas now truncated to run only from Kingston to Fairlight. This highly successful operation was followed on special occasions by the return to the main lines of both the smallest and the largest of NZR steam locomotives, immaculately restored.

Where it is impracticable to operate locomotives the alternative is static display with protection from destructive elements; *Josephine* set the pattern for this. The Minister of Railways later donated J^A 1274 to the City of Dunedin, now housed in an adjacent showcase. This locomotive, built in Dunedin's Hillside Workshops, was the last steam locomotive made in the country and the final such addition to the NZR fleet.

Briefly, there was a down side to the preservation story. Locomotives, enthusiastically put on display in parks and playgrounds, were ill-maintained and became hazardous. W^A 68, having been placed in a harsh seaside environment, was broken up for safety reasons. Most have now been removed to storage and subsequent restoration, few remain in an unprotected plinthed condition. H 199, the world's only surviving 'Fell' type locomotive, was given by the Minister of Railways to the people of Featherston, the town closest to the foot of the Rimutaka Incline after closure of that line in 1955. After a period of outside display it was restored and is now housed in the purpose built Fell Locomotive Museum.

At the end of the steam era a number of locomotives were purchased from NZR in running order, enabling long delivery trips to be made by steam hauled trains. Notable journeys were made by W^W 480 and W^W 644 from Greymouth to Auckland, and J 1234 from Dunedin to Paekakariki. Many of these locomotives, together with some acquired incomplete, have been restored to operating condition and are now certified for main line operation.

Industry, disposing of its steam locomotives, gave many former NZR locomotives to museums and preservation societies, thus accounting for the survival in preservation of most of the early designs of NZR tank engines. Some industrials were abandoned and have been recovered after lengthy periods of dereliction.

At various times it was the practice of the Railways Department to place derelict locomotives in riverbanks and on the seashore to control erosion. South Island dump-sites have been a fruitful source of more or less complete locomotives for restoration purposes. Uplifted from Branxholme near Invercargill was a considerable quantity of chassis parts for an intended renewal of class V locomotives 35 and 132. K 88 was disinterred from this site, this locomotive, initially restored to steam in 1981, has subsequently been returned to service complete with a new boiler. The dump at Mararoa Junction, near Lumsden, disgorged K 92, also restored to running order. P 25 and P 107 from Beaumont and W^B 292 and W^B 299 from Seddonville are being worked on with the intention of creating a complete member of each class. The contents of these dump-sites are generally well recorded, however, a recent discovery is the whereabouts of P 135, lost without trace after being written off NZR books in 1930. It has recently been found laying in Omoto Creek near Greymouth.

164 - Nostalgia

In summary, it can be said that a substantially complete range of NZR locomotive types is in existence on the ground, with perhaps some of the early twentieth century 4-6-0s still recoverable (see page 178). There are some notable omissions from the fleet. The world's first medium-gauge 'big' locomotive, the Avonside designed Canterbury J 2-6-0 of 1874 is not represented, neither are any of the early American tender machines of Baldwin manufacture, classes T and O 2-8-0 goods locomotives of 1879 and 1885 respectively, and the 2-6-2 passenger locomotive of 1885, class N. The greatest omission is that not one of the world's first true Pacific type, the Baldwin built class Q 4-6-2 of 1901, was saved from the cutter's torch.

The New Zealand Railway and Locomotive Society (NZRLS) was formed in 1944. In due course a number of provincial branches were incorporated with several undertaking preservation activities. In more recent years most branches have become independent. More specifically: NZRLS Auckland Branch became the Railway Enthusiasts Society in August 1958. NZRLS Otago Branch became the Otago Railway and Locomotive Society on 23 September 1982. NZRLS Wellington Branch became the Silver Stream Railway on 1 April 1983 and the Canterbury Branch became the Canterbury Railway Society on 9 June 1990.

The list gives for each locomotive the current owner, its location and how it was acquired, and a brief resume of its history in preservation. Reference should be made to Chapter Nine for those marked 'from industry'. Locomotives are identified by the 1890 number, except for the first three which went into industrial use before that scheme was introduced. The information contained hereafter was current at September 2002.

List compiled by R. W. McNaught and T. D. Selby

Number	Type	Owner, Current Location and History
Mills A	0-4-0T	West Coast Historical and Mechanical Society, Shantytown, Greymouth. From industry. Placed on static outside display, Greymouth, May 1960. To protected display at Shantytown, c.1986. Named *Opossum*.
C 126 (C 1 in 1882)	0-4-2ST	Westport Railway Preservation Society, Westport. From industry. Dumped at Te Kaha, Buller River, September 1929. Recovered December 1994, partial cosmetic restoration. On display in former NZR goods shed, Westport.
C 132 (C 2 in 1882)	0-4-2ST	Silver Stream Railway, Upper Hutt. From industry. Donated to Wellington Branch NZR&LS, to Seaview site Lower Hutt, 9 May 1972. To Silver Stream Railway, 26 July 1980. Overhauled and returned to use, April 1984. In regular service 2002.
1890 Number		
D 6	2-4-0T	Otago Railway and Locomotive Society. Ocean Beach Railway, Dunedin. From industry in working order, 22 September 1965. Stored in a partially dismantled condition at Ocean Beach Railway.
F 12	0-6-0ST	Canterbury Railway Society. Ferrymead Historic Park, Christchurch. From industry, incomplete, 1967. Donated jointly to Canterbury and Otago Branches NZR&LS as parts supply for sister locomotives F 13 and F 111. Protected storage.
F 13	0-6-0ST	Canterbury Railway Society. Ferrymead Historic Park, Christchurch. From NZR. Steamed from Arthur's Pass to Christchurch, 26 November 1967. Donated to Canterbury Branch, NZR&LS and transferred to Ferrymead, February 1968. Overhauled and returned to service, 9 June 1984. In use 1984-1999. Second overhaul commenced in April 2000. Named *Peveril*.

		PRESERVED LOCOMOTIVES (continued)
1890 Number	**Type**	**Owner, Current Location and History**
D 16	2-4-0T	Pleasant Point Railway and Historical Society. Pleasant Point, South Canterbury. From industry, 1973. To static display at Waitaki Farmers Freezing Co. Pukeuri Freezing Works, North Otago. To Timaru 23 March 1985, restoration commenced. To Pleasant Point, 30 May 1986. Recommissioned 13 May 1987. In regular service 2002.
R 28	0-6-4T	Buller District Council, Reefton, Westland. From industry, 1959. To outside display, February 1961. Later moved to protected display.
V 35	2-6-2	Tony Batchelor, Hooterville Heritage Charitable Trust, Waitara, Taranaki. Dumped Oreti River, Branxholme, Southland, June 1927. Parts recovered, January 1998. To Mainline Steam Trust depot, Parnell Auckland, thence to Waitara, January 2001. (Also various parts from V 125 and V 136, recovered from Branxholme May 1999).
A 62 (A 196 in 1906)	0-4-0T	Ian Insley, Avondale, Auckland. From Traffic to Maintenance Branch NZR, February 1906. Various working locations. Placed on static display at Otahuhu Workshops c.1929 for staff training. To Jack Ryder for display at his private museum c.1961. Acquired by Mr Insley, May 1996.
A 64	0-4-0T	Ashburton Railway and Preservation Society. Plains Railway, Tinwald, South Canterbury. From industry, 1965. Donated to Ashburton Steam & Model Engineering Club, to static display at Tinwald Domain, thence to AR&PS in 1971. Returned to operating condition, February 1973. Second overhaul completed in May 2000. In regular service 2002.
A 66	0-4-0T	Otago Railway and Locomotive Society, Dunedin. Leased to the Waimea Plains Railway Trust Board, Mandeville, Southland. From industry, 1949. Static display at Otago Early Settlers' Museum, Dunedin. To storage at Ocean Beach Railway, November 1973. Cosmetically restored for display at Caernarvon Restaurant, Dunedin, February 1981, fire damaged on 30 June 1988. Leased to Strath Taieri Lions Club for outdoor display at Middlemarch, March 1990. Leased to WPRTB and transferred to protected storage at Gore, November 2000.
A 67 (A 5 in 1892)	0-4-0T	Otago Railway and Locomotive Society. Ocean Beach Railway, Dunedin. From industry, steamed from Milburn to Dunedin, 2 September 1967. Under overhaul at various times, 1975-1989. In service 1990-1996. Second overhaul commenced October 1996, completed December 2001. In regular service 2002.
K 88	2-4-2	Ashburton Railway and Preservation Society. Plains Railway, Tinwald, South Canterbury. Leased to the K 88 Trust Board, Tinwald. Dumped Oreti River, Branxholme, Southland, June 1927. Recovered, January 1974. To Tinwald, June 1974. Restored to operating condition 1975-1981. Recommissioned 27 November 1982. Second restoration started in August 1996 with new welded boiler built in 1999 by Lyttelton Engineering. Completed February 2002 and recommissioned 30 March 2002. In service 2002. Named *Washington*.
K 92	2-4-2	Waimea Plains Railway Trust Board, Mandeville, Southland. Dumped Oreti River, Mararoa Junction, Southland, October 1928. Recovered by Fiordland Vintage Machinery Museum, Te Anau, June 1985. Partially restored to steamable condition, August 1991. Transferred to Dunedin for additional restoration work. In running condition by 1997. Ownership passed to Colin Smith of the Waimea Plains Railway Trust Board, February 2000. Transferred to Kingston, October 2000. Subsequent occasional service on the Kingston Flyer line.
K 94	2-4-2	Ashburton Railway and Preservation Society. Plains Railway, Tinwald, South Canterbury. Leased to the K 88 Trust Board, Tinwald, South Canterbury. Dumped Oreti River, Branxholme, Southland, June 1927. Recovered, March 1986, to Tinwald, 21 April 1986. Stored in dismantled condition.

166 - Nostalgia

ABOVE: The first NZR steam locomotive preserved in New Zealand is also the oldest. Fairlie E 175, *Josephine*, received a cosmetic restoration at the Otago Iron Rolling Mills in 1925 which included the installation of non-standard balloon stack funnels. The locomotive was initially displayed at the New Zealand and South Seas Exhibition in Dunedin before being placed on outside display at the Otago Early Settlers' Museum in 1927. (A. P. Godber Collection, Alexander Turnbull Library)

BELOW: The Ocean Beach Railway at St. Kilda in Dunedin is the earliest of the country's railway museums. In 1967 its second locomotive, A 67, became the first former NZR machine to be returned to operating condition. The 0-4-0 also has a claim to fame by being the first privately preserved locomotive to run on NZR track, when on 2 September 1967 it made the journey from Milburn to Dunedin under its own steam. St. Kilda, Dunedin, December 1967. (G. W. Emerson)

Nostalgia - 167

		PRESERVED LOCOMOTIVES (continued)
1890 Number	**Type**	**Owner, Current Location and History**
P 107	2-8-0	Project Steam, Dunedin. Dumped Clutha River, Beaumont, Otago, August 1932. Recovered, May 1992. Under restoration incorporating parts from P 25, also dumped at Beaumont and recovered at same time.
F 111	0-6-0ST	Otago Railway and Locomotive Society. Ocean Beach Railway, Dunedin. From industry in operating condition, March 1966. Overhauled c.1974 and returned to service 23 January 1975. Out of service by March 1979 and old boiler scrapped. Restoration commenced in 1998. New boiler required. Named *Rob Roy*.
V 132	2-6-2	Tony Batchelor, Hooterville Heritage Charitable Trust, Waitara, Taranaki. Dumped near Bealey, Canterbury, c.1930. Frame recovered in April 1998, to Mainline Steam Trust depot, Parnell, Auckland, thence to Waitara January 2001. (To be rebuilt using various parts from V 125 and V 136, recovered from Branxholme May 1999).
D 137	2-4-0T	Silver Stream Railway, Upper Hutt. From industry, November 1963. To outside display Hutt Park Motor Camp, 16 May 1964. Thence to Silver Stream Railway, August 1989. Protected storage, partially stripped.
D 140	2-4-0T	Canterbury Railway Society. Ferrymead Historic Park, Christchurch. From industry, 1960. Donated to Canterbury Society of Model and Experimental Engineers, November 1960, outside display. To Canterbury Branch, NZR&LS, 1967; moved to Ferrymead in 1968. Restoration commenced in October 1999.
D 143	2-4-0T	Silver Stream Railway, Upper Hutt. From industry, 1969. To Wellington Branch, NZR&LS, at Seaview site, April 1971. To Silver Stream Railway, 26 July 1980. Restoration commenced November 1987, suspended 1994. Named *Trout*.
B^B 144	4-8-0	Les Hostick, Hamilton. Leased to Ian Welch. Mainline Steam Trust, Parnell, Auckland. From NZR, December 1967. To protected storage at Waikato Branch NZR&LS Te Awamutu museum. To Mainline Steam Trust, Parnell, 28 July 1994. Restoration commenced, February 2001.
F 150	0-6-0ST	Otago Railway and Locomotive Society, Dunedin. Leased to Ashburton Railway and Preservation Society, Plains Railway, Tinwald. From NZR, January 1958. To outside display Newlands Park, Invercargill. Donated to Otago Branch NZR&LS, 30 June 1974. To AR&PS, September 1986. Stored on Plains Railway, partially dismantled condition, 2002.
F 163	0-6-0ST	Rail Heritage Trust of New Zealand. Loaned to Feilding and District Steam Rail Society, Feilding. From NZR traffic, 10 October 1964. Stored by NZR at various locations. Overhauled and returned to service by Vintage Rail, 28 June 1986. In main line service 1986-1999. Stored serviceable 2000-2001. Transferred to Feilding and District Steam Rail Society, 24 March 2002. Named *Ivanhoe*.
W^A 165	2-6-2T	Gisborne City Vintage Railway, Gisborne. From NZR, May 1961. Outside display Alfred Cox Park, Gisborne, 1964-1968. Moved to Young Nick's Park, Gisborne, 1968-1985. To Gisborne City Vintage Railway, October 1985. Restoration commenced June 1989, completed with new welded boiler built by Dispatch Engineering, December 1997. Main line certified, in regular service 2002.
D 170 (D 576 in 1912)	2-4-0T	Museum of Transport and Technology, Western Springs, Auckland. Leased to Rodney Community Tourist and Development Trust, Helensville, Auckland. From industry, 1960. To Hastings Model Railway Club, July 1960; thence to MOTAT, April 1961. Moved to Tokomaru Steam Museum, 1975, thence to Christchurch, 1981. Recovered and railed to Helensville, October 2000. Cosmetic refurbishment, outside display at Helensville railway station.

ABOVE: The oldest NZR steam locomotive restored to operating condition is the 1872 vintage F 13. Owned by the Canterbury Railway Society, it was in occasional use at Christchurch's Ferrymead Historic Park between 1984 and 2000 and has visited other heritage lines including the Weka Pass Railway. Nine examples of the class survive. Waipara, September 1999. (R. W. McNaught)

BELOW: Another early NZR design is the Avonside built class L 2-4-0 tank locomotive. Three examples are preserved including L 207 which is occasionally steamed at the Museum of Transport and Technology's Western Springs Railway. Western Springs, Auckland, November 1999. (R. B. Croker)

PRESERVED LOCOMOTIVES (continued)

1890 Number	Type	Owner, Current Location and History
E 175	0-4-4-0T	Otago Settlers' Museum, Dunedin. From industry, 1925. Cosmetically restored for display at New Zealand and South Seas Exhibition, Dunedin, 1925. Placed on outside display at the Otago Early Settlers' Museum, January 1927. Refurbished and placed in new glass-walled display hall, 21 March 1968. Named *Josephine*.
F 180	0-6-0ST	Museum of Transport and Technology, Western Springs, Auckland. From NZR, April 1965. Donated and moved to MOTAT, 15 April 1966. Outside display. Overhaul started in 1988 and suspended. Restoration commenced 1999. Named *Meg Merrilies*.
F 185	0-6-0ST	Bush Tramway Club. Pukemiro Junction, Waikato. From industry, 1972. To Bush Tramway Group at MOTAT, in use 1973-1977. To Bush Tramway Club at Pukemiro Junction, August 1977. Restored and recommissioned 21 October 1995. In regular service 2002.
W 192	2-6-2T	Rail Heritage Trust of New Zealand. Temporarily loaned to Canterbury Railway Society, Christchurch. From NZR traffic, July 1959. Cosmetically refurbished for NZR Centennial Display, November 1963. Restored to operating condition by NZR Addington Workshops staff for the Workshops Centennial, November 1979. Main line certified, in occasional service at Ferrymead Railway, 2002.
H 199	0-4-2T	Friends of the Fell Inc. The Fell Locomotive Museum, Featherston. Presented to Featherston Borough Council at opening of the Rimutaka Tunnel, 3 November 1955. Static outside display at Featherston, 1958-1984. Moved to purpose-built Fell Locomotive Museum, 10 March 1984. Fully restored by April 1989.
L 207	2-4-0T	Museum of Transport and Technology, Western Springs, Auckland. From industry. Donated to MOTAT, 1967 and delivered April 1971. Restored and returned to operation, 1977. In regular service 2002.
L 208	2-4-0T	West Coast Historical and Mechanical Society, Shantytown, Greymouth. From industry. Donated to Tauranga Historic Village, March 1974. Restored to operation, September 1976. Transferred to Shantytown, January 1999. Second overhaul commenced.
L 219	2-4-0T	Silver Stream Railway, Upper Hutt. From industry. To Wellington Branch, NZR&LS, at Seaview site, 22 November 1973. Restored to operating condition, August 1979. Transferred to Silver Stream Railway, 7 March 1980. Under overhaul November 1988-January 1990. Second overhaul commenced in 2001.
D 221	2-4-0T	Kaitaia District Council, Centennial Park, Kaitaia, Northland. From industry. Dumped in swamp, Kaingaroa, Northland, c1928. Recovered March 1967. Outside display, April 1967. Cosmetic refurbishment, 1999.
F 230	0-6-0ST	Hamilton City Council, Lake Park, Hamilton. From industry. Outside display c1957.
F 233	0-6-0ST	Glenbrook Vintage Railway, Waiuku, South Auckland. From industry, 1964. Donated to the Railway Enthusiasts Society and placed on covered display at RES Clubrooms, Onehunga, Auckland, 22 August 1964. Transferred to the GVR, 22 December 1984. Protected storage at Pukeoware. Named *Ada*.
F^A 250	0-6-2T	Waikato Branch, New Zealand Railway and Locomotive Society. Leased to Goldfields Steam Train Society, Waihi, Bay of Plenty. From industry, 1966. Donated to the Waikato Branch, NZR&LS, July 1967. Protected storage at Te Awamutu railway museum, 1967-1996. To Goldfields Railway, 11 April 1996. Stored at Waihi.

170 - Nostalgia

ABOVE: In 1897 Hillside Railway Workshops built W^A 165, its first locomotive. Withdrawn from stock after sixty-three years of service with the NZR, the 2-6-2 then languished in a park at Gisborne for a further quarter of a century. The locomotive was subsequently rescued and fully restored to operation by Gisborne City Vintage Railway. Gisborne, January 1998. (R. W. McNaught)

BELOW: Amongst the wide range of preserved former NZR tank locomotives are the useful high-boilered W^W class 4-6-4 machines. One of three rebuilt survivors, W^W 480 has recently resumed its former NZR identity following a major overhaul after twenty-five years of service on the Glenbrook Vintage Railway where it had operated as GVR N° 1. Pukeoware, March 2002. (R. W. McNaught)

PRESERVED LOCOMOTIVES (continued)			
1890 Number	Type	Owner, Current Location and History
W^B 299	2-6-2T	W^B Locomotive Group. Paekakariki. Steam Incorporated Museum, Paekakariki. Dumped by NZR in Mokihinui River, Seddonville, 5 January 1960. Recovered June 1989. To Silver Stream Railway, 20 October 1989. Then to Steam Incorporated, 27 July 1995. Restoration commenced, January 1996. (Parts of W^B 292 recovered at the same time, including the boiler, to be used in the restoration).
W^D 357	2-6-4T	Canterbury Railway Society. Ferrymead Historic Park, Christchurch. From industry. Donated to Canterbury Branch, NZR&LS and delivered 30 October 1966. Used at Ferrymead, March 1967 to August 1968, then stored until 1988. Restored and recommissioned, October 1988. In regular service 1988 to February 2002. Stored awaiting an overhaul.
W^F 386	2-6-4T	Steam Incorporated, Paekakariki. From NZR, October 1958. Purchased by Mayor of Taumarunui, to outside display near Taumarunui railway station, 8 November 1958. Made available to Steam Incorporated for restoration, transported in parts to Paekakariki, 27 August 1978. Part restored and project then suspended.
W^F 393	2-6-4T	Canterbury Railway Society. Ferrymead Historic Park, Christchurch. From NZR in operating condition. Donated to Canterbury Branch, NZR&LS, 1967. To Ferrymead, 6 May 1968. Never operated, initially outside display, then to protected storage.
W^F 403	2-6-4T	Nelson Railway Society, Founders Park, Nelson. From NZR, non-serviceable boiler. To Nelson City Council, 13 September 1973. Leased to Grand Tapawera Railroad group, Founders Park. Boiler removed for overhaul and subsequently condemned. Restoration commenced, 1999. Replacement W^F boiler obtained, November 2000.
A 423	4-6-2	Kevin and Paul Jowett, Huntly and Auckland. From NZR in operating condition. Ran Greymouth to Christchurch, 29 August 1970, Wellington to Frankton, 25-27 September 1970. Protected storage at Waikato Branch, NZR&LS Te Awamutu museum, October 1970.
A 428	4-6-2	Weka Pass Railway, Waipara, North Canterbury. From NZR, July 1969. To New Zealand Railway Preservation Society, then to A 428 Preservation Society. Stored Greymouth to August 1983. Thence to Weka Pass Railway and transferred to Waipara, 10 December 1983. Restoration completed August 1993. In operation on Weka Pass Railway since. In regular service 2002.
X 442	4-8-2	New Zealand Railway and Locomotive Society, Wellington. Leased to Feilding and District Steam Rail Society, Feilding. From industry, last run 21 November 1964. Donated to NZR&LS, 1968, to storage Timaru, 15 March 1968. To Linwood Depot, August 1973. Then to Ferrymead Historic Park, 1st October 1978. Covered storage 1979-2001. Transferred by sea and road to Feilding, 19-23 September 2002.
W^W 480	4-6-4T	Glenbrook Vintage Railway, Waiuku, South Auckland. From NZR in operating condition. Ran Greymouth to Auckland, 25 May-2 June 1969. Restored at Papakura, completed March 1976. Moved to Glenbrook, March 1976. Second restoration commenced September 1998, completed February 2002. In regular service 2002. Previously ran as GVR N° 1.
W^W 491	4-6-4T	Museum of Transport and Technology, Western Springs, Auckland. From NZR Otahuhu Workshops, boiler sectioned for staff training purposes. Donated to MOTAT, December 1974 and delivered March 1975. Outside display.
Y 542	0-6-0T	Museum of Transport and Technology, Western Springs, Auckland. From industry. Donated to MOTAT, May 1985 and delivered August 1985. In service 1986 to 1996. Overhaul commenced March 2001, completed March 2002. In regular service 2002.

Nostalgia - 171

172 - Nostalgia

ABOVE: Two examples of the class A Pacifics have been preserved, both built by A & G Price. A 428 has been the Weka Pass Railway's regular steam power since returning to service in 1993 after a full restoration. Waipara, September 1995. (R. W. McNaught)

BELOW: The 1930s era class C 2-6-2 shunting locomotives were strictly functional in looks with small driving wheels and a distinctive American style slope-back tender. C 847, one of two preserved, operates in regular service on the Silver Stream Railway, Silverstream, Upper Hutt. January 2002. (R. W. McNaught)

\multicolumn{3}{c}{**PRESERVED LOCOMOTIVES (continued)**}
1890 Number	**Type**	**Owner, Current Location and History**
B^A 552	4-8-0	Les Hostick, Hamilton. Leased to Ian Welch. Operated by Mainline Steam Trust, Parnell, Auckland. From NZR in operating condition, June 1969. Run Wellington to Frankton (from Palmerston North with A 423), 25-27 September 1970. Protected storage at Waikato Branch NZR&LS Te Awamutu museum, October 1970. To Parnell, 28 July 1994. Overhaul completed August 2000. Main line certified. In regular service 2002.
W^W 571	4-6-4T	Silver Stream Railway, Upper Hutt. From NZR in operating condition. Run Greymouth to Picton, 5-7 September; Wellington to Taita 14 September 1969. To Wellington Branch NZR&LS, Gracefield site. Transferred to Seaview site, April 1971. Thence to Silver Stream Railway, 13 May 1984. Restoration commenced December 1984, completed April 1988. Second overhaul completed February 1999. In regular service 2002.
A^B 608	4-6-2	New Zealand Railway and Locomotive Society, Wellington. Leased to Steam Incorporated, Paekakariki. From NZR, unserviceable condition. Donated to NZR&LS, 21 August 1967. Stored at various locations, thence to Ferrymead Historic Park, 1 October 1978. Covered display 1979-1993. Towed to Paekakariki, November 1993. Restoration commenced March 1998. Named *Passchendaele*.
W^W 644	4-6-4T	Glenbrook Vintage Railway, Waiuku, South Auckland. From NZR in operating condition. Ran Greymouth to Auckland, 30 March-5 April 1970. To Papakura, 5 April 1970. To GVR 1973, never operated. Restoration commenced, 1978. Stored dismantled 1978-2002. Restoration recommenced, April 2002.
A^B 663	4-6-2	Ian Welch, Wellington. Operated by Mainline Steam Trust, Christchurch. From NZR, incomplete. Stored at Dunedin as spare locomotive for Kingston Flyer, 1969-1983. Sold to Ian Welch, to storage Hutt Workshops, September 1984. Restoration commenced at Hutt Workshops, 1988. To Silver Stream Railway July 1992, completed May 1997. Converted to oil-firing. Main line certified. In regular service 2002. Named *Sharon Lee*.
A^B 699	4-6-2	Pleasant Point Railway and Historical Society, Pleasant Point, South Canterbury. From NZR, March 1968. Stored at Timaru, to Pleasant Point, 28 November 1970. Protected display at railway station, then restored to operating condition, November 1975. In regular service 2002.
A^B 745	4-6-2	Tony Batchelor, Hooterville Heritage Charitable Trust, Waitara, Taranaki. Buried under fill after track washout at Hawera, 16 July 1956. Recovered without the tender, 11 November 2001 and moved to Waitara in December 2001 for restoration.
A^B 778	4-6-2	Invest South Limited. Leased to Kingston Flyer Steam Train Limited. From NZR in operating condition, July 1969. Returned to special stock for Kingston Flyer tourist train service, 22 December 1971. Leased to Kingston Flyer Ltd and operated between Kingston and Fairlight, December 1982 to March 1997. Returned to Tranz Rail stock, May 1997. Sold to Invest South Ltd, 1 May 2002. In regular service 2002.
W^AB 794	4-6-4T	New Zealand Railway and Locomotive Society, Wellington. Leased to Feilding and District Steam Rail Society, Feilding. From industry. Donated to NZR&LS, 1968. To storage Timaru, 15 March 1968, then to Linwood August 1973. To Ferrymead Historic Park, 1 October 1978. Covered storage 1979-1997. Towed to Feilding March 1997. Restoration commenced April 1997, completed December 2001. Main line certification pending.
A^B 795	4-6-2	Invest South Limited. Leased to Kingston Flyer Steam Train Limited. From NZR in operating condition, July 1969. Returned to special stock for Kingston Flyer tourist train service, 22 December 1971. Leased to Kingston Flyer Ltd and operated between Kingston and Fairlight, December 1982 to March 1997. Returned to Tranz Rail stock, May 1997. Sold to Invest South Ltd, 1 May 2002. In regular service 2002

ABOVE: The largest NZR designed tank locomotives which ran in New Zealand were the W^{AB} class 4-6-4 machines, that initially were used on both main line goods and passenger services. In later years they hauled suburban trains at Wellington and Auckland. One of two survivors, W^{AB} 794 has been restored for main line operation by the Feilding and District Steam Rail Society. Feilding, January 2002. (D. C. Whyte)

BELOW: The K series 4-8-4 type locomotives are regarded by many as the apex of New Zealand steam power. The improved class K^A machines are represented by three preserved examples. One is Ian Welch's K^A 942 that for most of the 1990s wore a replica of the as-built streamlining. In the early years of the decade the tender was decorated with a 1930s period nationalistic slogan. Springfield, July 1992. (G. T. Radcliffe)

Nostalgia - 175

\multicolumn{3}{c}{**PRESERVED LOCOMOTIVES (continued)**}
1890 Number	**Type**	**Owner, Current Location and History**
W^AB 800	4-6-4T	Jointly owned by Silver Stream Railway, Waikato Branch NZR&LS and Les Hostick. From NZR, May 1967. To Waikato Branch NZR&LS Te Awamutu museum, December 1967. Protected storage.
A^B 832	4-6-2	Museum of Transport and Technology, Western Springs, Auckland. Leased to Glenbrook Vintage Railway, Waiuku, South Auckland. From NZR, December 1967. Donated to MOTAT, delivered 2 October 1971. Stored outside 1971 1996. To Glenbrook Vintage Railway, 17 December 1996. Covered storage.
C 847	2-6-2	Silver Stream Railway, Upper Hutt. From NZR, October 1968. To Wellington Branch NZR&LS, Seaview site, December 1974. To Silver Stream Railway, 13 May 1984. To Glenbrook Vintage Railway, 8 April 1990. Restoration completed February 1994, used on GVR. To Silver Stream Railway, 16 July 1998. In regular service 2002.
C 864	2-6-2	Canterbury Railway Society. Ferrymead Historic Park, Christchurch. From NZR, May 1968. To Canterbury Branch NZR&LS, arrived Ferrymead 29 January 1972. Returned to operation 17 June 1972, occasional use to 1990. Stored unserviceable 1990-2002.
K 900	4-8-4	Museum of Transport and Technology, Western Springs, Auckland. From NZR, October 1966. Donated to MOTAT, 1967. Outside display Pacific Steel Ltd., Otahuhu, March 1969. To outside display MOTAT, 20 December 1975, then to protected display.
K 911	4-8-4	Ian Welch, Wellington. Mainline Steam Trust, Plimmerton. From NZR, from Hutt Workshops stationary boiler use, incomplete, June 1989. Stored Gracefield, 1989-1998. To Mainline Steam Trust Upper Hutt, September 1998. Restoration commenced, October 1998. To Plimmerton, December 2000. To incorporate other parts including a K^B trailing bogie.
K 917	4-8-4	Steam Incorporated, Paekakariki. From NZR, from Hutt Workshops stationary boiler use, incomplete, June 1989. To Steam Incorporated, stored Gracefield 1989-2001. To Paekakariki, 2 April 2001. Stored.
K^A 935	4-8-4	Silver Stream Railway, Upper Hutt. From NZR, February 1968. Stored at Waikato Branch NZR&LS Te Awamutu museum, thence to Wellington Branch NZR&LS Seaview site, 18 August 1972. Returned to steam, 22 September 1973. To Silver Stream Railway, 13 May 1984. Under overhaul March 1996-May 1999. In regular service 2002.
K^A 942	4-8-4	Ian Welch, Wellington. Mainline Steam Trust, Plimmerton. From NZR, February 1972. Stored Paekakariki, 1974-1986, thence Otaki, 1986-1989. To Glenbrook Vintage Railway, November 1989. Overhauled by GVR, January - July 1990. In service 1990-2000. To Plimmerton, October 2001. Restoration commenced March 2002. Named *Nigel Bruce*.
K^A 945	4-8-4	Steam Incorporated, Paekakariki. From NZR, December 1967. Purchased by Sir Len Southward, 1968. Stored at Taumarunui 1968-1975. To Paekakariki, 29 June 1975. Donated to Steam Incorporated, 1981. Restoration commenced January 1983, completed April 1985. In service 1985-1995. Stored awaiting overhaul from June 1995. Second overhaul commenced April 1998.
K^B 968	4-8-4	Ferrymead Trust, Christchurch. Leased to Ian Welch, stored at Mainline Steam Trust, Christchurch. From NZR, March 1969. Purchased by Ferrymead Trust, 1970. Stored Linwood Depot 1969-1975, 1976-1978, industrial use as stationary boiler, 1975-1976. To Ferrymead Historic Park, 1 October 1978. Protected display. First steamed at Ferrymead 17 March 1979, thereafter occasionally until 1985. To Mainline Steam Trust, Sockburn, 29 July 1995. Stored awaiting restoration.

176 - Nostalgia

ABOVE: Numerically the J series 4-8-2 tender locomotives are the most common type of steam locomotive preserved in New Zealand. Included in this group are three of the original North British built examples. One of these, Ian Welch's J 1236, has been restored as an oil-fired J^B variant complete with front mounted twin air compressors as originally fitted. Pukeoware, March 2002. (R. W. McNaught)

BELOW: The improved Hillside built class J^A, most of which were fitted with roller bearing connecting and coupling rods, is well represented with six preserved including both operational and static display examples. One of the last quartet built in 1956, J^A 1271 was returned to main line operation in 1997 after a major restoration by Steam Incorporated. Paekakariki, August 2000. (R. W. McNaught)

		PRESERVED LOCOMOTIVES (continued)
1890 Number	Type	Owner, Current Location and History
J 1211	4-8-2	Ian Welch, Wellington. Operated by Mainline Steam Trust, Plimmerton. From NZR, November 1971. Sold to private buyers. Run from Christchurch to Picton, 21-22 April 1973; Wellington to Palmerston North to Paekakariki, 19 May 1974. Sold to Ian Welch, June 1976. Stored Paekakariki, 1976-1985. Operated on Bay of Islands Vintage Railway, 1985-1986. Overhauled, in service, October 1988. Converted to oil-firing 1998. Second overhaul, 1999. Main line certified. In regular service 2002. Named *Gloria*.
J 1234	4-8-2	Steam Incorporated, Paekakariki. From NZR, November 1971. Sold to Steam Incorporated members. Run from Dunedin to Timaru, 18 November 1972; Timaru to Christchurch, 20 April 1973; Christchurch to Picton, 21-22 April 1973. Wellington to Palmerston North to Paekakariki, 19 May 1974. Limited use at Paekakariki, 1974-1984. Overhauled, in service February 1992. Leased to Railway Enthusiasts Society, April 1998. Main line certified. Occasional use on the Glenbrook Vintage Railway, 2002.
J 1236	4-8-2	Ian Welch, Wellington. Operated by Mainline Steam Trust, Parnell, Auckland. From NZR, November 1971. Sold to Railway Enthusiasts Society. Towed to Wellington, then run Wellington to Auckland, 31 March-3 April 1972. Onsold to A. Bucher, then P. Baker. To outside display, Museum of Transport and Technology, 20 December 1975. Sold to Ian Welch, 1990. To Mainline Steam Trust, Auckland. Restoration commenced February 1991, returned to service July 2001. Converted to oil-firing and reclassified J[B]. Main line certified. In regular service 2002. Named *Joanna*.
J[A] 1240	4-8-2	Ian Welch, Wellington. Mainline Steam Trust, Parnell, Auckland. From NZR, November 1971. Sold to Peter Coleman; moved to his farm near Blenheim, February 1972. Sold to Ian Welch, towed to Mainline Steam Trust, Auckland, September 1991. Stored in an unserviceable condition.
J[A] 1250	4-8-2	Philip Goldman, Auckland. Leased to Railway Enthusiasts Society, Auckland. From NZR, November 1971. Towed to Wellington, thence ran (with J 1236) Wellington to Auckland, 31 March-3 April 1972. Stored Glenbrook Vintage Railway, 1973-1982. Overhauled and returned to service, October 1982. NZR main line service 1985-1992. Full restoration commenced March 1995, completed October 1998. Main line certified. Undergoing boiler repairs, 2002. Named *Diana*.
J[A] 1260	4-8-2	Ashburton Railway and Preservation Society. Plains Railway, Tinwald, South Canterbury. From NZR, November 1971. Stored Ashburton 1972-1973, to Tinwald, 16 February 1973. Limited service on Plains Railway 1981-1985. Leased to the Weka Pass Railway, 1986-1988. To Tinwald, protected storage. Overhaul for restricted Plains Railway use commenced, 1995.
J[A] 1267	4-8-2	Waikato Branch, NZRL&S and various individual owners. From NZR, November 1971. Towed Christchurch to Wellington, April 1972. Ran Wellington to Frankton, 21-23 July 1972. To Waikato Branch NZR&LS Te Awamutu museum, 24 July 1972. Protected storage.
J[A] 1271	4-8-2	Steam Incorporated, Paekakariki. From NZR. Stationary boiler, Dunedin, December 1976. Sold to Russell Gibbard and Reid M[c]Naught in incomplete condition. Towed Dunedin to Wellington, March 1978. Restoration commenced January 1992, completed October 1997. Main line certified. In regular service 2002.
J[A] 1274	4-8-2	City of Dunedin. Otago Settlers' Museum, Dunedin. From NZR, November 1971. Last NZR steam locomotive built, December 1956. Donated to City of Dunedin after refurbishment at Hillside Workshops, 1975. To covered display, 26 July 1975.
J[A] 1275	4-8-2	Les Hostick, Hamilton. Leased to Ian Welch. Mainline Steam Trust, Parnell, Auckland. From NZR, August 1968. To protected storage Waikato Branch NZR&LS Te Awamutu museum, 1970. To Mainline Steam Trust, Parnell, 28 July 1994. Restoration commenced June 2001.

178 - Nostalgia

INTO THE FUTURE

Compiled by R. W. McNaught

The preceding table of preserved NZR steam locomotives lists all known examples 'saved' for posterity. Their physical condition ranges from completely restored through to essentially complete but awaiting an overhaul to, at the most extreme case, little more than a collection of parts from a specific steam locomotive that have been recovered from a dump site.

Already some historically significant examples, notably two Rogers class K 2-4-2 type tender locomotives numbers 88 and 92, have been restored to running condition after many years buried in Southland riverbanks. However, there are still a number of 'buried treasures' awaiting recovery in the immediate future. Below is a list of the most likely candidates to possibly join their already preserved NZR kin in the years to come.

1890 Number	Type	Current Location, Condition and Ownership Status
U^B 17	4-6-0	Oamaru, Otago (partially exposed in foreshore embankment). Frame, running gear, boiler and tender parts. Hooterville Heritage Charitable Trust.
P 60	2-8-0	Branxholme, Southland (in Oreti River bank). Frame and running gear only. Ohai Railway Board Heritage Trust.
V 126	2-6-2	Mararoa Junction, Southland (in Oreti River bank). Substantially complete with tender. Ohai Railway Board Heritage Trust.
V 127	2-6-2	Mararoa Junction, Southland (in Oreti River bank). Substantially complete with tender. Ohai Railway Board Heritage Trust.
P 133	2-8-0	Branxholme, Southland (in Oreti River bank). Frame, running gear and boiler. Ohai Railway Board Heritage Trust.
U^B 282	4-6-0	Oamaru, Otago (buried in foreshore embankment). Frame, running gear, boiler and tender parts. Hooterville Heritage Charitable Trust.
L^A 312	4-4-0T	Omoto, Westland (submerged in Grey River). Substantially complete. Reefton Historic Trust Board.
U^B 330	4-6-0	Omoto, Westland (buried in railway embankment). Substantially complete with tender. Hooterville Heritage Charitable Trust.
U^B 331	4-6-0	Omoto, Westland (buried in railway embankment). Frame, running gear and boiler. Hooterville Heritage Charitable Trust.
U^C 361	4-6-0	Omoto, Westland (buried in railway embankment). Frame, running gear and boiler. Hooterville Heritage Charitable Trust.
U^C 365	4-6-0	Omoto, Westland (dumped on top of railway embankment). Substantially complete with tender. Hooterville Heritage Charitable Trust.
U^C 369	4-6-0	Omoto, Westland (submerged in Grey River). Substantially complete with tender. Reefton Historic Trust Board.
U^C 370	4-6-0	Omoto, Westland (submerged in Grey River). Substantially complete with tender. Reefton Historic Trust Board.

CHAPTER ELEVEN

NUMBER PLATES and MAKER'S PLATES of the NZR STEAM LOCOMOTIVES

By W. W. PREBBLE

For a period of nearly ninety years from 1882 to the end of the steam era on New Zealand Railways, the number plate was inextricably linked with the locomotive and its allocated road number throughout its working life.

New Zealand Railways generally took delivery of a locomotive from either its own workshops or an outside builder with at least two sets of plates; the maker's plate(s) and the cabside number plates. The maker's plates gave details of the locomotive builder, origin, date of manufacture and sequential number. The cabside number plate however conveyed the road number of the locomotive and often the locomotive class. Occasionally locomotives were delivered or specified with a further plate; the smokebox number plate.

While originally intended as an identification and operational aid to the NZR, these plates have contributed significant information to the observer, photographer and researcher along the way, as well as providing just a few red herrings! It is the intention of this chapter to detail the evolution of these plates alongside the numbering system and the locomotives to which they were affixed.

THE ORIGIN OF THE NZR CABSIDE NUMBER PLATE

Name plates actually preceded number plates. From the early 1870s there were examples of locomotives sporting cast plates bearing the official locomotive name. Some of the most well known being *Josephine, Fox, Ada* and *Snake*. More frequently names were painted on the tanks.

Throughout the 1870s and early 1880s it was the practice of the various isolated sections to show the locomotive class and road numbers by painting these on the locomotive. Favourite positions were the front and rear headstocks, the side or saddle tanks, bunker rear and the cabside. Often the class and number were painted each side of the maker's plate which usually resided on the tanks or cabside. Obviously a more permanent form of identification was required - enter the number plate.

THE FIRST NUMBER PLATES

The first number plates appeared about the time of the 1882 renumbering, of which two variations have emerged. The first variation was affixed, in the South Island, to the class V (nee class N) locomotives allocated to the Hurunui-Bluff section in the 1882-1890 period. These plates were very simple affairs, being oval with, initially, the class letter N, a fullstop, and the locomotive number following. Later, when these locomotives were reclassified V the class letter and full-stop were omitted from the number plate. There were subtle variations within the various N and V plates. This gives rise to conjecture that these number plates were wooden as a pattern would have faithfully reproduced consistent brass or bronze castings.

The second variation occurred in the North Island when some of the class E, F and R locomotives allocated to the Wanganui-New Plymouth section in the period 1882-1890, were fitted with plates similar to the classes N and V. While these plates generally were of the same style and showed the class and number in large lettering across the plate, they differed principally through being thinner than the South Island plates and through the inclusion of some extra wording. Situated above and below the locomotive number was the lettering "NZR". It is likely that this was the first time this abbreviation was used on locomotives as it was only in the 1880s that the department begun to be referred to as "New Zealand Railways". Unlike the classes N and V plates, there was a degree of consistency about their appearance and were likely cast of brass or gunmetal.

Short-lived however these plates would be, as 1890 saw many of these locomotives renumbered with consequent withdrawal of the number plates. Another era was about to begin.

THE 'STAR' PLATES

From around 1890 when the final numbering scheme was instituted, a new design of plate originated. These became known as the 'star' number plates, so called as they featured a very prominent star cast either side of the locomotive classification. Affixed to the tank side of sidetank locomotives and cabside of both saddle-tank and tender locomotives, these plates displaced the maker's plates previously situated at these positions. This subsequently caused one of the maker's plates to be affixed to the rear of the bunker or tender (one can only assume the 'spare' maker's plate was put into the scrap heap for melting down and reuse).

The 'star' plates were fitted broadly to locomotives of the B, C, D, F, H, J, P, and R classes. Photographic evidence indicates that the fitment of these plates was principally confined to the North Island locomotives.

However, three locomotives allocated to the Greymouth section are known to have had 'star' plates fitted while in service during the 1890 period. It is possible that the isolated Westland sections were under the jurisdiction of Wellington as it was easier to ship equipment from Westland to Wellington than to Canterbury at the time. Unfortunately, the period when the 'star' plates were abolished cannot be accurately defined.

ABOVE: An example of the 'star' number plates used in the early 1890s; these were fitted to various locomotives in North Island service and on the Greymouth section. This plate, albeit minus the road number, survived on C 166 working on the Castlecliff Railway until 1956.

THE NZR STANDARD CABSIDE NUMBER PLATE

What was next to emerge would become the standard NZR number plate. From its inception about 1890 to the end of steam in 1971 and beyond, this design would remain unchanged for over eighty years. Unfortunately, original documentation does not exist but it is probable that the design and castings originated at Addington around the same time that the North Island workshops were affixing 'star' plates. Exactly when the 'star' number plates were replaced by the standard cabside number plate for both islands is unclear.

The standard NZR cabside number plate of the steam era was cast in leaded gunmetal (commonly referred to as bronze). Early practice was to leave the plate background polished but by 1908 it became the practice for the background to be painted vermilion.

Initially plates were cast without the locomotive classification but H. H. Jackson, the Chief Mechanical Engineer of the time, amended blueprint 2785 in December 1914 to incorporate the locomotive classification at the top of the plate. This drawing shows the first letter as being one inch high and any subsequent classification letters as three-quarters of an inch high. An underscore was shown below the second classification letter. However, the only plates to be so treated were some affixed to the classes W^A, W^{AB}, W^F, W^G and W^W.

The first plates to be cast with classification letters were the class A^A of 1914. Any locomotives number plates devoid of classification letters were treated during the locomotive's next overhaul, the operation involving the soldering of the class letters to the existing plate. Often these had a tendency to be knocked off or to fall off in service, usually resulting in the letters being brass riveted to the plate. However, there were some plates which escaped having class letters added, these being all of the class H and some members of the classes F, U^C and W^D.

A further twist was the reclassification of some locomotives. Usually reclassification resulted in the locomotive retaining its original number and number plate; the non-applicable original classification was ground off and new classification letters were soldered on. Examples include W^S to W^{AB}, W^G to W^W and J to J^B. Oddly, W^{AB}'s converted to A^B's had new plates cast even though the locomotives retained their original numbers.

ABOVE: Number plate W^A 288 features an underscore under the 'A'. Despite the official NZR drawing showing this underscore, only some plates of classes W^A, W^{AB}, W^F, W^G and W^W were cast to include this.

Throughout the years the scars of service showed in many ways; W^{AB}'s with their wide tanks invariably incurred gouges from the corners of wagons, repositioning of cab appliances, seat brackets or tablet exchangers resulted in extra holes being drilled through plates, and many plates on side tanks suffered cracks around their mounting holes as fitters would heavily peen the rivets in an attempt to stem the constant water leaks. Dutifully though, any number plate that was missing or badly damaged was promptly replaced.

The standard NZR drawing clearly showed both the dimensions for the number plate and the lettering font. This however has resulted in a degree of interpretation by the various workshops that cast NZR number plates over the years and some notable features may be traced as each workshop reproduced these variations from their own patterns.

BALDWIN CASTINGS

The 1901 batch of locomotives ordered by New Zealand Railways from Baldwin were shipped with standard NZR number plates; these were the 1901 classes N, Q, U^B and W^D. Standard; that is in the broadest sense. It would appear that Baldwin were supplied with the NZR number plate blueprint which showed the number 213. This allowed Baldwin to reproduce the overall shape, size and double border with accuracy, as well as the numerals 1, 2 and 3.

Obviously the rest of the numerals were drawn by Baldwin or were left to Baldwin's pattern makers, as these numerals differ considerably from the standard font. Of interest, stamped on the reverse of each of these plates is Baldwin's unique form of locomotive identification.

ABOVE: One of Baldwin's cast plates from the 1901 batch of locomotives, U^B 337 exhibits a '7' which is quite unlike the standard font used by the NZR.

182 - Number Plates and Maker's Plates

A & G PRICE LTD. CASTINGS

Commencing locomotive building for the NZR in 1904, A & G Price delivered each of their locomotives complete with cabside number plates. Again, some interpretation appears to have been made of the NZR drawing. The A & G Price number plates differed considerably to the NZR cast equivalents. They were thinner, lighter, slightly smaller and all the numerals lacked serif; this lack of serif gave the A & G Price plates a particularly plain appearance in comparison with the equivalent NZR castings.

Nevertheless, A & G Price number plate casting proved to be very consistent throughout the twenty four years of locomotive building for NZR.

ABOVE: Comparative examples of plates cast by A & G Price and NZR workshops. A^B 760, cast by the NZR, exhibits the standard font whereas A^B 702, cast by A & G Price, is 'sans-serif'. Note the differences between the numbers 7 and 0.

NORTH BRITISH LOCOMOTIVE CO. LTD. CASTINGS

The North British batches of A^B's were devoid of plates from the builders, these being cast in New Zealand. It wasn't until the 1939 class J and 1951 class J^A that North British locomotives were delivered complete with cabside number plates. As the classes J and J^A were numbered in the 1200 series, this necessitated fitting four numerals across the number plate, impossible with the existing numeral font. The outcome was a reduction in the width of each numeral by approximately one inch.

While North British reproduced fairly accurately the standard NZR cabside number plate, the ellipse of the plate differed slightly. They also exhibited a more yellow colouring when polished, due to these plates being cast in brass (an alloy of copper and zinc) rather than the traditional bronze used in other plates.

ABOVE: Different elliptic shape (squarer in the shoulders) and brass composition are unique to the North British class J number plates. In this instance the plate has had the 'B' classification suffix soldered on after the locomotive's conversion to an oil burner.

NZR WORKSHOP CASTINGS

The New Zealand Railways cast number plates for locomotives built in their workshops or for locomotives imported without number plates. With a number of workshops each erecting locomotives and casting plates, some variation was likely to arise as each pattern maker subtly used his hand to produce the patterns. Addington, Hillside, Hutt, Newmarket and Petone all cast number plates and while generally the font remained consistent there were some variations, particularly from Hillside.

Petone for example used a rather different 6 or 9 when casting the plates for the classes H, W^B and A^A. This very same pattern emerged on K^A plates 945, 946 and 959 cast by Hutt, indicating that at least some of the patterns were moved from Petone to Hutt in the late 1920s.

Cabside plates on K^A 940-943 and latterly 944, when it returned to North Island service after its spell in the South, had all the hallmarks of being cast at Hillside. In these instances the pattern for the letter K was identical to those on the K^B plates. Additionally, the figures had been set lower on the plate in typical Hillside fashion and there were distinguishing differences within the double border.

There were other examples: for the South Island J^A locomotives Hillside attempted to emulate the numerals used by North British on the J plates. This resulted in some rather unusual numbers. Furthermore, a different font was used for some of the converted W^{AB} number plates cast by Hillside.

Fittingly, at the end of steam Hillside workshops cast some of the last number plates. These were replacement plates for the two *Kingston Flyer* locomotives, A^B 778 and A^B 795, the original plates having been removed from the locomotives in 1969 for sale in the usual manner.

ABOVE and BELOW: An example of variations that occurred within the various NZR workshops. Classification letter font and placement of the numbers are just two of the subtle differences distinguishing the casting shop. In this instance the plate for K^A 936 was cast by Hutt and that for K^A 944 was cast by Hillside.

THE SMOKEBOX DOOR NUMBER PLATE

Use of the round smokebox door number plate actually predates the cabside number plate in New Zealand. Its use may be traced to the popularity on many railroads within the United States, and would appear to have been regarded as 'standard equipment' from most of the locomotive builders within that country.

For New Zealand Railways, the honour of a locomotive being passed out with a smokebox door number plate was reserved for main line locomotives. As main line locomotives were eventually displaced into secondary service or extensively rebuilt, generally the smokebox door numberplate would be removed.

Unlike the standard NZR cabside number plate, the smokebox door number plate evolved over the years, starting with standard American designs and eventually culminating in a New Zealand design many years later. Certainly the use of smokebox door number plates would appear to have a direct correlation with the influence that American locomotive design had during that period.

An obvious anomaly however was the absence of a smokebox door number plate on the 1951 North British class J^A, as at the time both the class J and South Island class J^A were fitted with smokebox door number plates. This is inexplicable as NZR specification 437 of February 1951 to North British clearly lists the standard NZR smokebox number plate drawing

THE ROGERS SMOKEBOX DOOR NUMBER PLATE

It all started in 1878 when the Rogers Locomotive and Machine Works of Paterson, New Jersey, shipped to New Zealand the 2-4-2 class K, resplendent with a smokebox door number plate. This plate was deeply dished with a heavy brass bezel incorporating the two digit road number. Most of the plates appear to have been removed by the time the locomotives were reboilered.

184 - Number Plates and Maker's Plates

Following the class K were the two 2-4-4T locomotives for the Rakaia and Ashburton Forks Railway in 1878. These were acquired by the Government in 1881, given the class Q classification and the plates numbered.

THE BALDWIN SMOKEBOX DOOR NUMBER PLATE

Immediately after the Rogers locomotives was the delivery in 1879 of the NZR T class from Baldwin Locomotive Works of Philadelphia, Pennsylvania. These locomotives incorporated what was to become Baldwin's very famous smokebox number plate. Within a double border around the perimeter Baldwin included their name and location, leaving a large area in the middle for affixing the locomotive road number.

This was the commencement of a trend; over the next thirty-five years Baldwin would ship ninety-five locomotives to New Zealand Railways, encompassing classes T, O, N, U^B, W^B, W^D, Q and A^A, each proudly displaying the classic Baldwin front number plate.

Generally, most Baldwin smokebox door number plates in NZR service incorporated the road number, especially prior to cabside number plates becoming standard. There were of course exceptions; with numbers either soldered or riveted to plates and there were occasions when they were absent such as the class A^A plates which were always devoid of numbers. Examples also exist of given locomotives over a period exhibiting considerably different number fonts on the plate, proof that numbers did at times succumb to the laws of gravity.

Amazingly, some of these plates were retained on locomotives well after the engines had passed their prime. Examples of this were some of the class Q retaining their plates into the 1940s and some of the Westport based class W^B still proudly displaying their Baldwin front number plates during the early 1950s.

THE STANDARD NZR SMOKEBOX DOOR NUMBER PLATE

Considerable time was to pass between Baldwin's delivery of the class A^A in 1914 and the emergence of the next smokebox door number plate. Approved by the then Locomotive Superintendent, P. R. Angus, the New Zealand Railways designed their first smokebox door number plate to adorn the new K class locomotives in 1932. This was the start of a standard design which would be featured on all future main line steam locomotives, with two exceptions.

Incorporating the classification letters at the top with road numbers through the centre and 'NZGR' neatly wrapped along the bottom circumference of the double border, this was undoubtedly an attractive plate with its bright red background. A threaded hexagonal nut on the back anchored them to the smokebox door.

LEFT and RIGHT: K 926, cast at Hutt, exhibits the standard NZR number plate font while K^B 969 shows the unusual '9' associated with many of the K^B front plates. Interestingly this '9' is identical to that shown on the standard NZR blueprint yet was only used on the K^B and K^A 940-944 plates.

It is interesting to note that Hutt cast all the K plates plus those for K^A 930-939 and K^A 945-964. However, plates for K^A 940-944 were cast at Hillside, the unusual Hillside numeral '9' and other numerals being evident on those five plates. K^A 944 wore two Hillside cast plates during its service, firstly from the period it was built until being shipped to the South Island, then a second plate was cast by Hillside for its return to North Island service.

The unusual '9' was evident on all the class K^B locomotives as they were outshopped in their original streamlined guise. During the period of destreamlining these locomotives temporarily lost their smokebox door number plates, these being reinstated some years later. However, the original plates were not used, new plates were cast and fitted, again often incorporating that odd '9' or '6'.

Destreamlining of the class J, which had been built without smokebox door number plates, resulted in new plates being cast for these locomotives. At that time J 1200 to 1229 resided in the North Island and received plates cast by Hutt. J 1230 to 1239 were Dunedin based and plates for these were cast by Hillside. The result was two sets of different looking plates as the Hutt 'J' and '2' patterns were rather different from those of Hillside.

From 1952 a number of the class J smokebox door number plates had a 'B' classification suffix added to signify conversion of these locomotives to oil firing. Addition of the suffix would seem to have not been controlled by a drawing as placement of the 'B' occurred at random on these plates.

What had become the standard NZR smokebox door number plate finished when Hillside produced their final run for the class J^A in 1956.

ABOVE: Variations between the casting shops were obvious. Cast by Hutt, the plate for J 1214 exhibits obvious detail differences of both the 'J' and '2' from that for J^A 1271 which was cast by Hillside.

THE 'G' SMOKEBOX DOOR NUMBER PLATE

Conversion of the three Beyer Peacock built Garratt-type locomotives into six 4-6-2 class G locomotives by Hillside in 1937 found them emerging with a distinctive smokebox door number plate. This plate was somewhat larger than the standard and affixed at the back with three mounting faces as opposed to the single hexagonal mounting on the standard plate. It could be best described as a Hillside version of the popular Baldwin smokebox door number plate as it incorporated Hillside's name and the letters 'NZR' within a double border around the perimeter, while the classification and locomotive number was placed in the centre.

It is not known if this plate was designed by the Chief Mechanical Engineer's office as a new standard plate or whether it was the imaginative work of Hillside workshop. Drawings of this plate, which would solve this mystery, have not been located. Either way, only six were produced for the class G and no further castings were produced for other locomotives.

THE NZR MAKER'S PLATE

Essentially the 'Birth Certificate' of any locomotive, the maker's plate records the parentage, year of erection and sequential number. While this information may have been of use on many railway systems, the New Zealand Railways had evolved a system of locomotive identification for the purposes of overhauls which was based on either the road number, which was shown on the number plates, or the boiler number which was recorded on the boiler pressure plate attached to the boiler backhead.

Accordingly, for the New Zealand Railways the maker's plate was more a form of ornamentation. During overhauls it was not unusual for maker's plates to be lost, particularly if boiler swaps or smokebox repairs were undertaken. It was therefore common for locomotives to run devoid of one or more maker's plates. The general exception was tank locomotives which normally had the plate(s) attached to the bunker; an area not usually requiring engineering, resulting in most tank locomotives retaining their maker's plate(s) through to the end of service.

There were traps for the unwary. Boiler swaps often involved lifting the boiler from the locomotive with smokebox intact. The boiler was later repaired and often returned to another locomotive, effectively transferring the maker's plate from one locomotive to the other. Similarly, locomotive tenders were often swapped at depots or workshops, again effectively transferring any maker's plate on the tender rear from one locomotive to the other.

THE 'M' REBUILT PLATE

Unlike other countries where it was common to combine the road number and maker's plate details on a single plate, with one exception this did not occur on New Zealand Railways. The exception occurred with M 4 whereby the wording "Rebuilt At Addington Workshops" was applied to the number plate. None of the other three M class plates were similarly altered, nor were these locomotives allocated maker's numbers from the NZR sequence.

THE NZR REBUILT PLATE

Throughout the years as traffic and operating patterns changed or locomotive shortcomings were identified, the NZR undertook a surprising number of locomotive rebuilds or conversions. In doing so it became general policy for rebuilt or converted locomotives to have fitted what draughtsman R. Pye Smith labelled the 'rebuilt plate'.

Drawn by R. Pye Smith in 1892 for F^A 242 and later rebuilds or conversions, these plates were generally affixed to the bunker rear of the locomotives. Somewhat smaller than the standard NZR maker's plate, the year and workshop name was changed to suit. In the instances of tender to tank locomotive conversion (W^A and W^E class), the plate lettering was changed from 'rebuilt' to 'converted'. The only workshop to place the maker's number on the plate was Addington; Hillside, Newmarket and Petone all omitted the sequential numbers from these plates.

Generally New Zealand Railways treated rebuilt locomotives as 'new' locomotives and allocated maker's numbers from the NZR series. For the researcher though the most frustrating thing about 'rebuilt' plates was the lack of consistency in their use. For example, the F to F^A/F^B rebuilding project was spread through five workshops, the NZR issued maker's numbers to all affected locomotives. However, only some locomotives (Numbers 9, 10, 186, 242, 244 and 251) are known to have received 'rebuilt' plates.

A similar situation occurred with the L/L^A rebuilds. Of the seven locomotives rebuilt, only 206, 264 and 266 had 'rebuilt' plates, 91 and 205 lacked any maker's plates, 265 had a standard NZR maker's plate on the bunker rear, and 267 displaying both 'rebuilt' plates on the smokebox with a standard NZR maker's plate on the rear.

ABOVE: Placed on the bunker rear of W^E 376, this 'converted' plate, a variation of the 'rebuilt' plate, were usually devoid of builder's number. Addington, Hillside, Newmarket and Petone cast plates with their own workshop name to adorn various rebuilt or converted locomotives.

One further interesting example is the conversion of J 120 into W^A 120. Converted plates were affixed to the bunker sides bearing Addington's name. Certainly Addington built the boiler but the locomotive conversion was undertaken at Hillside. As with all of the J to W^A and the B to W^E conversions, the NZR never issued maker's numbers to these locomotives.

Number Plates and Maker's Plates - 187

THE HILLSIDE W^AB CONVERTED PLATE

It was during 1947-48 that Hillside converted eight W^AB's into A^B's. It is known that at least five of these locomotives (786, 787, 791, 792 and 795) had a rather different maker's plate affixed. An interesting departure from the standard NZR maker's plate, these plates had the words 'W^AB Converted' added directly below the sequential number and date, and the word 'Built' had been modified to read 'Rebuilt', thus the plate read 'Rebuilt Hillside Workshops'.

An error occurred when the rebuilt plates cast for A^B 792 were given maker's number 230. Number 230 was already allocated to W^AB 770 but the error was not corrected until boiler repairs resulted in removal of the maker's plate.

Three further W^AB to A^B conversions were passed out by Hillside in 1957 but all of these locomotives were devoid of maker's plates.

THE STANDARD NZR MAKER'S PLATE

First appearing on the bunker side of W 192 in 1889, this design remained basically unchanged until the last maker's plates were cast for J^A 1274 in 1956. Cast in leaded gunmetal and painted bright red, they were affixed by the various workshops in positions which differed by locomotive class or workshop. Further variation occurred in regard to the number of plates per locomotive; this varied from none at all to four per locomotive.

ADDINGTON WORKSHOPS MAKER'S PLATES

Rebuilds: 12
Locos Built New: 114
Total Built: 126

Addington became regarded as the home of the NZR locomotive and produced some undoubtedly famous engines. From W 192's completion in 1889 through to 1897, Addington affixed one maker's plate to each of the bunker sides of the classes W, W^A and F^A. With the building new of the six class F^B in 1902 and 1903, Addington changed the position of the maker's plates and instead affixed a solitary maker's plate to the rear of the bunker of these locomotives.

Preceding this, Addington commenced building the first home-grown tender locomotives in 1894; the U class. This started a long tradition of Addington placing the maker's plate on the rear of the tender, a tradition that would cease when Addington built its last steam locomotive over thirty years later.

Again, for the class B in 1899, Addington placed a solitary maker's plate on the rear of the tender. By this stage Addington was over committed and had transferred the W^A programme to Hillside, causing some disorder in the series of maker's numbers which until then had been controlled in an orderly fashion by Addington. This was to cause Hillside to issue W^A 288 with maker's number 27 which meantime had been issued by Addington to B 304. To rectify this, Addington subsequently allocated B 304 maker's number 43 but the maker's plate remained unchanged, B 304 retaining maker's plate number 27 on the rear of the tender.

Ten class W^F followed in 1904 and 1905 with one maker's plate being affixed to each side of the bunker.

Then commenced a period of intense activity for Addington which would last to the end of steam

ABOVE: Addington's latter day steam era plate is typified here on their last built steam locomotive, A^B 785. The workshop name has now been included on the plate, previously being cast as 'Built At Railway Workshops'.

locomotive building in 1926, a twenty year period when they would complete seventy-five locomotives.

At the time of building the famous A class Pacific's in 1906, an alteration was made to the maker's plate; the word 'Railway' was deleted and replaced by the workshop name, thus now reading 'Built At Addington Workshops'. Following were two separate builds of the compound class X, totalling eighteen locomotives. Next was a batch of ten class B^A, and then Addington's famous class A^B, a run that would eventually total thirty-eight locomotives. All of these locomotives had the Addington maker's plate affixed to each side of the smokebox and also on the rear of the tender. Of all the class A^B locomotives built, only the Addington built A^B's had a maker's plate in this location.

During 1917-18 Addington built the first two class W^{AB} locomotives using some of the components previously cast for the last two A^B locomotives of the second batch. Because three plates were cast for each A^B locomotive, these two W^{AB}'s found themselves decorated with one maker's plate on each side of the cab plus one on the bunker rear (Hillside and A & G Price W^{AB}'s were all devoid of a maker's plate on the bunker rear).

Addington ceased their tradition of placing maker's plates on the rear of their steam locomotives with the completion of their last steam loco, A^B 785 in 1926.

NEWMARKET WORKSHOPS MAKER'S PLATES

Rebuilds: 9
Locomotives Built New: 1
Total Built: 10

The necessity to expedite the F to F^A and L rebuild programme in the early 1890s resulted in Newmarket completing a number of rebuilds.

Newmarket's only claim to actually building a new locomotive rests with F^A 276. Allocated builder's number 37 of 1896, F^A 276 sported a standard style maker's plate which differed by having a slightly different elliptical shape and finer lettering. As usual for the time, the plate was devoid of the workshop name.

ABOVE: Fitted to Newmarket's only locomotive built new, F^A 276, this plate differs slightly from the standard NZR pattern by having a different elliptical shape and finer lettering.

PETONE WORKSHOPS MAKER'S PLATES

Rebuilds: 7
Locomotives Built New: 4
Total Built: 11

Petone was responsible for erecting many of the overseas-built locomotives shipped to New Zealand in 'knocked-down' form and also undertook some of the class F/F^A and L rebuilds. It has to its credit however only a small number of locomotives built new.

In 1903 Petone built three new class L locomotives. All three were allocated builder's numbers and standard maker's plates were affixed to the bunker sides. Unfortunately L 219 was allocated number 52 which had previously been issued by Addington to F^A 374 in 1902. This was rectified in 1913 by allocating maker's number 162 to L 219 and casting replacement maker's plates.

ABOVE: The second or 'true' maker's plate for L 219 is shown here. While this plate was cast in 1913 it correctly shows the year the locomotive was built.

The only other new locomotive completed at Petone was the infamous E 66. Again maker's plates were affixed to the bunker sides. As was the practice for the period, all of Petone's standard maker's plates were devoid of the workshop name.

HUTT WORKSHOPS MAKER'S PLATES

Rebuilds: NIL
Locomotives Built New: 77
Total Built: 77

Late to appear on the scene, Hutt was built to replace the ageing Petone Workshops in the late 1920s and was set up principally as a locomotive erection and heavy repair workshop.

Often referred to as Woburn, Hutt commenced their first building job in close co-operation with Hillside, with each workshop completing a batch of twelve class C heavy shunters. Fitted with standard maker's plates to the smokebox right hand side, the Hutt class C differed in detail from the Hillside equivalents as Hutt also placed a further maker's plate above the rear headstock on the tender toolbox.

Hutt then commenced the class K 4-8-4 building programme which required Hillside to provide extensive castings. As with the class C, Hutt placed a maker's plate on the smokebox right hand side and the tender rear, the left hand side of the smokebox being devoid of a maker's plate.

Upon completion of the class K, Hutt then commenced their part in the K^A building programme which involved both Hillside and Vulcan Foundry of Manchester supplying Hutt with various components. Hutt was also responsible for the manufacture of various components and the ultimate erection of all the locomotives. This time the locomotives wore a streamlined casing and Hutt placed maker's plates on both sides of the streamlining on a flat surface in the smokebox area. Again a maker's plate was affixed to the rear of the tender.

During the de-streamlining process, which occurred later, it appears that many K^A's lost their maker's plates, these not being refitted to the smokebox sides.

ABOVE: Typical of all standard NZR maker's plates cast by Hutt, the workshop name was never used, instead retaining the 'railway workshops' designation favoured in earlier years by other workshops.

Hutt's industrious, but short (twenty year), period of locomotive building concluded with the completion of two Baker valve gear K^A's, 958 and 959, in 1950. By exception neither of these locomotives were fitted with maker's plates.

Throughout the period of steam locomotive manufacture Hutt followed the earlier standard pattern of maker's plate, casting their plates 'Railway Workshops', unlike Addington and Hillside who had long before added their name to the plates.

HILLSIDE WORKSHOPS MAKER'S PLATES

Rebuilt: 21
Locomotives Built New: 165
Total Built: 186

Hillside may be attributed with producing the greatest number of locomotives of any workshop in New Zealand, the greatest number of tank locomotives produced and, of course, as the last builder of steam locomotives in New Zealand. From commencement of building W^A's in 1897 until completion of the W^{AB}'s in 1926, Hillside had built only tank locomotives, a total of one hundred and twelve.

190 - Number Plates and Maker's Plates

Starting with their first locomotive, W^A 165 of 1897, Hillside affixed the standard NZR maker's plate to the bunker rear. All other Hillside W^A locomotives had the maker's plates attached to each side of the bunker.

In 1907 Hillside commenced production of a batch of sixteen class W^F locomotives. It was at this time Hillside modified their maker's plates, replacing the word 'Railway' with 'Hillside', thus reading 'Built At Hillside Workshops'. These plates were affixed to both sides of the bunker, although W^F 403 carried a solitary maker's plate on the bunker rear for most of its life, the result of a collision with P 133 at Dunedin.

A large run totalling seventy W^G and W^W locomotives was then produced over a period of nine years. All locomotives had a standard maker's plate affixed to the bunker sides but some of the plates cast during World War One had the final date either left off or amended before outshopping. Manpower shortages, material shortages and a decree by the Government of the day that components could not be imported from enemy countries, meant that the specified Schmidt superheaters could not be used. The delay in securing alternative Robinson's superheaters to complete the batch from W^W 668 through to 681 plus 685 resulted in their late completion at Hillside. In these instances the final number of the year was soldered or brass riveted onto the plate just prior to completion. This also happened at other times and it is not uncommon to find NZR maker's plates so treated.

Twenty W^S and W^{AB} heavy tank locomotives were then produced between 1923 and 1926. The first ten had maker's plates fitted to the bunker sides while the second batch of ten had maker's plates affixed to both the bunker sides and smokebox sides, a total of four plates per locomotive.

The production of the Hillside class C followed in 1930. While Hutt labelled their locomotives with a maker's plate on the smokebox right hand side and tender rear, Hillside contented themselves with a solitary maker's plate on the smokebox right hand side.

Next followed the Garratt rebuild programme of six 4-6-2 class G locomotives. This extensive rebuild resulted in Hillside allocating builder's numbers and casting standard plates. As before, a solitary maker's plate was affixed to the smokebox right hand side.

On the heels of the class G came the K^A building project with some associated work done on behalf of Hutt. Much of this work dovetailed into the six K^B locomotives allocated to Hillside for completion. Unlike the Hutt K^A's, Hillside did not affix any maker's plates to the streamlined sheathing, thus the K^B's ran devoid of smokebox maker's plates throughout their lives. A solitary maker's plate was fitted to the rear of the tender.

Finally for Hillside was the batch of thirty-five J^A locomotives. Material shortages from broken supply lines found the first seven locomotives being completed in 1947 with 1945 and 1946 maker's plates. In what may be considered a departure from Hillside practice on tender locomotives, Hillside placed maker's plates on both sides of the smokebox. Confusion arose when four J^A's (1265-1268) were built out of sequence for Christchurch. Hillside cast maker's plates with numbers 379-382 instead of 388-391; the latter numbers subsequently were never used. When Hillside resumed building more Dunedin division J^A's commencing with J^A 1256, the correct numbers for this group were used (379-382), thus duplicating these numbers.

ABOVE: As evident on this plate from W^A 68, Hillside used the 'railway workshops' designation prior to 1907. Cast without a final year of manufacture, the '3' has been made of brass separately and soldered on prior to the locomotive's completion.

BELOW: Showing the 'Hillside' designation, this plate from W^W 680 was cast in 1917. Presumably due to the effects of war delaying completion, the '7' has been ground off the date suffix and a separate brass '9' soldered on.

Finally, Hillside cast their last maker's plates for a new steam locomotive, J^A 1274, in 1956. If unnumbered rebuilds are taken into account, New Zealand Railways had by then produced over 400 steam locomotives, most of which had proudly displayed their maker's plates and number plates from passing out of the workshops until meeting with 'rotten row'.

BELOW: Q 345 resting at Frankton, proudly displaying her Baldwin smokebox number plate. August 1922. (W. W. Stewart)

CHAPTER TWELVE

A GOOD MANY BRAINS AT WORK

By R. D. GRANT, F.I.P.E.N.Z (Retired)

WHO DESIGNED OUR EARLY LOCOMOTIVES?

Who indeed, for the early 3 foot 6 inch gauge locomotives were a fairly heterogeneous lot. Charles Rous-Marten writing in the "Railway Magazine" in 1899 supposed "that there must have been a good many brains at work, seeing that within a very brief period after the start, the New Zealand Railways found themselves the proud possessors of no fewer than twenty different types of engine". To a degree he was correct.

The first locomotives ordered by the General Government in 1871 were initially schemed by District Engineer W. N. Blair of the Public Works Department's (PWD) Dunedin Office. Engineer-in-Chief John Carruthers, fresh from railway construction in Canada, USA, Russia and Mauritius took up his appointment in mid 1871 and it was his hand that steered the Department until 1878. The Government's consulting engineers in London, Messrs. Hemans and Bruce had their input into designs. The Otago Railways initially engaged Robert Fairlie as their consulting engineer and he too has left his mark. The greatest contributions to early New Zealand locomotive design came from the builders themselves, notably Neilson and Company, the Avonside Engine Company, the Rogers Locomotive and Machine Works and the Baldwin Locomotive Works.

There was a rationale in the choice of the locomotives for the operating conditions perceived in the various sections of railway initially constructed. The Hope Gibbons fire of 1952 destroyed practically all the early PWD correspondence. While much can be explained and inferred from other sources, the complete account remains to be unravelled.

The railway from Dunedin to the Clutha River crossing was among the first projects of the 1870 Public Works and Immigration Scheme. Practically all the arrangements for the work, the location of the line, its construction, the provision of locomotives and rolling stock, were initially undertaken by the Dunedin District Office of the PWD, under Mr. W. N. Blair, while the Department itself was in the process of formation. Blair, whose specification notebooks are currently held in National Archives (reference W17/1 and W17/2), was obviously most interested in locomotives and railway plant. As well as recording current locomotive specifications, the notebooks are a mine of information on locomotives and railway construction, both in New Zealand and overseas.

The requirement for locomotives, approved by John Blackett, the acting Engineer-in-Chief, in April 1871 and forwarded through the Agent General in London to Hemans and Bruce to arrange construction, specified a six-coupled tank locomotive suitable to run on 40 pounds per yard rail, of loaded weight of 17 tons and capable of hauling a gross load of 100 tons over 1 in 50 grades. Curves of 10 to 12 chains radius needed to be negotiated. Cylinders $10^{1/2}$ inches diameter by 18 inches stroke, wheels 3 feet diameter, wheelbase 10 feet 6 inches and a boiler heating surface of about 500 square feet were specified. A sketch drawing of the general arrangement of the locomotive accompanied the outline specification.

Hemans prepared a single general arrangement drawing and drew up a general specification to enable competitive tenders to be called from locomotive builders. The preferred tenderer, Neilson and Company, then prepared detailed working drawings for Hemans' approval before construction could commence. A typical Scottish ogee tanked locomotive resulted. Neilson built five of them initially, and their working drawings were adopted as standard by both the consulting engineers and the PWD. In all, eighty eight of these very useful engines were built to Neilson's drawings by various builders between 1872 and 1888. When classification was introduced, these became class F. Over the next few years, some variations on the F resulted and it would be as well to deal with these now.

The Dunedin and Clutha locomotives had been designed for 10 chain curves. As further railway surveys progressed into more broken country, notably the west slope of the Rimutakas, the deep valleys of the Palmerston North to Wanganui line and the Tuapeka (Lawrence) branch to the Gabriel's Gully goldfields, it became obvious that curves down to five chains radius would have to be resorted to in order to keep construction costs within economical bounds. The 10 feet 6 inch rigid wheelbase of the F design could handle this only with difficulty. Excessive tyre wear, and worse, derailments were the order of the day.

Several solutions to this problem were put in hand, but that which concerns us now were the January and March 1875 contracts which called for twenty-six F type locomotives in which a half inch lateral play was to be given to the leading axle by means of Cartazzi's patent radial axleboxes. Both contracts were undertaken by the Avonside Engine Company, Bristol and they were fitted with Widmark's radial axle box, a scheme almost identical with the Cartazzi. Mr. Widmark was Avonside's chief draughtsman. This F variation was classified O, although the actual classification seems to have become confused between various sections of railway. Whether further F's were built in this way or subsequently altered to a more flexible wheelbase, I am unable to say at present.

As a further variation, one of the Avonside locomotives, O 40, ran for a while with the leading coupling rods removed, thus being a 2-4-0ST. Whether it produced a better result other than a loss of adhesive weight, I do not know.

A 2-4-0T had been considered for the easier sections of the Dunedin and Clutha Railway until it was realised that the 0-6-0T was capable of all that was required. A 2-4-0T design keeps recurring in the early years. The first revival was for a 2-4-0T otherwise identical to the F design and taken to specification stage by Hemans for the Picton to Blenheim Railway in January 1872. However, that month instructions were sent from New Zealand to cancel the specification and to prepare one for what became the class C 0-4-0ST. Possibly the same specification was resurrected later that year for four locomotives for the comparatively straight and easily graded Rakaia to Ashburton section. The Picton to Blenheim specification had called for a leading truck of "two wheels, thirty inch in diameter on a Bissell bogie or other approved system of radiating the wheels on curves". The consulting engineers substituted a four-wheeled Bissell truck as being more suitable for the higher speeds expected on the Canterbury Plains. Black Hawthorn were the builders and the locomotives, apart from cosmetic differences, were identical with the Neilson 0-6-0ST's. The 4-4-0ST's were classified G and were noted as fast enough with light trains but liable to lose their feet with a heavy load.

The final 2-4-0T variation on the F were the "locomotive tank engines, $10^{1/2}$ inch cylinder, 4 wheels coupled with Bissell's bogie at the leading end" as Hemans and Bruce's specification of May 1877 put it. The consultants drawing, N° 3611, shows a neat 2-4-0 side tanker and further drawings show the arrangements for a two wheeled Bissell truck.

Again, the boiler, cylinders, wheels etc. were to be identical with the F's and Neilson's original drawings for these as adopted by the PWD. These were enumerated and specified, though some allowance could be made in positioning the cylinders to accommodate the Bissell truck. Again Avonside were the successful tenderers, Widmark's radial axle box was substituted for the Bissell truck, the cylinders stayed in place and to improve stability at speed the coupled wheelbase was lengthened. The class L, as they became, were successful suburban tank engines, particularly in the Wellington area.

Thus we have a number of classes; F, O, G and L, all of which were variations on a theme by Neilson; or was Blair the composer?

Another early order, that of January 8 1872, was for locomotives for the 'feeder railways' of Canterbury, these being branches from the main line originally planned as horse tramways. Rails of only 30 pounds per yard were intended and this required a very light locomotive to haul passenger and goods trains of only 50 tons or so on comparatively level lines. In this service, the class A 0-4-0T's were perfectly successful and the fertile plains of Canterbury were thus opened up for agriculture. Dubs and Company of Glasgow, were responsible for this design.

A similar case where the design was completely left to the manufacturer was that for the class C 0-4-0ST's. It appears that no drawing was supplied by either the PWD or by Hemans and Bruce. The outline specification of January 23 1872 asked for ten four-wheeled contractors engines, weighing 12 tons in working trim with a wheelbase of not more than six feet. The few specifics noted that the cylinders were to be $9^{1/2}$ inches by 18 inches, wheels 30 inch diameter and boiler pressure 130 pounds per square inch. Possibly 'off the shelf' manufacturers standard types were sought. Neilson and Company got the contract.

In slow moving construction service, the engines were adequate enough but once they were passed into general traffic they rapidly got a bad name for unsteady riding even at moderate speeds, being known as 'grasshoppers'. The ailment was cured by adding a trailing truck. Even so, many of the C's were relegated to shunting service as soon as steadier locomotives were available.

194 - A Good Many Brains at Work

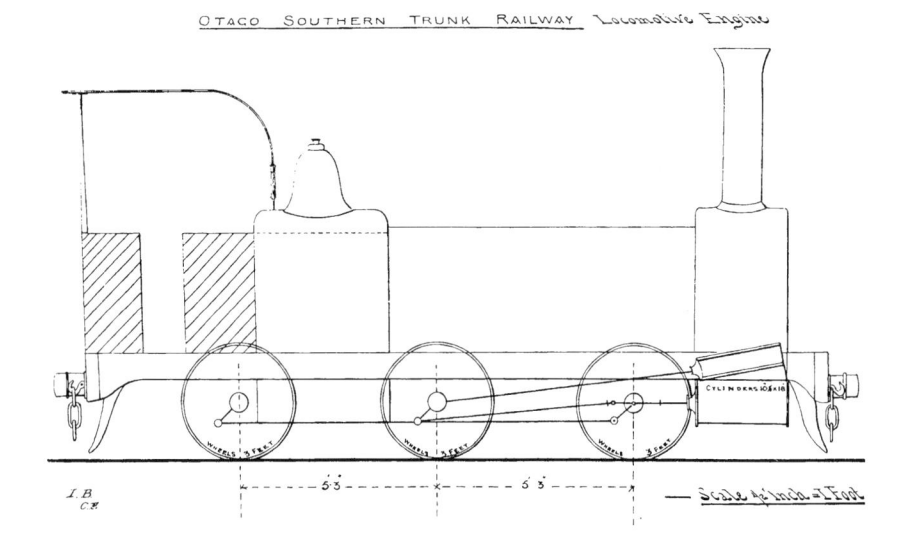

LEFT: The Dunedin Office of the Public Works Department produced the concept sketch for a locomotive for the Otago Southern Trunk Railway in April 1871. John Blackett, the acting Engineer-in-Chief, approved it, signing it "J.B.,C.E.".
AJHR D6 1871, Hocken Library, Dunedin

RIGHT: The Avonside version of class F, known in Otago as class O, was fitted with Cartazzi's lateral-motion leading axleboxes. F 40 ran experimentally with the leading siderods removed to test its suitability for working express trains. Palmerston, about 1879.
(W. W. Stewart Collection)

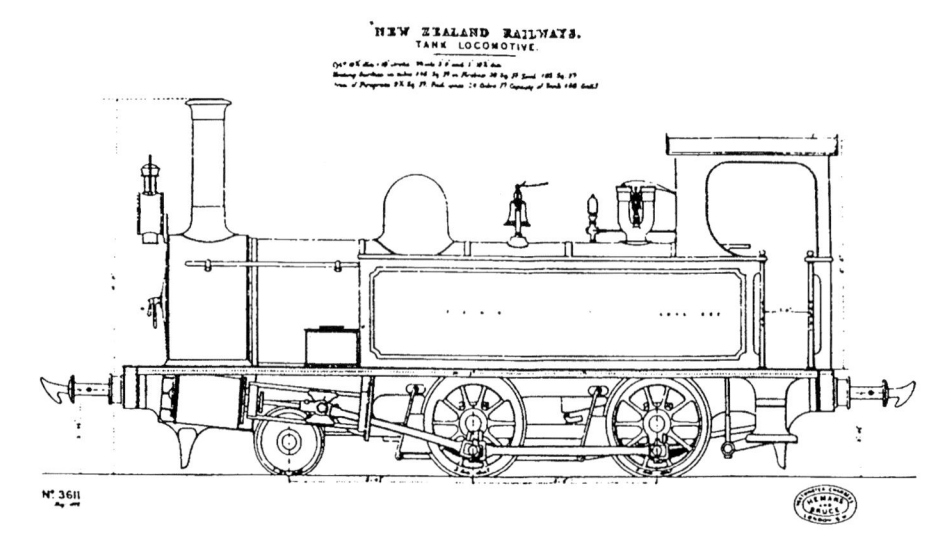

LEFT: Hemans and Bruce, consulting engineers' drawing No 3611 was used to invite tenders for the future class L 2-4-0T. The Avonside Engine Company's draughtsmen would prepare working drawings from the consultant's specification and this drawing. The class L as built is illustrated on page 52.
(National Archives File W17/2)

Much more care was taken in the specification for the small Bissell-trucked 2-4-0 side tankers of 1874; the class D. An outline general arrangement drawing was prepared along with a fairly complete specification. Again Neilson got the contract and prepared detailed drawings to Hemans' approval. It has been claimed by C. Hamilton Ellis in his "Some Classic Locomotives" that the D design was similar to Beyer Peacock's successful 2-4-0T's for the 3 foot 6 inch gauge Norwegian Railways. While prudent designers take careful note of their fellows' successful designs, the similarity of the steeply inclined outside cylinders was probably about the total of the points of resemblance. These would have been so placed in both designs to clear the Bissell truck when traversing a sharp curve. They were successful little engines with a good turn of speed while able to tread lightly on 30 pound branch line rails. They continued on light services well into the twentieth century.

The origins of the first 'big locomotives', the so called 'Canterbury goods' 2-6-0's, class J, remains a story yet to be unravelled. By 1873, traffic on the 5 foot 3 inch gauge Canterbury Railways was already heavy, notably with the port traffic to and from Lyttelton. These were the 'bonanza wheat' days when New Zealand exported grain grown on the lands newly accessible by rail. The broad-gauge locomotives were of greater power than any of the narrow-gauge locomotives. Canterbury interests were only too ready to point this out. In their opinion, narrowing the gauge could only contribute to further seasonal transport chaos.

The origins of what was in fact one of the largest narrow-gauge 2-6-0's in the world at the time of its construction can at present only be guessed at. What evidence there is points to the Avonside Engine Company of Bristol as not only the detailed designers and constructors but probably the originators of the concept of a large 2-6-0. What instructions they were given and what was the basis of the contract we do not know.

The company had recently built 4-4-0, 2-6-0 and 4-6-0 locomotives for the 3 foot 6 inch gauge Toronto, Grey and Bruce and Toronto and Nipissing Railways in Canada. While these were British built, the general design of all three types was American in concept and layout and the resemblance to our J is quite marked. Cylinder placing, wheel spacing and general details follow American practice while the plate frames and parallel sided boiler follows British practice. The 14 by 20 inch cylinders were as large as those of any narrow gauge 2-6-0 of the day anywhere. The drawings were approved by John Carruthers as standard PWD plans. Further contracts were then opened to other builders and Stephenson, Dubs, Neilson and the Vulcan Foundry all built J's.

The Fell locomotives of 1875, thanks to full discussions on them at the Institution of Civil Engineers, we know to be entirely an Avonside design based on a performance specification. Practically the only requirement was that two locomotives coupled together must be capable of hauling 100 tons exclusive of their own weight up an incline of 1 in 15 while the boiler pressure must be 130 pounds per square inch as with other New Zealand locomotives.

At the time, the Fell centre rail system was the only practical means of working a steep gradient other than a rope-worked incline. Fell railways had operated over the Alps via the Mont Cenis Pass from 1868 and were also running in Brazil. In spite of this, Fell had not perfected a completely reliable locomotive for his system and tended to favour two cylinder derived-drive machines whose complication practically invited regular mechanical breakages.

The Avonside Company were under no illusions about the earlier Fell locomotive shortcomings. Mr. Wilson, the manager of the company, in discussing the New Zealand engines said "The usual drawings could not be supplied. Fell central rail locomotives had been manufactured before, chiefly on the Continent, but they had all been more or less failures. A few odd tracings of parts of these machines were seen but they were entirely put aside and these four engines were designed 'de novo'. The largest share of the credit was due to Mr. H. W. Widmark, chief draughtsman of the Avonside Company". These, and the repeat order from Neilson and Company in 1886, were the only completely successful Fell locomotives ever built. Meantime rack railways on both the Riggenbach and the Abt systems were established all over the world over the next two decades while no further Fell line was ever built. Fell's system could have been just as successful if Fell himself had only spent the time to "take the bugs" out of his system.

Robert Fairlie's contribution to New Zealand locomotive history included both his double and single Fairlie bogie engines, but his more enduring legacy was the introduction of Walschaert valve gear which he favoured. Following the famous trials on the narrow-gauge Ffestiniog Railway with the double engine *Little Wonder* in 1870, the Fairlie principle was widely acclaimed and Fairlie himself was sought after as a consulting engineer for railways worldwide. Among these was the Dunedin and Port Chalmers Railway Company. While the water level route was undemanding, it caused no surprise to anyone that the company's motive power were Fairlie double locomotives, *Josephine* and *Rose*.

The double boiler locomotive with greater boiler power and the use of all wheels for adhesion was in its element on steep gradients with sharp curvature. The initial cost in relation to a conventional locomotive of similar power was high indeed as might be expected with the doubling up of most components. Regardless of this, Fairlie in his consulting work generally specified his double locomotives whatever the terrain. The Fairlie Engine and Rolling Stock Company designed both his double and single bogie locomotives for construction by outside firms and this is the aegis under which his locomotives for New Zealand were built.

Fairlie continued an association with the Otago Railways. When the Port Chalmers line was bought out by the Government, an early project was the motive power for the light branch railways which were to be laid with only 28 pounds per yard iron rail. On November 14 1873, Macandrew, the Otago Provincial Superintendent, sent particulars to the Otago Agent in Edinburgh of the "light locomotive to be constructed under the direction of R. F. Fairlie Esq. in accordance with his system of the Double Bogie ... The locomotive now ordered is intended for one of our light branch lines and if it turns out as I expect will no doubt be the forerunner of a great many of the same sort".

The Fairlie Engine Company's smallest standard design, that for a 9 inch by 16 inch cylinder double engine locomotive was put in hand by the Avonside Engine Company. On completion in September 1874, an independent consulting engineer, Mr. Robert May, was to trial it and report. We do not know what the original specifications were but Mr. May considered the weight of the locomotive to be far in excess of that which was ordered. Macandrew's opinion was that it was too heavy to be used on the Awamoko Line (Duntroon branch) for which it was intended. Macandrew perhaps would have been wiser to have followed Canterbury's lead and ordered further class A 0-4-0T's for the Awamoko, Waiareka and Outram branches. The cost of an A locomotive would have been only a third of the £2840 that the Fairlie cost. A class D 2-4-0T was borrowed from the General Government to work the branch. The Fairlie, which became class B *Lady Mordaunt*, had already been shipped and strange to say later spent some time on the 30 pound per yard rails of the Sheffield branch in Canterbury with no reported ill effects to the track.

In the meantime, James Davidson of the Otago Foundry had the Hunslet Engine Company design a light 8 inch by 15 inch cylinder six-coupled saddle tank and construct certain parts towards the assembly of three engines in Dunedin as a private speculation. One of them went to the Awamoko. The price was £1200 each. One went to the Kaitangata Coal Co. while the remaining two were later classified P following the abolition of Provincial Governments.

There was a real need for Fairlie locomotives with the sharper curvature and steeper grades that had to be adopted in the Dunedin, Wellington and Wanganui areas, and as we have seen these were to give the class F 0-6-0ST's a certain amount of grief. A General Government order of 1874 called for six double Fairlies and was routed through the Agent General and consulting engineers, Hemans and Bruce. The drawings, and probably much of the specification, were the work of the Fairlie Engine and Rolling Stock Company though finally it was Hemans' and Bruce's specification that went out to tender.

The locomotives were in many ways more up to date versions of the Port Chalmers locomotives and again were a Fairlie Engine Company standard design with 10 inch by 18 inch cylinders and 3 foot 3 inch wheels. Walschaert valve gear was fitted as was that for the overweight light lines *Lady Mordaunt*. Fairlie was among the first in Britain to realise the possibilities of this arrangement. The new Fairlies, along with the Port Chalmers engines, became class E. Again Avonside got the contract. The locomotives were delivered to the three railway sections concerned, although later it became more advantageous to concentrate all the double Fairlies on the Wanganui section where they worked well into the twentieth century until superseded by class W^A 2-6-2T's.

A more conventional type was the Single Fairlie which was still a double bogie engine which again articulated separately from the main engine frame. A deep and most effective firebox was possible, thanks to the bogie configuration. The Single Fairlie was just as capable of negotiating sharp curvature as a double engine and could be designed to exert considerable power. Its cost was only about two thirds of that required for a commensurate double engine, in fact not a great deal more than that for a conventional locomotive. Fairlie did not exploit this design to its fullest. In the writer's opinion it had a great potential on difficult lightly constructed railways, though the Americans were soon to demonstrate that there were even simpler means of constructing powerful locomotives that could still hold the track on difficult alignments.

A Good Many Brains at Work - 197

RIGHT: This preliminary sketch for the class R 0-6-4T was probably prepared by the Fairlie Engine and Rolling Stock Company for Public Work Department approval prior to being handed to the consulting engineers.

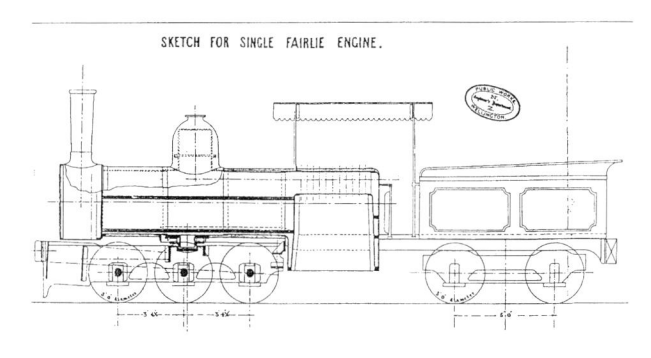

RIGHT: Almost certainly a consultant's drawing accompanying an invitation to tender. This detailed drawing quotes PWD order "Memo 105/77". The class R is illustrated on page 53.
(Both drawings from the E. J. McClare Collection)

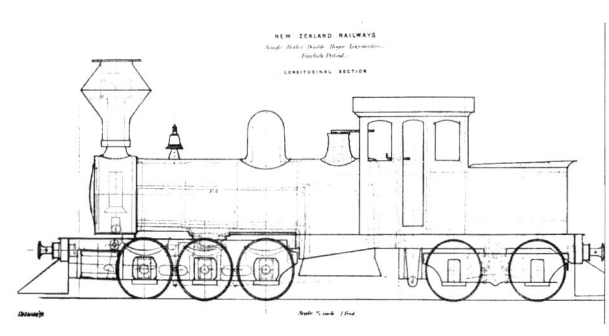

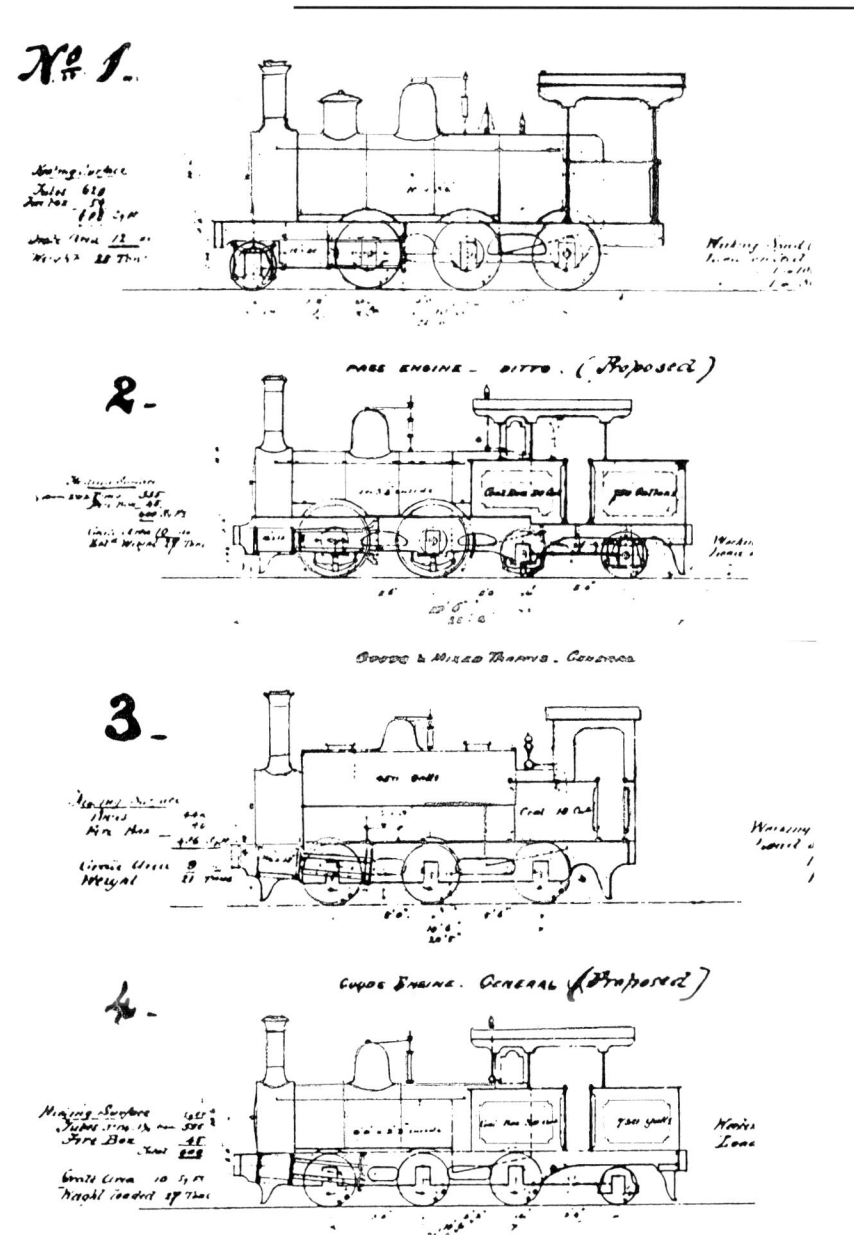

LEFT: The four drawings, numbers 1-4, are H. P. Higginson's first design essay for main line locomotives. Nº 2, the 0-4-4T passenger locomotive was developed into the 0-4-2 tender locomotive in the second version, whilst the 0-6-2T goods locomotive eventually appeared as class F^A in 1897.
(Developed from a mutilated PWD Drawing, W. G. Lloyd Collection)

198 - A Good Many Brains at Work

The original Single Fairlies of 1869 were a product of the Great Southern and Western Railway's Inchicore Works in Ireland. While the design was well reported to the Institution of Civil Engineers in 1873, Britain's railways with their easy curvature and gradients had little requirement for such machines. In America, the type was taken up by William Mason and 'Mason Bogies', as the type was known in the USA, could be found on New England branch lines, Long Island suburban service and the lightly tracked heavily graded trails of the Colorado Rocky Mountains.

The order for eighteen six-coupled Single Fairlies of December 1877 is believed to have originated in a personal preference from John Carruthers, the PWD Engineer-in-Chief. When the order was passed to the consulting engineers, Hemans, Falkner and Tancred as the consulting firm had now become, the consultants wrote back recommending double engines as being more suitable for this particular order. Carruthers stuck to his guns and the Fairlie Engine Company prepared the drawings. Hemans called for tenders. The lowest bid of £1760 was that of Sharp Stewart and Company who had successfully built Fairlie Engines in the past. Robert Fairlie was consulted about the tenders and Sharp Stewart's bid was passed over in favour of that of the Avonside Engine Company at £1840 each. There is probably a story behind this as Sharps never built another Fairlie engine. Be that as it may, the single Fairlies, class R, were a thorough on-going success on difficult routes, powerful good steamers and well liked by their crews. What amounted to a repeat order with improvements, class S, followed two years later.

By 1876, the linking by rail of the three South Island cities of Christchurch, Dunedin and Invercargill was close at hand. Passenger locomotives would be required and Harry P. Higginson, Superintending Engineer for South Island Railways, outlined his proposals for these on PWD drawing 5403 of November 25 1876. These were a rigid framed 0-4-2 tender engine with 12 inch by 20 inch cylinders and 48 inch driving wheels for the Canterbury Plains section and for Otago, a Bissell-trucked 2-4-0 tender engine of similar power but with 42 inch drivers. Higginson's pupillage had been with Sir William Fairburn and the proposals were reminiscent of Fairburn's very conservative locomotive designs. How these concepts were translated into the racy and up to date Rogers 2-4-2 is discussed in detail in Gerald Petrie's book "In the Beginning".

The credit for the introduction of American locomotives is often ascribed to Allison D. Smith, previously manager of the Wellington section, who was appointed Locomotive Engineer at Christchurch on April 10 1877 at age 23, replacing J. G. Warner who had resigned. Smith had served a locomotive engineering pupillage with the North British Railway under Thomas Wheatley. Before leaving for New Zealand he spent some weeks with the Westinghouse Continuous Air Brake Company, and while crossing America "Spent six weeks in visiting the best workshops in the USA. The information gained may no doubt be useful to the railways of this colony" as he put in his application for employment in the PWD.

The initial pair of American locomotives in New Zealand had their genesis in a report by John Carruthers to the Minister of Public Works, Edward Richardson of 30 May 1876, in which he said "It would, I think to be an advantage to get a couple of engines from America as an experiment. Although generally roughly finished, American engines do good work." Carruthers had spent some years on railways both in the USA and Canada before coming to New Zealand, notably on the Great Western Railway of Canada. The latter was an English financed concern which used American built 4-4-0's on passenger trains while British built rigid-framed inside-cylinder 0-6-0 tender locomotives, complete with wooden pilots and kerosene headlights, hauled freight trains across Ontario. His report was approved and an order for two locomotives was placed soon afterwards.

Allison D. Smith at the time was employed as traffic manager of the Wellington to Masterton railway which at that time extended to Upper Hutt only. Apart from his journey across America, he had no experience of American locomotives at all. Smith arrived in Christchurch in time to erect our first American locomotives and along with the other Canterbury locomotives was responsible for their day-to-day running and maintenance. He became an enthusiastic champion of American locomotives for New Zealand conditions.

All American locomotive builders were desperate for orders following the financial 'Panic of 1873' which effectively stopped investment in railroads and railroad plant. The Rogers Locomotive Works took to looking overseas for locomotive orders and engaged Mr. Walton W. Evans, a very respected New York railroad consulting engineer to assist them in this. In late 1876, Evans had written to the Victorian Government offering to design, arrange the building, oversee construction and ship to destination locomotives from the Rogers Works to the specification and requirements of the Victorian Railways. It seems very likely that a similar offer was made to the New Zealand Government, and that the design requirements set out by Higginson formed the basis for discussion.

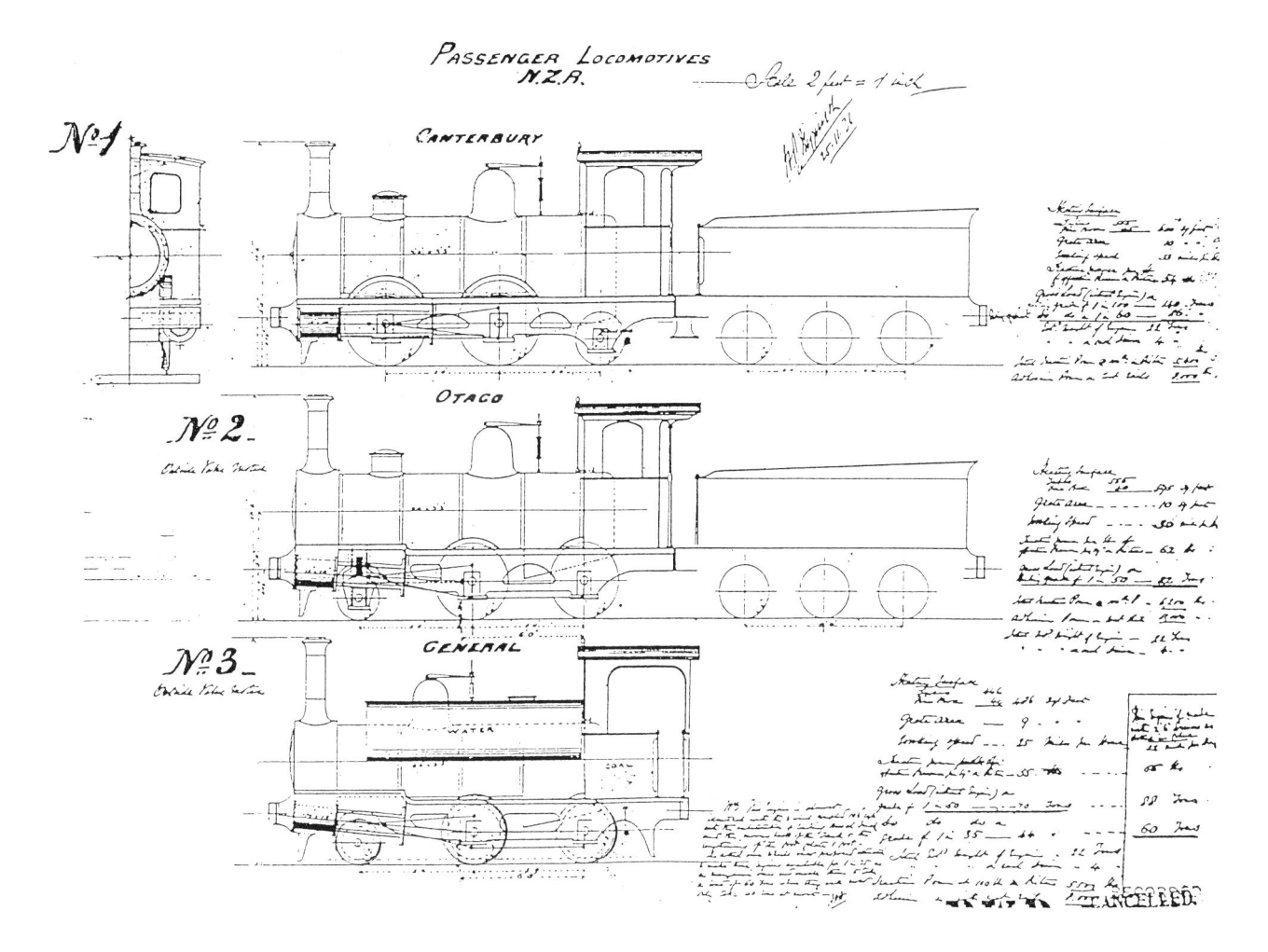

ABOVE: The second version, PWD Drawing 5403, signed by Harry Higginson on 25 November 1876 showing his proposals for South Island passenger Locomotives. Nº 1, a typically British plate-framed 0-4-2 locomotive was developed in America with bar-frames and a leading bogie to become the class K 2-4-2. Only Nº 3, the 2-4-0T was constructed more or less as shown as the class L. (PWD Drawing, A. C. Bellamy Collection)

BELOW: Class K locomotive *Lincoln* at Christchurch locomotive depot, 1879. (Moffatt Collection, Canterbury Museum)

We know that Evans was given the order for two locomotives, and while the 2-4-2 wheel arrangement is a long way off Higginson's somewhat archaic 0-4-2, the intended dimensions of cylinders, driving wheels, boiler diameter and length, the heating surfaces, the deep firebox, grate area and the expected tractive effort are very close, indeed in many cases identical to the final dimensions of the class K 2-4-2.

The K's were designed by William H. Hudson, the superintendent of Rogers works and incorporated many of his innovations to truck design, springing and his patented arrangement of compensated springing throughout, from the front Bissel truck to the driving wheel springs and on to the rear swinging truck. They are described in Forney's "Catechism of the Locomotive" as 'Hudson Double Ender Locomotives' and in the Rogers' catalogue as class DE. Speedy with a light load, they powered our first expresses until increasing train loads made six-coupled locomotives essential.

Even before the initial Rogers locomotives had arrived in New Zealand, a repeat order for six further machines was cabled to Evans. The *Dunedin Star* said of the locomotives "they will be capable of doing 25 to 35 miles per hour. Six of them will be used between Christchurch and Dunedin and two between Dunedin and Invercargill."

William Conyers, himself a locomotive man with experience at Kitson and Company, Hudswell Clarke and the East Indian Railway came to Southland to erect the standard-gauge locomotives for the Southland Provincial Council in 1863 and was appointed manager of the Otago Railways in May 1874. An early responsibility as such was to arrange for locomotives to work the Southland Railways when they were regauged to three feet six inches. Four six-coupled tank locomotives with 13 inch by 20 inch cylinders were ordered from the Hunslet Engine Company. The design was an excellent one, the engines being only slightly less powerful than the class J moguls. In January 1877 Conyers was appointed to the Public Works Department as Superintending Engineer for South Island Railways, succeeding Higginson who had resigned to take up private practice. Soon afterwards Smith was appointed to assist him as Locomotive Engineer, Christchurch. The following year the Working Railways Department, still attached to the Public Works Department, was formed and Conyers became Commissioner (or General Manager) for the South Island. A separate Railways Department was in the process of forming.

Conyers, no doubt with Smith's enthusiastic recommendations, ordered six American freight locomotives. Goods traffic was increasing markedly on the new trunk route as Conyers successfully competed with coastal shipping which hitherto had almost a monopoly on inter-settlement freight. Again this order appears to have been routed through Evans and was placed with the Baldwin Locomotive Works. Their standard class of 15 inch by 18 inch cylinder 2-8-0, Baldwin class 10-24-E was chosen. Baldwin's standard classes were already being assembled of preplanned component parts that suited various sizes and types of locomotive such that detailed working drawings of the particular locomotive order were not generally needed. The individual design work of the components was already worked out and all that was required was for a skeleton elevation of outlines only to be prepared and upon it references to the various cards, sketches and templates used in the construction for the particular order would be noted.

At the same time as the New Zealand order was being put through the works (class T), a batch of identical locomotives for the three feet gauge Denver and Rio Grande Railroad (D & RG class 56) was also under construction. For their day, the T's were powerful if slow brutes. The *Christchurch Press* of November 2 1880 records that a train of one hundred and seven loaded wagons totalling some 900 tons was taken from Heathcote to Christchurch at a speed of 10 miles per hour.

In that year the Public Works Department partially relinquished control of the railways. A separate Railways Department was established in its own right. A General Manager, J. P. Maxwell, was appointed on October 12 1880 with Smith becoming the initial Locomotive Superintendent. The New Zealand Government Railways Department was a going concern.

Charles Rous-Marten was quite right in his surmise that a good many brains were at work in choosing New Zealand's first locomotive types. There is no doubt that the numbers of types of locomotives in service could have been reduced by half at least if the differing interests, provincial governments, consulting engineers *et al* had all been brought together to a common purpose. At the same time it must be said that the best of the roster, the single Fairlies, the class J 2-6-0's, the class K passenger engines and the Baldwin consolidations were thoroughly efficient and up-to-date locomotives for their time, while the smaller engines, the ubiquitous class F 0-6-0ST's, the branch line class D 2-4-0T's and even the tiny light railway class A 0-4-0T dwarfs were appropriately chosen for the work they were intended to perform.

PHOTOGRAPH INDEX

Ada		14
Auckland section	Nº 1	9, 120
Auckland section	B 10	10
Auckland section	B 51	10
Auckland section	C 51	42
Auckland section	F 8	15
Auckland section	F 9	120
Auckland section	J 56	43
Auckland section	L 12	15
Auckland section	R 53	43
A 62		48
A 65 (diesel rebuild)		160
A 67		166
A 178		90
A 178 (rebuilt)		90
A 428		172
A^A 650		101
A^A 653 (rebuilt)		101
A^B 608		125
A^B 617		102
A^B 788		103
A^B (number unknown)		139
Bluff Harbour & Invercargill Rly.	Nº 1	4
Borthwicks & Co.	D 138	149
Branxholme locomotive dump		157
B 302		74
B 302 (modified)		74
B 303		75
B 303 (reboilered)		75
B^A 148		98
B^A 499		98
B^B 55		99
B^B 619		99
B^C 463		95
Canterbury Frozen Meat Co.	C 5	146
Canterbury Railways	Nº 21	24
Canterbury Railways	Nº 28	24
Castlecliff Railway	W^A 67	152
Christchurch		45
C 5 Canterbury Frozen Meat Co.		146
C 53 South Otago Freezing Co.		146
C 847		172
C 851		107
Dunedin & Port Chalmers Rly.	Nº 2	16
D 1		100
D 6 McDonald's Lime Co.		148
D 16 Waitaki Farmers' Freezing Co.		148
D 138 Borthwicks & Co.		149
D 140 Kempthorne Prosser		149
D 197		48
DS 2 Tasmanian Government Railways		153
E 66		100
E 175		166

F 13		168
F 40		194
F 74		49
F 226		127
F 248		49
F^A 41 Whakatane Board Mills		152
F^A 157		66
F^A 186		66
G 55 (4-4-0ST)		51
G 96 (4-6-2)		106
G 98 (4-6-2+2-6-4)		106
Hurunui-Bluff section	R 29	37
Hurunui-Bluff section	C 6	162
H 200		51
Invercargill Roundhouse		31
Josephine		16, 166
J 84		131
J 121		56
J 1212 (four photos)		114, 115
J^A 1243		143
J^A 1271		176
J^A 1274		116
J^A 1283		116
J^A Locomotive line-up		105
J^B 1236		176
Kaipara section	D 16	125
Kempthorne Prosser	D 140	149
K 87		199
K 94		57
K 900		110
K 900 (modernised)		110
K 919		111
K^A 935		111
K^A 942		174
K^A 955		143
K^A 958		112
K^B 970		112
Lincoln		199
L 207 (2-4-0T)		168
L 207 (4-4-2T)		84
L 219		52
L^A 267		67
L^A 313		67
M^{ac}Callum Mhor		120
McDonald's Lime Co.	D 6	148
Mazepa		121
Mount Egmont		121
M 89 (0-6-0T)		121
M 90 (2-4-4T)		52

Napier section	A 41	40	
Napier section	J 41	40	
NZ Midland Railway Co.	Nº 2	45	
N 27		61	
N 27 (rebuilt)		61	
N 353		84	
N 354 (dumped)		156	
N 453		94	
Ohai Railway Board	X 442	153	
Otago Railways	Nº 1	131	
Otago Railways	Nº 10	124	
Otago Railways	Nº 20	21	
Otago Railways	Nº 25	29	
Otago Railways	Nº 27	124	
O 99		62	
O^C 458		95	
Passchendaele		125	
Peveril		168	
P 269		62	
Q 51		57	
Q 343		82	
Q 344		82	
Q 345		191	
Q 346		83	
Q 350		83	
Rob Roy		124	
R 28 (derelict)		157	
R 271 (dumped)		156	
R 273		53	
Saladin		21	
Schnapper		125	
Snake		9, 120	
South Otago Freezing Co.	C 53	146	
Steam crane Nº 103		160	
S 214		53	
Tasmanian Government Railways	DS 2	153	
Taupiri Coal Co. (Hurunui-Bluff)	C 6	162	
T 102		56	
U 237		72	
U 237 (rebuilt)		72	
U^A 176		77	
U^B 17		81	
U^B 282		80	
U^B 329		135	
U^B 330		80	
U^B 371		81	
U^C 369		135	
U^C 369 (reboilered)		77	
U^D 464		94	
V 126		60	
V 132		60	
Waitaki Farmers' Freezing Co.	D 16	148	
Wanganui section	E 22	42	
Weka		124	
Wellington & Manawatu Railway	Nº 6	45	
Wellington section	H 6	127	
Wellington section	H 37	121	
Wellington section	S 6	37	
Whakatane Board Mill	F^A 41	152	
W 192		63	
W 192 (rebuilt)		63	
W 192/W 238		118	
W^A 67	Castlecliff Railway	152	
W^A 68 (display)		161	
W^A 137		71	
W^A 165		170	
W^A 217		70	
W^A 220		70	
W^A 262		88	
W^A 289		71	
W^{AB} 791		103	
W^{AB} 794		174	
W^B 298 (scrapping)		161	
W^B 299		76	
W^D 327		76	
W^E 375		88	
W^F 386		86	
W^F 389		139	
W^F 843		86	
W^G 491		87	
W^H 449		93	
W^J 466		93	
W^S 771		102	
W^W 480		170	
W^W 488		87	
X 442	Ohai Railway Board	153	
X 588		91	
X 591		91	
Y 544		107	

Frontispiece - J^A 1274 photo: correct date of photo is 6 December 1956.

Page 11 - Section Numbers listing: should be Wellington 30-38.

Page 32 - Rakaia and Ashburton Forks Railway: the two locomotives were built by Rogers Locomotive Works, Paterson, New Jersey, USA.

Page 68 - W^E 376 and W^E 377: Addington and Hillside Workshops reversed.

Page 69 - First line listing for A 409: correct Maker's Number is 83/07.

Page 77 - U^A class locomotives were built from new with piston valves.

Page 94 - U^D class locomotives had the largest diameter driving wheels on the 3 feet 6 inch gauge NZR system.

Page 118 - Note 50: J^A 1256 - 1259 had maker's plates attached later. These displayed the correct numbers, duplicating the plates cast for J^A 1265 - 1268.

Page 132 - Dubs maker's no. 885: 1882 system column, should be Gy. C1.

Page 134 - Neilson maker's no. 1772: 1882 system column, should be Gy. C2

Page 135 - The U^C illustration is an NZR photograph.

Page 137 - NZR maker's numbers 388-391; refer to correction page 118.

Page 152 - W^A 67 was the largest and last of four former NZR locomotives purchased by the Castlecliff Railway Company…

C 166 and C Belmont were purchased via other intermediate owners.

Page 164 - C 126: should be Westport C 2 in 1882 number column.

Page 164 - C 132: should be Greymouth C 1 in 1882 number column.